SHORTORDER

ADOBE

Photoshop® 5.5

MICHAEL LENNOX

Short Order Adobe® Photoshop® 5.5

Copyright © 2000 by Hayden Books

FIRST EDITION

FIRST PRINTING—1999

International Standard Book Number: 0-7897-2044-2

Library of Congress Catalog Card Number: 9965639

01   00   4   3   2

Printed in the United States of America

Trademarks

All terms mentioned in this book that are known to be trademarks or service marks have been appropriately capitalized. Hayden Books cannot attest to the accuracy of this information. Use of a term in this book should not be regarded as affecting the validity of any trademark or service mark.

Adobe and the Adobe logo are trademarks of Adobe Sytems Incorporated.

Warning and Disclaimer

Every effort has been made to make this book as complete and as accurate as possible, but no warranty or fitness is implied. The information provided is on an "as is" basis. The author and the publisher shall have neither liability nor responsibility to any person or entity with respect to any loss or damages arising from the information contained in this book.

EXECUTIVE EDITOR
Beth Millett

ACQUISITIONS EDITOR
Karen Whitehouse

DEVELOPMENT EDITOR
Beth Millett

MANAGING EDITOR
Thomas F. Hayes

PROJECT EDITOR
Lori A. Lyons

COPY EDITOR
Kay Hoskin

INDEXER
Larry Sweazy

PROOFREADERS
Maryann Steinhart
Mary Ellen Stephenson

TECHNICAL EDITOR
Christina Weisbard

INTERIOR DESIGN
Karen Ruggles

COVER DESIGN
Aren Howell

COPY WRITER
Eric Borgert

LAYOUT TECHNICIAN
Brad Lenser

OVERVIEW

Introduction 1

1   Opening, Placing, and Saving Images 6

2   Using the History Palette 30

3   Resolution and Size Issues 40

4   Image Modes 52

5   Selecting 78

6   Transforming Selected Areas 100

7   Painting 110

8   Using Layers 132

9   Layer Effects and Techniques 150

10   Putting Type in an Image 170

11   Using Channels and Masks 186

12   Image Adjustments and Corrections 196

13   Color Correction 216

14   Working with Paths 232

15   Using Filters 246

16   Paper Publishing 266

17   Electronic Publishing 280

18   Achieving Consistent Color 304

19   Automating Photoshop 314

20   Protecting and Sorting Your Images 324

Index 336

Color insert

CONTENTS

Introduction 1

  Who This Book Is For 1

  About Photoshop .1

  How to Use This Book 3

  About *Short Order* 4

1 Opening, Placing, and Saving Images 6

  Creating a New Image 8

  Handling an ICC Profile Mismatch 9

  Opening a Kodak PhotoCD File 11

  Opening an EPS or Adobe Illustrator File 13

  Opening a PDF 14

  Placing an EPS or PDF 15

  Saving Files 16

  Saving a JPEG 18

  Saving a GIF 20

  Saving a PNG 23

  Saving a TIFF 24

  Saving an EPS 25

  Saving a DCS 2.0 File 27

  Saving a Copy of an Image 29

2 Using the History Palette 30

  Using the History Palette 32

  Saving Snapshots 33

  Creating a New File from a Snapshot or
  History State 34

  Working with Nonlinear History 35

  Painting with Previous Versions of the File
  with the History Brush 36

  Painting with Nonlinear History 38

3 Resolution and Size Issues 40

  Changing the Size of an Image 42

  Choosing an Interpolation Method when
  Resampling 44

  Choosing a Resolution 45

Changing the Resolution 47

Changing the Canvas Size 48

Cropping an Image 49

4 Image modes 52

Converting from RGB to CMYK 54

Previewing Out-of-Gamut Colors 56

Dealing with Out-of-Gamut Colors 57

Dealing with Out-of-Gamut Colors with
Masks 59

Converting to Indexed Color 61

Converting to Indexed Color Using
ImageReady 65

Using RGB Instead of Indexed Color for
Text and Resampling 67

Using DitherBox to Control Dithering 68

Modifying a Color Table in ImageReady 70

Converting to Grayscale 72

Converting to Duotone 73

Converting to Bitmap Mode 75

5 Selecting 78

Constraining Selection Sizes 80

Adding, Subtracting, and Selecting
Overlapping Areas 82

Making a Color-Based Selection with the
Magic Wand Tool 83

Making a Selection Based on Contrasting
Areas 84

Making a Color-Based Selection with the
Color Range Command 86

Transforming a Selection Boundary 88

Expanding and Contracting a Selection 89

Making a Border Around a Selection 90

Fading a Selection 92

Saving a Selection 93

Loading a Saved Selection 94

Using Channels to Make Selections 95

Creating a Mask for Objects Without
Clearly Defined Edges 96

6 Transforming Selected Areas 100

Measuring Distances and Angles 102

Adding Perspective .103

Straightening an Image 105

Removing Keystoning 107

Specifying Numeric Values for a
Transformation 108

7 Painting 110

Choosing How Paint Should Blend 112

Editing an Existing Brush 114

Making a New Brush Shape 116

Saving and Loading a Brush Set 117

Smudging and Finger Painting 118

Erasing Areas of a Layer to Transparency . . .119

Filling an Area with a Pattern 121

Painting with the Pattern Stamp 122

Creating Geometric Shapes 123

Painting with Previous Versions of an
Image 124

Creating Artistic Effects with Previous
Versions of an Image 126

Creating Shaped Gradients 128

Customizing Gradients 130

8 Using Layers 132

Changing Layer Properties 134

Linking Layers 135

Aligning Layers 136

Merging and Flattening Layers 137

Choosing a Layer Blend Mode 138

Preserving Transparency 140

Creating Shadows for Objects 141

Selecting Nontransparent Pixels on a
Layer 144

Copying Layers from One Image to
Another 145

Controlling a Layer's Blend If Options
for Compositing 146

Removing Halos from Layers 148

9 Layer Effects and Techniques 150

Filling Text or an Object with an Image 152

Creating a Layer Mask with a Selection 154

Creating and Editing a Layer Mask
by Painting 156

Moving a Layer Mask 157

Removing or Disabling a Layer Mask 157

Creating a Drop-Shadow or a Cut-Out
Effect 158

Creating a Glow 161

Creating a Bevel and Emboss Effect 162

Applying a Solid Color Fill to a Layer 164

Applying a Gradient or Pattern to a Layer . .165

Applying a Preset Layer-Effect Style to
a Layer 167

Copying Layer Effects to Other Layers 168

Breaking Layer Effects into Their
Component Layers 169

10 Putting Type in an Image 170

Placing Text 172

Editing Text 175

Adjusting Leading 176

Adjusting Kerning and Tracking 177

Adjusting the Baseline Shift 179

Applying Special Effects to a Text Layer 179

Creating Wood Text .180

Creating Metal Text .182

Creating Carved Text 184

11 Using Channels and Masks 186

Saving Selections as Channels 188

Loading Channels as Selections 190

Managing Saved Selections 191

Selecting with Painting Tools Using Quick
Mask Mode 193

Splitting and Merging Channels 195

12 Image Adjustments and Corrections 196

Checking Parts of the Image with the
Eyedropper and Samplers 198

Determining the Tonal Range of an Image
with the Histogram .200

Adjusting the Tonal Range with Levels 201

Adjusting the Tonal Range with Curves 203

Removing Dust and Scratches 206

Copying Adjacent Areas with the
Rubber Stamp Tool .208

Blurring Areas 210

Sharpening Areas 211

Sharpening an Image 212

Lightening Areas 214

Darkening Areas 215

13 Color Correction 216

Changing the Saturation in an Area 218

Removing a Color Cast with Variations 219

Removing a Color Cast with Levels 221

Removing a Color Cast with Curves 222

Changing Color with Hue/Saturation 223

Changing Color with Selective Color 226

Changing Color with Replace Color 227

Creating an Adjustment Layer 228

Pulling Detail Out of Shadows 230

Correcting High-Key and Low-Key
Images 231

14 Working with Paths 232

Creating, Selecting, and Editing Paths 234

Saving a Work Path .236

Saving an Image with a Clipping Path for
Use in a Page-Layout Program 236

Saving a Path for Use in an Illustration
Package 238

Converting a Path into a Selection 239

Converting a Selection into a Path 240

Filling a Path 241

Stroking a Path 242

Blurring an Object Along a Path 243

15 Using Filters 246

Using Other Plug-ins 248

Fading a Filter's Effect 249

Applying a Blur 250

Creating Depth-of-Field Effects 252

Using Artistic Effects 254

Creating a Comic-Book Effect 256

Applying Texture to an Image 258

Applying a Displacement Map to an
Image 260

Changing the Lighting in an Image 262

Adding Noise 264

16 Paper Publishing 266

Choosing a CMYK Model and Conversion
Method 268

Creating Spot Color Channels 272

Applying Trapping 275

Choosing an Appropriate File Format 276

Setting Halftone Screens 276

Creating Transfer Functions 278

Adding Crop Marks, Registration Marks,
and Calibration Bars .279

17 Electronic Publishing 280

Saving GIFs for the Web 282

Saving JPEGs for the Web 285

Saving PNGs for the Web 287

Saving Images with Transparency 290

Using the Web Palette 291

Creating Seamless Backgrounds 292

Laying Out a Web Page in Photoshop and
ImageReady 294

Slicing Images and Creating Imagemaps 296

x

Creating Button Rollovers 299

Creating Animations .301

18 Achieving Consistent Color 304

Characterizing Your Monitor with Adobe
Gamma 306

Choosing an RGB Profile 309

Choosing a Grayscale Profile 311

Changing Your Image's Profile 312

19 Automating Photoshop 314

Loading and Saving an Action Set 316

Running an Action 316

Running Selective Commands and
Controlling User Input 317

Recording an Action 318

Editing Actions 319

Inserting a Stop in an Action 319

Inserting a Path in an Action 320

Inserting a Menu Item in an Action 321

Running Actions on Groups of Images 322

Creating and Using Droplets 323

20 Protecting and Sorting Your Images 324

Entering Copyright Information, Captions,
and Keywords 326

Embedding and Reading a Watermark 329

Creating Thumbnails 331

Creating Contact Sheets 332

Creating Picture Packages 333

Creating a Web Photo Gallery 334

Index 336

ABOUT THE AUTHOR

Michael Lennox is a writer, teacher, and designer who has been working with computer graphics for the past 12 years. As a Certified Technical Trainer, he has provided Photoshop training for dozens of companies, including IBM, Intel, and Netscape. He specializes in Photoshop and AutoCAD. He is an Adobe Certified Training Provider in Photoshop and helped design the Photoshop 5.0 proficiency exam for certification by Adobe. In addition, he co-authored the *Adobe Photoshop 5.0 Certification Guide* for Adobe Press.

ACKNOWLEDGMENTS

Thanks to Andrea Swenson, my wife, for her constant love and support. Thanks to my family for their encouragement and advice. I'd like to thank Charles Barnard for his insights, suggestions, and lengthy discussions about Photoshop, computer graphics, and other delightfully esoteric topics. Thanks also to hundreds of students who keep Photoshop vibrant and alive as we discover together the accessibility of art in the age of the computer. Finally, warm thanks to Beth Millett, Christina Weisbard, Karen Whitehouse, and the rest of the people behind the scenes at Hayden who make all of this possible.

SPECIAL THANKS

Figure 5.38, page 96 and Figure 12.6, page 200
Courtesy of Glenn Williams Photography
1006 W. Ben Holt Drive
Stockton, CA 95207

Figure 5.22, page 89
Courtesy of Dennis McDaniel and Haeger, Inc.
811 Wakefield Drive
Oakdale, CA 95361

Images of the Seattle skyline, pages 126-127, and C.1, C.2, and C.3 in the color insert
Courtesy of Chris Swenson
718 Sequoia Ave
San Mateo, CA 94403

TELL US WHAT YOU THINK!

As the reader of this book, you are our most important critic and commentator. We value your opinion and want to know what we're doing right, what we could do better, what areas you'd like to see us publish in, and any other words of wisdom you're willing to pass our way.

As a Publisher for Hayden Books, I welcome your comments. You can fax, email, or write me directly to let me know what you did or didn't like about this book—as well as what we can do to make our books stronger.

Please note that I cannot help you with technical problems related to the topic of this book, and that due to the high volume of mail I receive, I might not be able to reply to every message.

When you write, please be sure to include this book's title and author as well as your name and phone or fax number. I will carefully review your comments and share them with the author and editors who worked on the book.

Fax: 317-581-4666

Email: hayden@mcp.com

Mail: John Pierce
        Hayden Books
        201 West 103rd Street
        Indianapolis, IN 46290 USA

INTRODUCTION

Who This Book Is For

Short Order Adobe Photoshop 5.5 was created for people interested in quick solutions to the tasks and problems you encounter in Photoshop every day. Using step-by-step examples and plenty of illustrations, you'll learn to put intermediate to advanced tasks and commands to work for you—in short order.

If you have worked with Photoshop before and want to step up your skills, this book will teach you tricks used by professional graphic designers that are sure to enhance your artwork. You will find that this book is particularly helpful as a quick reference, as well as a guide to expanding your Photoshop horizons to include cutting-edge techniques and learning the new features of Photoshop 5.5 and ImageReady 2.0.

About Photoshop

Photoshop is the industry standard for the manipulation of raster-based images. Web designers, photographers, and other graphics professionals use Photoshop every day to prepare images for Web pages, for print, and for use in hundreds of other imaging applications. Photoshop's vast array of features, powerful special effects, and seamless integration with other widely accepted Adobe products make Photoshop an effective and necessary tool.

What You Can Do with Photoshop

On the surface, many of Photoshop's tools and commands are simple and easy to use. Under the surface, however, are compound techniques and infinite layers of complexity. Some of the things you can do with Photoshop include:

- Customize images with special effects, editing tools, and text
- Composite image elements

- Correct and retouch photographs
- Batch process series of images
- Create professional Web graphics
- Prepare images for process printing, including spot colors
- Import and export images in a variety of file formats

What's New in Photoshop 5.0 and 5.5

Photoshop 5.0 added many new features that built upon an already incredibly strong foundation laid by previous versions of Photoshop. Photoshop 5.5 is an incremental upgrade, adding useful tools for general Photoshop users and essential tools for those creating Web graphics, including the addition of ImageReady 2.0. Here are just a few of the highlights of Photoshop that you will find out about when you read this book:

- Editable type layers let you change text in an image at any time.
- The History palette provides the ability to go beyond one Undo and to work with previous versions of an image.
- Support for spot-color channels and DCS 2.0 make Photoshop even easier to use when preparing images for process printing.
- New color management features and support for ICC color profiles help you achieve consistent color between devices and platforms.
- Elegant layer effects help you create some of the most commonly used graphic techniques, such as glows and drop shadows.
- Actions and new automation tools simplify the creation of macros and make it easier to share, modify, and apply the actions to batches of images.

Photoshop 5.5 with ImageReady 2.0 also adds exciting functions for Web designers and other graphics professionals, including:

- The long-awaited support for animated GIFs has arrived, and setting them up is as easy as creating layers.

- JavaScript rollovers and image slices are easy to create, and ImageReady can even automatically generate the HTML.

- Combined with the background eraser, the Extract command makes separating foreground objects from their backgrounds much simpler and speeds up the creation of complex masks.

- Improved text handling, additional layer effects, and a streamlined process for saving images for the Web with customizable and repeatable optimization levels.

Almost all the procedures in this book work in Photoshop 5.0. Some are Photoshop 5.5 or ImageReady 2.0 specific, and these are indicated with icons to let you know where you can find that functionality. All the dialog boxes shown are from Photoshop 5.5. If you are using Photoshop 5.0, you may see minor differences in the dialog boxes and some extra steps included for Photoshop 5.5 users.

How to Use This Book

The step-by-step instructions throughout this book provide recipes for image effects and techniques. In most cases, there are other ways to accomplish the same effect. Use the recipes to get started, and you'll soon find yourself adding new ingredients and combining techniques to tap some of Photoshop's infinite variety.

Watch the tips for suggestions about how you can start to experiment and shortcuts to make you more efficient. These shortcut tips should serve as memory joggers for the experienced user and as points to commit to memory for the novice.

The notes, also placed throughout the book, offer explanations to clarify task-specific details and to provide commentary on some of Photoshop's more challenging aspects.

If a picture is worth a thousand words, then you'll find no shortage of visual verbiage here. As is characteristic of the *Short Order* series, there are plenty of screenshots to guide you through the tasks, along with plenty of callouts that emphasize specific features of Photoshop's dialog boxes and palettes.

This book includes directions for both Macintosh and Windows platforms. In this day and age, software is becoming increasingly interchangeable; after you have launched the software, there are very few differences, regardless of where you're using the program. This means that you have the ultimate flexibility in skills and resources: If this book shows screen shots in a platform you're not familiar with, don't worry—it will still apply. Keyboard shortcuts are provided for both platforms. You'll find Macintosh shortcuts in parentheses and Windows shortcuts in brackets, like this: (Command-Shift-P) [Control+Shift+P].

About *Short Order*

Treat *Short Order Adobe Photoshop 5.5* as your Photoshop quick-reference. The book is divided into chapters that contain collections of related tasks. Everything you need is in one place so that you can quickly find the answer to your problem and get back to work. Although this book is not meant to be read sequentially from cover to cover, there is a general order to the way that the chapters have been organized so that you can find what you need quickly.

Chapters 1 through 4 help guide you through the basics of handling raster-based images. Opening and saving in a wide range of file formats, changing an image's size, and working with image modes lay the foundation for working with images in Photoshop. The History palette chapter demonstrates techniques for working with previous versions of an image.

Chapters 5 and 6 guide you through the tools and techniques for creating selections and then transforming them.

Chapter 7 helps you master the painting tools and use them effectively in a variety of images.

Chapters 8, 9, and 10 help you make the most out of layers, layer techniques, and type in an image.

Chapter 11 expands on selection and painting techniques to help you create and save selections and to work effectively with channels.

Chapters 12 and 13 guide you through image retouching and color correction.

Chapter 14 again increases the range of selection and painting techniques by adding the functionality of paths.

Chapter 15 helps you choose and use filters and special effects in your image.

Chapters 16 and 17 examine the opposite ends of Photoshop's publishing spectrum: paper publishing and Web publishing.

Chapter 18 provides guidelines for achieving consistent color throughout your image workflow.

Chapters 19 and 20 demonstrate Photoshop's macros, automation tools, and sorting and copyright options.

From Web designers in need of small, simple graphics to artists creating dazzling special effects for a series of print ads, *Short Order Adobe Photoshop 5.5* strives to break through the complexities of Photoshop and deliver what you really need, when you really need it.

CHAPTER 1

In this chapter you learn how to...

Create a New Image

Handle an ICC Profile Mismatch

Open a Kodak PhotoCD File

Open an EPS or Adobe Illustrator File

Open a PDF

Place an EPS or PDF

Save Files

Save a JPEG

Save a GIF

Save a PNG

Save a TIFF

Save an EPS

Save a DCS 2.0 File

Save a Copy of an Image

Photoshop can open and save a large variety of image formats. Some of the file formats, such as BMP and PICT, are plat-form specific. Others are widely used for accomplishing particular output purposes, such as GIF and JPEG for the Web and EPS for printing. Still others, such as TGA and PCX, are used by specific industries to work with other software and to meet hardware requirements.

OPENING, PLACING, AND SAVING IMAGES

You probably already know what types of files you need to use. If you are uncertain, check the documentation of any other applications you will be using with the files. Even if another application supports more than one format available from Photoshop, you should experiment to determine the best option. Although alpha channels may be supported by a file format, for example, applications other than Photoshop may not read that information. If you need to preserve the alpha channel information, you may need to use a different format.

Although the Photoshop native file format (PSD) is read by only a few other image-editing applications, it is the only format that supports multiple layers. The Photoshop native file format also is used by ImageReady. When you save from ImageReady, the file contains additional information that is ignored by Photoshop, such as URLs, slices, and rollover settings. ImageReady can open many of the same formats that can be opened by Photoshop. Other than saving in one of the Web formats, however, images can be saved only in the Photoshop native format. If you need to save an ImageReady file in another format, open the file in Photoshop.

Creating a New Image

When you create a new image in Photoshop, you have the opportunity to determine some of its most important features from the start.

1. Choose File→New. The New dialog box appears (1.1).

2. Enter a filename for the new image. If you choose to leave the image untitled, you are prompted for a filename the first time you save the image.

3. Choose a height and width for the image. You can set the dimension in a variety of units. If you have image data stored on the Clipboard, the size of that data is used as the default.

4. Choose a resolution for the image. If you are creating an image for onscreen display, choose 72 pixels per inch (ppi). If you are creating an image that will be printed, determine the appropriate resolution by multiplying the screen frequency by 1.5 to 2 times.

5. Choose an image mode for the image. If you will use an image mode not listed in the New dialog box, create the image first, and then convert it using Image→Mode.

6. Choose a color for the background layer in the image, or choose Transparent.

7. Choose OK.

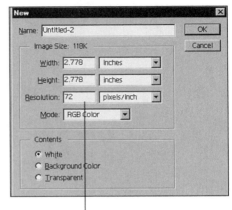

1.1

Calculating resolution using a precise screen frequency multiplication factor (that is, 1.5 to 2.0) is particularly important when storage space is an issue. Some users choose standard resolution settings (72, 150, and 300 ppi) that are sometimes larger than the 1.5 to 2.0 multiplication rule and choose the most appropriate setting for the image's final output, varying from these standard resolutions only when required by the print or service bureau. You also may need extra image detail (resolution), depending on what you do with the image in Photoshop (compositing, scaling, transformations, and so on). See Chapter 3, "Resolution and Size Issues," for more information.

Handling an ICC Profile Mismatch

1.2

For CMYK images, do not use the Convert to CMYK working space option, because important color information such as black generation and trapping can be lost in a color shift from one CMYK profile to another. Instead, select Ask when Opening or use the Convert to RGB or Convert to Lab option. The CMYK profile setup information is reapplied when you convert an RGB or lab image to CMYK mode.

Images created in Photoshop 5.0 and later can contain embedded ICC color profiles, or descriptions of the working space in which the image was created. Because the working color space is defined precisely, the image's color information can be translated and displayed correctly on any properly characterized monitor or printer.

You can choose how Photoshop should handle mismatches and which profile should be assumed for those files lacking embedded profiles so that the color information in the file is displayed correctly by Photoshop on your system. Changing the profile setup affects every file you open in Photoshop.

1. Choose File→Color Settings→ Profile Setup. The Profile Setup dialog box appears (1.2).

2. Choose an assumed profile to be used when opening untagged RGB, CMYK, and grayscale images.

   For more information about choosing color profiles, see Chapter 18, "Achieving Consistent Color." For information about choosing color profiles for CMYK images, see Chapter 16, "Paper Publishing."

continues

Handling an ICC Profile Mismatch continued

3. Choose a method to use when opening an untagged image or an image that uses a profile that differs from the working space.

Choose Ignore to disregard embedded profile information. The file opens without any conversion.

Choose Ask when Opening if you want Photoshop to prompt you each time an image is opened with a profile mismatch (**1.3**).

Choose Convert to convert the file to the selected color space.

1.3

 I P

If you are going to use a grayscale image for onscreen display, you can use the Convert to Grayscale option. If the grayscale image is going to be printed, use the Ask when Opening option so that you can choose a profile conversion method when the file is opened.

 I P

You can set RGB mismatches to convert to the RGB working space for most images. Because some color shifting may occur, which may be unacceptable if the original file contains precise RGB values, select Ask when Opening so that you can choose a profile for conversion to the RGB working space.

Opening a Kodak PhotoCD File

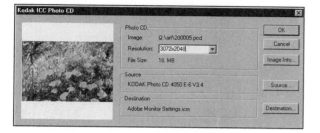

1.4

1.5

Kodak PhotoCD files are placed on a CD in several resolutions, depending on the type of CD. When you open an image from a Kodak PhotoCD, you can control the display and color mode by using the Kodak Precision Color Management System (KPCMS) installed with Photoshop. When you open a Kodak PhotoCD image, you should select source and destination ICC profiles to use for the color space conversion.

1. Choose File→Open. In the Open dialog box, choose Kodak ICC PhotoCD as the file type, or choose All Formats.

2. Select a Kodak PhotoCD file to open and choose Open. The Kodak ICC PhotoCD dialog box appears **(1.4)**.

3. In the Resolution box, choose a resolution for the file you are opening. Note that Pro Photo CDs have an additional high resolution, 4096×6144.

4. If the image is in portrait orientation, choose Landscape if you want to rotate the image when it is opened.

5. To view the original file source and scanner information for the image, choose Image Info. You can use this information **(1.5)** when selecting an appropriate color profile in the next step. Click OK.

continues

Opening a Kodak PhotoCD File continued

6. Choose Source to select the color profile used when the image was scanned. If you do not know the correct profile, or if the Image Info dialog box is blank, try using the Color Negative profile. Consult your PhotoCD provider for accurate information and instructions. Select a profile and choose Open **(1.6)**.

7. Choose Destination to select an ICC color profile for the intended output device and Photoshop color mode. Select a CIELAB profile to maintain the widest possible gamut and to most closely match Kodak's YCC color model. Select a profile and choose Open **(1.7)**.

1.6

1.7

 I P

*If you have installed the Kodak PhotoCD Acquire Module **(1.8)**, you can use its additional capabilities, such as sharpening, cropping, and tonal scale adjustments, to alter the image in the YCC color model before opening it in Photoshop.*

You can download the latest version of the Acquire Module and CMS transforms from http://www.kodak.com/global/en/ service/software/photoCDSoftware.shtml

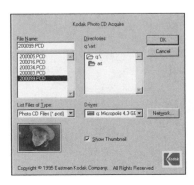

1.8

Opening an EPS or Adobe Illustrator File

Vector artwork

1.9

Rasterized vector artwork

1.10

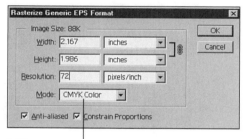

1.11   **To minimize color shifts when opening or importing Adobe Illustrator or EPS data, make sure that you choose an appropriate image mode in the Rasterize Generic EPS Format dialog box or that your Photoshop image is already in the correct image mode.**

1.12

If you want to import vector information as paths in Photoshop, copy it in your illustration program and paste it into Photoshop. Photoshop prompts you to select how you want to insert the information.

If you open an EPS or Illustrator file that contains vector information **(1.9)**, Photoshop must convert the vectors into rasters **(1.10)**. Then you can edit the pixels just as you would any Photoshop image. After you rasterize an image, you cannot easily covert it back into vectors.

1. Choose File→Open. In the Open dialog box, choose Photoshop EPS or Generic EPS as the file type, or choose All Formats.

2. Select an EPS or Adobe Illustrator file and choose Open.

3. Choose a width and height for the image **(1.11)**. By default, the image's current size is listed. If you want to constrain the relationship between width and height, choose Constrain Proportions.

4. Choose a resolution to use when rasterizing the file. For images that appear onscreen, choose 72 ppi. For images that will be printed, determine the resolution by multiplying the screen frequency by 1.5 to 2.

5. Choose an image mode to use for the image.

6. If you do not want to anti-alias the file, clear the Anti-Aliased check box.

7. Choose OK.

Opening a PDF

A Portable Document Format (PDF) file can contain both text and graphics. When opening a PDF file, the text must be rasterized.

1. Choose File→Open. In the Open dialog box, choose Generic PDF as the file type, or choose All Formats.

2. Select a PDF file and choose Open. The Generic PDF Parser dialog box appears (1.13).

3. Use the arrows under the thumbnail window to select a page to open, and then choose OK.

4. In the Rasterize Generic PDF dialog box, choose a width and height for the image. If you want to constrain the relationship between width and height, choose Constrain Proportions.

5. Choose a resolution to use when rasterizing the file. For images that appear onscreen, choose 72 ppi. For images that will be printed, determine the resolution by multiplying the screen frequency by 1.5 to 2.

6. Choose an image mode to use for the image. If you know the image mode of the PDF file, use the same image mode for the Photoshop file to minimize color shifts.

7. Choose OK.

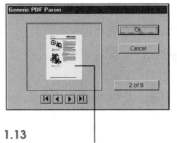

1.13
If the PDF file does not have thumbnails generated for each page, no thumbnail is displayed.

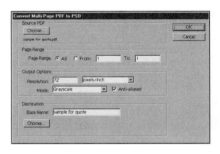

1.14
If you want to create separate Photoshop files from each page of a multipage PDF file, choose File→Automate→Multi-Page PDF to PSD.

Placing an EPS or PDF

1.15

Vector images can be transformed before they are rasterized.

1.16

You can place an Encapsulated PostScript (EPS) or Portable Document Format (PDF) file into an existing Photoshop document. When you place an EPS file, it must be rasterized if it contains vector information. However, before you rasterize, you can scale and rotate the image. Unlike pixels in Photoshop, vector images maintain their quality, and do not become jagged when manipulated.

1. In a Photoshop document, choose File→Place.

2. In the Place dialog box, select the type of file you want to place.

3. The file is inserted into the image with active transformation handles (1.15). Click and drag a handle to resize the imported graphic.

4. After you resize the graphic, double-click inside the graphic to commit the change (1.16).

Saving Files

Photoshop can open 23 different common image file formats and save images in most of the same formats. When you choose Save As, only some of the file formats are available, depending on the mode and contents of your image (1.17). Tables 1.1 through 1.3 should help you determine why a specific format is not available when saving. Photoshop native files (PSD format) support all image modes, 24 channels, and paths. Also, PSD is the only format that supports any layer information other than the background. Either flatten your image or—preferably—use the Save a Copy command.

 I P

When exporting to the Web, use JPEG for photographs and GIF for flat color images and animations. Use DCS 2.0 whenever you want to save spot color channels.

 I P

Companies other than Adobe also create plug-ins that enable you to save files. There are plug-ins to save images in formats that can be read by proprietary software and plug-ins that save in standard formats (JPEG, for example) but determine the information to be saved differently.

Table 1.1   Web File Formats

File Format	Supported Image Modes	Channels Supported	Paths Supported
GIF	Bitmap, Indexed Color (with or without transparency), Grayscale	No	No
JPEG	Grayscale, RGB, CMYK	No	Yes
PNG	Bitmap, Indexed Color (with or without transparency), Grayscale, RGB	One in grayscale and RGB, to define areas of transparency	No

Table 1.2   Prepress File Formats

File Format	Supported Image Modes	Channels Supported	Paths Supported
DCS 1.0	CMYK	No	Yes
DCS 2.0	CMYK, Multichannel	One alpha multiple spot color	Yes
EPS	All but Multichannel, (Indexed Color without transparency)	No	Yes
PDF	Bitmap, Grayscale, Indexed Color (without transparency), RGB, CMYK, Lab	No	Yes
TIFF	Bitmap, Grayscale, Indexed Color (without transparency), RGB, CMYK, Lab	In grayscale, RGB, and CMYK	Yes

Table 1.3   Other File Formats

File Format	Supported Image Modes	Channels Supported	Paths Supported
BMP (Windows)	Bitmap, Grayscale, Indexed Color (without transparency), RGB	No	No
IFF	Bitmap, Grayscale, Indexed Color (without transparency), RGB	No	No
PCX	Bitmap, Grayscale, Indexed Color (without transparency), RGB	No	No
PICT	Bitmap, Grayscale, Indexed Color (without transparency), RGB	One in RGB	No
PICT Resource	Bitmap, Grayscale, Indexed Color (without transparency), RGB	One in RGB	No
PIXAR	Grayscale, RGB	One	No
Raw	Grayscale, Duotone, Indexed Color transparency), RGB, CMYK, Lab, Multichannel	In grayscale, RGB, and CMYK	No
Scitex CT	Grayscale, RGB, CMYK	No	No
TGA	Grayscale, Indexed Color (without transparency), RGB	One in 32-bit RGB	No

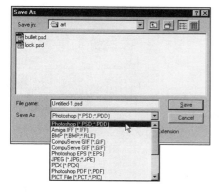

1.17

(T) I P

If you are a Macintosh user and are providing your files to Windows users or placing your files on a Web page, be sure to include file extensions. Press the Option key while choosing the file format in the Save As dialog box, or turn on file extensions permanently by choosing Append File Extensions in Preferences→Saving Files.

If you are a Windows user and are given a file that does not have a file extension, you can use Open As to open the file if you know the image format used. Macintosh users also can open images as a specific format by choosing Open→Show All Files. Select the file to import and select the file format from the list.

You also may be prompted to enter the image size if it cannot be determined from the file.

If the file does not open, the format you selected might not be the actual format of the file.

Saving a JPEG

When you save a Joint Photographic Experts Group (JPEG) file, you must choose a level of compression. JPEG compression is *lossy*, meaning that image data is discarded. You can save JPEG images in RGB and CMYK modes. Path information is stored with a JPEG image.

1. If the image contains only the background layer, choose File→Save As. If the image contains more than one layer, choose File→Save a Copy. When you select JPEG as the file type, the Flatten Image check box is selected automatically and cannot be changed.

2. If you use Save a Copy, enable the Exclude Non-Image Data check box to discard information beyond the actual pixel information, such as paths and file information.

3. Enter the name of the file and choose OK. The JPEG Options dialog box appears **(1.18)**.

4. If the image you are saving contains layer transparency, you can choose a color in the Matte drop-down list box to blend transparent and opaque pixels **(1.19)**.

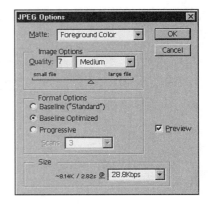

1.18

1.19

Table 1.4   JPEG Format Options

Options	Pros	Cons
Baseline "Standard"	Recognized by most Web browsers	
Baseline Optimized	Optimized color quality; Reduced file size	Not recognized by browsers
Progressive (also need to select the number of scans)	Image displayed progressively as it downloads.	Larger file sizes; Not recognized by all browsers

5. Choose an image quality, from 1 to 10. If you choose a low image quality, more image information is discarded and there may be noticeable arti-facting. If you select a higher quality, less information is lost but the files are larger.

6. Choose a bandwidth setting in the Size section to see an approximate size and down-load time.

7. Choose the format options for the JPEG. See Table 1.4 for the advantages and disadvantages of each type. When finished, choose OK.

 I P

Some Java applications do not correctly read JPEG images with thumbnails. If you do not want to save a thumbnail of the image, enable the Exclude Non-Image Data check box in the Save a Copy dialog box. This also reduces the size of the file.

 I P

Before creating a JPEG, save a Photoshop native version of the file to preserve all image data and layer information.

Saving a GIF

Photoshop supports two types of Graphics Interchange Format (GIF) files: CompuServe GIF and GIF89a. The CompuServe GIF format can be created from images in Bitmap, Grayscale, and Indexed Color modes. The CompuServe GIF saved from Photoshop supports interlacing, but not transparency. To create a GIF that contains transparency, use the Export GIF 89a plug-in. The GIF 89a exported from Photoshop enables you to export images from Indexed Color or RGB mode.

See (1.20) and (1.21) for an example of noninterlaced versus interlaced. (1.22) shows a file with a transparent background.

GIF files that contain transparency support only one level of transparency. That is, either a pixel is completely opaque or completely transparent. You cannot create gradual transparency in a GIF file.

For more information about saving files for the Web, see "Saving GIFs for the Web" on page 282 in Chapter 17, "Electronic Publishing."

1. Choose File→Export→GIF89a Export. The GIF89a Export Options dialog box appears (1.23).

2. If the image you are exporting is in RGB mode, choose a palette and number of colors to use when converting the image

1.20

1.21

1.22

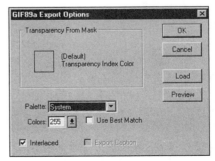

1.23

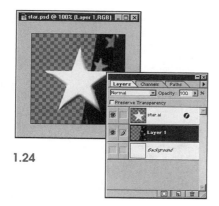

1.24

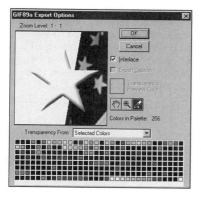

1.25

to Indexed Color mode. You can use an adaptive palette derived from the colors in the image, a system palette, or load a custom palette. If the image contains 256 or fewer colors, the exact palette also is available. If you select the system palette or a custom palette, enable the Use Best Match check box. For more information, see "Converting to Indexed Color" on page 61 in Chapter 4, "Image Modes."

When exporting an image in RGB mode, transparency is determined by transparent areas on the visible layers. Turn off any layers that you do not want to export (**1.24**).

Choose Preview to display a preview of the image, its transparency, and color table.

3. If the image you are exporting is in Indexed Color mode, the GIF89a Export Options dialog box displays the color table and a preview of the image (**1.25**).
Transparency can be specified by an alpha channel, selected colors, or the transparency that exists in the image.

To create an alpha channel to use as the transparency, select the area you want to remain

continues

Saving a GIF continued

visible and choose Select→
Save Selection before choosing
File→Export→GIF89a Export.
In the GIF89a Export Options
dialog box, choose the alpha
channel you created from the
Transparency From drop-down
list. Note that even though an
alpha channel may contain levels of gray, the transparency
has a hard edge.

To create transparency from
colors selected in the GIF89a
Export Options dialog box,
pick the colors in the image
preview or from the color table
swatches with the add eyedropper. Press (Command)
[Ctrl] to change the add eyedropper to the subtract eyedropper to deselect colors for
transparency. The preview
window in the GIF89a Export
Options dialog box shows the
image and uses a key color to
indicate the areas of transparency (1.26).

4. Choose OK.

5. Enter the name of the file that
   you want to export and choose
   Save.

For more information, see "Saving
GIFs for the Web" on page 282 in
Chapter 17, "Electronic Publishing."

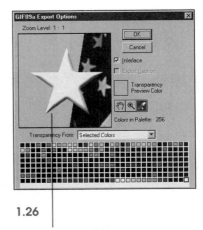

1.26

**By default, the key color for the
transparency is gray; but you
can change it to a color that
contrasts with those in the image
by clicking on the swatch next to
Transparency Preview Color.**

Saving a PNG

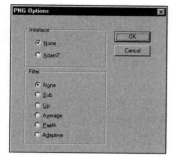

1.27

Table 1.5   PNG Filter Types

Filter Type	Uses
None	Compresses the image without a filter. Use this option for images in Indexed Color and Bitmap mode.
Sub	Optimizes compression of images with even horizontal patterns or blends.
Up	Optimizes compression of images with even vertical patterns.
Average	Optimizes compression of low-level noise by averaging the color values of adjacent pixels.
Paeth	Optimizes the compression of low-level noise by reassigning adjacent color values.
Adaptive	Applies the best-suited filter to the image. Select Adaptive if you are unsure which filter to use.

The Portable Networks Graphics (PNG) format is a patent-free alternative to the GIF. The PNG format supports RGB, Grayscale, Indexed Color, and Bitmap image modes, uses lossless compression, and can have multiple levels of transparency defined by an alpha channel. Files saved in the PNG format cannot be read by all browsers, although most 4.x and later browsers have built-in support for PNG files.

1. Choose File→Save As. If the file contains more than one layer, flatten the layers first or choose File→Save a Copy. From the list of file types, choose PNG.

2. If you use Save a Copy, enable the Exclude Non-Image Data check box to discard information beyond the actual pixel information, such as paths and file information.

3. Enter the name of the file you want to create; choose Save.

4. In the Interlace section of the PNG Options dialog box (1.27), select Adam7 to enable bidirectional interlacing to display the image in increasing detail as it is downloaded.

5. In the Filter section, choose a filter to prepare the image for compression. Table 1.5 lists the filter choices.

6. Choose OK.

Saving a TIFF

The Tagged Image File Format
(TIFF) supports most of the image
modes you can create in Photoshop.
TIFFs also support alpha channels
and paths.

1. Choose File→Save As. If the
   image contains more than one
   layer, flatten the layers or
   choose File→Save a Copy
   (1.28). From the list of file
   types, choose TIFF.

2. Enter the name of the file you
   want to create and choose
   Save.

3. In the TIFF Options dialog box
   (1.29), select the byte order you
   want to use: Macintosh or IBM
   PC. Some page-layout programs require a specific byte
   order to read the file.

4. Choose LZW Compression if
   you want to export the file
   using Lemple-Zif-Welch (LZW)
   compression.

5. Choose OK.

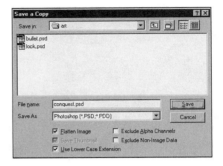

1.28

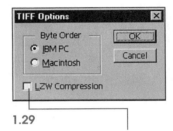

1.29

**LZW compression works particularly
well with images that contain large
areas of a single color. Using LZW
compression creates smaller files that
may take longer to open.**

Saving an EPS

1.30

A higher color depth cre-
ates a larger image. If you
choose None for the pre-
view, most page-layout
programs display the EPS
file as a gray box when
imported.

Table 1.6   EPS Encoding Options

	ASCII	Binary	JPEG
Platform	Windows	Macinstosh	JPEG (also need to select the amount of compression)
			Printers must use PostScript Level 2 or higher
Pros	Widely supported	Smaller files	Control over image compression (Maximum Quality discards the least amount of image data, but produces the largest file size.)
Cons	Larger files	Not supported by all page layout applications or printers	Not supported by all page layout applications or printers; JPEG is a a lossy compression (so some image data is lost)

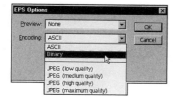

1.31

Encapsulated PostScript (EPS) files can contain both raster and vector information. When you save an EPS file from Photoshop, you can include clipping paths and preview information for use in a page-layout application. Clipping paths enable you to control the areas of transparency and opacity when the image is placed in a page-layout application. For more information about clipping paths, see "Saving an Image with a Clipping Path for Use in a Page-Layout Program" on page 236 in Chapter 14, "Working with Paths." You also can include printing information, such as the halftone screen and transfer function.

1. Choose File→Save As. If the file contains more than one layer, flatten the layers or first choose File→Save a Copy. From the list of file types, choose Photoshop EPS.

2. Enter the name of the file you want to create and choose Save.

3. In the EPS Options dialog box (1.30), choose a preview type from the Preview drop-down list.

4. From the Encoding drop-down list (1.31), choose an encoding type. See Table 1.6 for more information on these options.

continues

Saving an EPS continued

5. Enable the Include Halftone Screen check box to save the image's halftone information, such as screen frequency and the angle of the screen with the file **(1.32)**.

6. Enable the Include Transfer Function check box if you adjusted the transfer information to compensate for dot gain between image and film on a miscalibrated imagesetter. For more information, see "Creating Transfer Functions" on page 278 in Chapter 16, "Paper Publishing."

7. If you are saving an image in Bitmap mode, an additional check box, Transparent Whites, will make the white pixels in the image transparent.

8. Enable the PostScript Color Management check box if you are printing to a PostScript printer and have not already specified the printer's color space. Colors in the image are converted to match the color space of the printer.

9. Choose OK.

1.32

Include Halftone Screen check box

 I   P

PostScript Color Management is supported for CMYK images by printers that use PostScript Level 3. To use PostScript Color Management on a Level 2 printer, convert the image to Lab mode before saving.

Saving a DCS 2.0 File

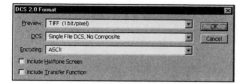

1.33

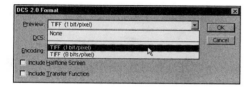

1.34

Desktop Color Separation (DCS) files are a derivation of the EPS format. The DCS format supports only CMYK and Multichannel modes. Like the EPS, you can include clipping path information in a DCS file. The greatest advantage of the DCS format is its support for channels and, in particular, spot color channels (once alpha channel supported). It is the only format other than the Photoshop native format that supports spot color channels. When you create a DCS file, each channel can be exported as a separate EPS file. Each EPS file can be used to create film for a printing plate.

1. Choose File→Save As. If the file contains more than one layer, flatten the layers or choose File→Save a Copy. From the list of file types, choose Photoshop DCS 2.0.

2. Enter the name of the file you want to create and choose Save.

3. In the DCS 2.0 Format dialog box (1.33), choose a preview type from the Preview drop-down list (1.34). A higher color depth creates a larger image. If you choose None for the preview, most page-layout programs display the EPS file as a gray box when imported.

continues

Saving a DCS 2.0 File continued

4. From the DCS drop-down list (**1.35**), choose how the file or files should be created. You can create single or multiple EPS files. You also can create a grayscale or color composite EPS file. Single files and those without composites use less space. If you choose a multiple file option, each color channel is saved in a separate EPS file.

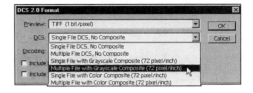

1.35

5. From the Encoding drop-down list (**1.36**), choose an encoding type. See Table 1.7 for more information.

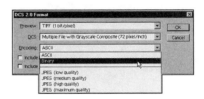

1.36

6. Enable the Include Halftone Screen check box to save the image's halftone information, such as screen frequency and the angle of the screen with the file.

7. Enable the Include Transfer Function check box if you adjusted the transfer information to compensate for dot gain between image and film on a miscalibrated imagesetter. For more information, see "Creating Transfer Functions" on page 278 in Chapter 16, "Paper Publishing."

8. Choose OK.

Table 1.7   DCS Encoding Options

	ASCII	Binary	JPEG
Platform	Windows	Macinstosh	JPEG (also need to select the amount of compression) Printers must use PostScript Level 2 or higher
Pros	Widely supported	Smaller files	Control over image compression (Maximum Quality discards the least amount of image data, but produces the largest file size)
Cons	Larger files	Not supported by all page layout applications or printers	Not supported by all page layout applications or printers; JPEG is a a lossy compression (so some image data is lost)

Saving a Copy of an Image

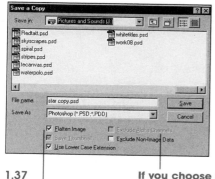

1.37

If you choose a format other than Photoshop native, this option is selected automatically and cannot be deselected.

If you choose a format that does not support alpha channel information, this option is selected automatically and cannot be deselected.

The Save a Copy command saves a copy of the current file with a new filename and leaves the current file open for editing with its original name. The Save a Copy command enables you to save in any format that supports the image mode of the current image, flattening layers or discarding alpha channels as necessary for the format.

1. Choose File→Save a Copy.

2. In the Save a Copy dialog box (1.37), choose the type of file you want to save from the Save As drop-down list.

3. Enable the Flatten Image check box to flatten the layers in the image.

4. Enable the Exclude Alpha Channels check box to discard alpha channels in the saved file.

5. Enable the Exclude Non-Image Data check box to discard information beyond the actual pixel information, such as paths and file information.

6. Choose Save.

 I P

Use the Save a Copy command to save a file at different stages of development while preserving the original file. Using the Save As command would require you to close the copy of the original and then reopen the original.

CHAPTER 2

In this chapter you learn how to...

Use the History Palette

Save Snapshots

Create a New File from a Snapshot or History State

Work with Nonlinear History

Paint with Previous Versions of the File with the History Brush

Paint with Nonlinear History

Purge Undo and History Information

Photoshop's History palette enables you to return to previous versions of an image while working on it. The History palette gives you "multiple undo" capabilities in addition to the normal Undo and Redo commands.

By default, Photoshop keeps track of the previous 20 actions. You can change the number of actions that Photoshop stores to any value between 1 and 100, but each state requires

USING THE HISTORY PALETTE

additional resources. If you are working on large images, decrease the number of states to improve performance. If you are working on small images or have plenty of system resources, you might increase the number of stored states so that travel further back into a document's history. Keep in mind that each open document has its own set of history states.

As you continue working with an image, the oldest history states are dropped from the list. A snapshot is a saved history state that remains as long as the document is open. Snapshots enable you to capture moments in a document's history starting from the moment you open the file. By default, Photoshop creates an initial snapshot. You can return to the way an image looked when you first opened it, even if you have saved your changes after initially opening the document. You can create as many snapshots as you need, but remember that Photoshop must keep track of every snapshot.

History states are not saved with the image, but Photoshop provides several tools that enable you to recover history information by painting or by creating new documents from a history state.

Using the History Palette

You use the History palette to move among history states, save snapshots, and set the source for the History brush. By default, the History palette is set to use linear history, so when you select a state, subsequent states are grayed out. If you change the image from the selected state, subsequent states are discarded. For more information about how Photoshop manages a document's history, see "Working with Nonlinear History," later in this chapter.

History states are named for the tool or command used to create them.

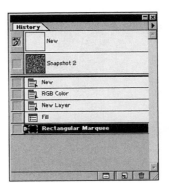

2.1

1. To move backward in a document's history, select a previous state by clicking. All subsequent states are grayed out **(2.1)**. If you make any changes, the grayed-out states are discarded, and the history begins again from the selected state **(2.2)**. Choose Undo to immediately return to the previous state and restore the discarded history states.

2. To move forward in a document's history, select a history state that occurs after the currently selected state.

2.2

 I P

To move backward in the history, press (Option-Command-Z)[Alt+Ctrl+Z]. To move forward, press (Shift-Command-Z) [Shift+Ctrl+Z]. Note that these keyboard shortcuts are variations on the keyboard shortcut for Undo, (Command-Z)[Ctrl+Z].

Saving Snapshots

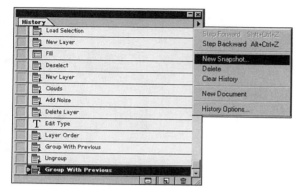

2.3

2.4

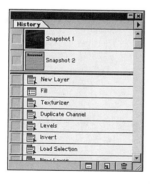

2.5

You can rename a snapshot in the History palette by double-clicking it.

With a snapshot, you easily can recover the entire image or selectively combine areas of the snapshot with the edited image to create completely new effects. Like a history state, a snapshot is not stored with the drawing.

Create a snapshot of an image before experimenting or before using a painting tool (because each brushstroke creates a history state).

1. Click the Create New Snapshot button at the bottom of the History palette. A new snapshot appears in the snapshot area of the History palette.

2. If you want to create a snapshot that contains the information from only the current layer or from a merged version of the visible layers, choose New Snapshot from the History palette menu (2.3). Enter a name for the snapshot, and choose which layer option you want to use in the New Snapshot dialog box (2.4).

 I P

You can select a history state or snapshot as the source for the History brush and for filling with a history using the Fill command.

See the section "Painting with Previous Versions of the File with the History Brush," later in this chapter, for an example of this technique.

Creating a New File from a Snapshot or History State

History states and snapshots are not saved with an image. As soon as you close an image, any history information is eliminated. You can save copies of images as you work on them by using a snapshot or history state. This capability can be useful to compare different versions of a file.

1. In the History palette, choose the snapshot or history state that you want to save to a new file.

2. Click the Create New Document from Current State button at the bottom of the History palette **(2.6)**. A new document is created.

The original document remains open, and you can place the document created from the snapshot next to it for comparison. Keep in mind that the original document displays the current history state or snapshot, so if you are comparing, change the state of the original document.

Note that the new document begins with a fresh History palette.

2.6

Click the Create New Document from Current State button to save a new file based on the currently selected state or snapshot.

 I   P

You can duplicate any state except for the most recent by holding down (Option)[Alt] and clicking on a state. You also can duplicate snapshots as states by holding down (Option)[Alt] and clicking on a snapshot.

Working with Nonlinear History

2.7

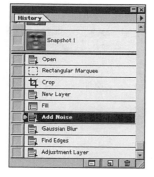

2.8

2.9

By default, Photoshop treats history in a linear fashion. When you select a history state, all subsequent states are dimmed **(2.7)**. If you make a change to the image from that state, all the subsequent states are eliminated. Each history state in the image is linked causally to those that precede it.

If you use a nonlinear history, when you choose a history state and make a change, all the subsequent states remain **(2.8)**. The new action is added to the list of history states, but you still can return to points along the other history path.

A nonlinear history can be useful when you are experimenting with procedures. You can try one procedure, return to the original state of the image, and try a different method. You then can compare the results of each procedure after each step by selecting the history states.

1. Choose History Options from the History palette menu. The History Options dialog box appears **(2.9)**.

2. Enable the Allow Non-Linear History check box.

If you previously used linear history, the history states remain. If you select a state, none of the states dim. If you make changes from a previous state, all subsequent states remain.

Painting with Previous Versions of the File with the History Brush

Using the History brush, you can paint with the effects of a filter or other image adjustment over another version of the same image. This feature gives you significant control over the area of a filter's effect (2.10). (See also C.5 in the color insert.) Use the History brush to apply the change selectively to areas of the image after undoing the change to the image by stepping backward in the History palette.

2.10

Be sure to create a merged snapshot, or the History brush paints from a layer in the snapshot to the same layer in the image.

1. In the History palette, select the source for the History brush by clicking in the box next to the snapshot or history state (2.11).

2. Choose the History brush from the toolbox. Double-click the History brush in the toolbox to set its options (2.12). You can select Impressionist to paint from the history state or snapshot with a copy of the history in an Impressionist style (2.13).

2.12

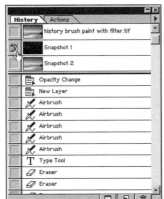

2.11

ⓣ I P

In addition to using the painting tools, you can select an area of the image and fill it with the selected history state or snapshot by choosing Edit→Fill→History.

2.13

2.14

3. Select a brush size.

4. Paint in the image. Wherever you paint, the selected history state or snapshot is applied **(2.14)**.

 I P

Painting with the History brush gives you considerable control over filters and image adjustments. Make an adjustment, create a snapshot, and then choose Undo. You then can select the snapshot as the history source and paint or fill the temporarily altered image in any blending mode or opacity.

Painting with Nonlinear History

When applying a filter, you can select specific areas in the image to be affected before applying the filter. Or, by using nonlinear history and the History brush, you can apply the filter selectively after running it.

You can use similar techniques with other filters (such as Smart Blur and Unsharp Mask) or image adjustments (such as Levels or Hue/Saturation).

This technique enables you to apply the Dust & Scratches filter by painting with the history state without destroying fine detail, such as hair or fur. The Dust & Scratches filter is useful for removing errors introduced when scanning or fixing problems with the original photograph (2.15). For more information about using the Dust & Scratches filter, see Chapter 12, "Image Adjustments and Corrections."

1. From the History palette options, choose Allow Non-Linear History.

2. Choose Filter→Noise→Dust & Scratches. In the Dust & Scratches dialog box (2.16), choose a radius and threshold that eliminate the errors in the image. You can afford to choose a large radius that begins to blur other details in the image, because you will be selectively painting with the filter (2.17).

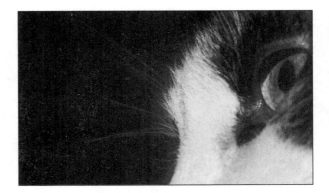

2.15

2.16

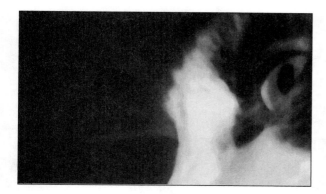

2.17

2.18

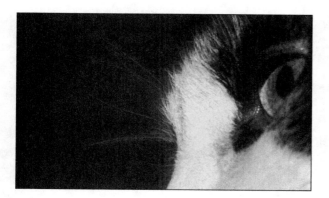

2.19

3. In the History palette, go back one step (2.18).

4. Set the source for the History brush to the Dust & Scratches state.

5. Select the History brush in the toolbox and paint in the areas to which you want to apply the Dust & Scratches filter (2.19). Because nonlinear history is enabled, painting does not eliminate the Dust & Scratches history state.

 I P

The main disadvantage of working with nonlinear history is that it is difficult to keep track of the relationships between earlier and later states. Take extra care when working with nonlinear history.

 I P

You could accomplish this same technique with linear history by creating a snapshot of the Dust & Scratches state, going back one step in the history, and using the snapshot as the source for the brush.

©HAPTER 3

In this chapter you learn how to...

Change the Size of an Image

Choose an Interpolation Method when Resampling

Choose a Resolution

Change the Resolution

Change the Canvas Size

Crop an Image

W hether you create an image for a Web page or for print, you always must be aware of the size of the image. The pixel dimensions directly relate to the size of the image file. The pixel dimensions also affect how long an image takes to download in the case of a Web page. In the case of a printed image, the pixel dimensions are determined by the appropriate print resolution. In all cases, the goal is for an image to contain just enough

RESOLUTION AND SIZE ISSUES

detail for its intended use. If an image contains too few pixels, it will look boxy when viewed in print or blurry when viewed on a Web page. If the image contains too many pixels, the image will take too long to download, and in the case of print images, the image will take up more space than necessary and take longer to print.

Closely related to the pixel dimensions of the image is the image's resolution. The resolution of an image is the number of *pixels per inch* (ppi). A 4"×5" image with a resolution of 300 dpi has pixel dimensions of 1200×1500 for a total of 1,800,000 pixels. A 4"×5" image with a resolution of 150 dpi has pixel dimensions of 600×750 for a total of 450,000 pixels. An image with half the resolution has one-fourth the number of pixels. Both images print the same size, but the printed size of the pixels differs by a factor of 4.

Your final output determines what your resolution needs to be, based on the relationship between the pixels in the image and the printed dots.

Changing the Size of an Image

You can increase or decrease the size of an image in Photoshop by adjusting the pixel dimensions or by changing the resolution (the number of pixels in each inch). Changing an image's pixel dimensions is called resampling. Increasing the number of pixels in an image is resampling *up*, whereas decreasing the number of pixels is downsampling.

Whenever you downsample an image, pixel information is discarded and cannot be recovered after the file is saved and closed.

1. Choose Image→Image Size. The Image Size dialog box appears **(3.1)**.

2. Enabling the Constrain Proportions check box scales the image equally in both directions **(3.2)**. If you want to adjust the horizontal and vertical dimensions independently, clear the Constrain Proportions check box. If the new dimensions you enter are not proportional, the resulting image is stretched **(3.3)**.

3. Make sure that the Resample Image check box is enabled if you want to change the pixel dimensions of the image.

4. Choose whether you want to use pixels or a percentage change by selecting Pixels or Percent from the Width and Height drop-down lists.

If you hold down the (Option)(Alt) key, the Cancel button changes to Reset to return the values to their original settings.

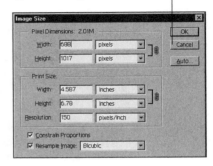

3.1

3.2

3.3

An approximated file size is displayed when resampling.

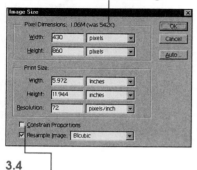

3.4

You can set the default interpolation method used when resampling by choosing File→Preferences→ General. This setting is used as both the default in the Image Size dialog box and whenever resampling occurs because of a transformation.

5. Enter the new horizontal and vertical dimensions for the image. If the Constrain Proportions check box is enabled, changing one value updates the other. When resampling, an estimate of the resulting file size appears in the Image Size dialog box (3.4).

6. Choose OK when finished or Cancel to disregard the changes.

T I P

Photoshop images are limited to either 30,000 pixels horizontally and vertically, or a file size of 2GB—whichever value is reached first.

T I P

When you change the pixel dimensions in an image, the file size changes geometrically. Decreasing the pixel dimensions by half produces a file size that is one-quarter of the original, for example. Doubling the pixel dimensions quadruples the file size.

Choosing an Interpolation Method when Resampling

Whenever you resample an image, Photoshop must fill in missing pixel data or replace groups of pixels. Photoshop uses a mathematical approximation process called inter-polation to determine the colors of pixels based on surrounding pixel information. You can choose an interpolation method based on the contents of an image **(3.5)**.

Photoshop uses one of three interpolation methods:

- **Bicubic.** The slowest and most accurate method when resampling continuous-tone images **(3.6)**. The bicubic method averages the color or gray values of 16 surrounding pixels and adds that average value to the image. It then uses a calculation-intensive algorithm to produce the smoothest tonal gradations.

- **Bilinear.** The medium method in both accuracy and speed **(3.7)**. The bilinear method averages four neighboring pixels, using a less-sophisticated algorithm than the bicubic method.

- **Nearest neighbor.** The fastest method and least accurate when resampling continuous-tone images **(3.8)**. Some noticeable jaggedness can occur. The nearest-neighbor method copies the value of one pixel and uses that value to create a pixel next to it. This method often is used when resampling artwork with crisp edges.

One pixel. The original image is 82 pixels by 82 pixels.

3.5

The original image resampled up 400 percent. Note that the gradient has been smoothed.

3.6

3.7

Four pixels. The image looks identical to the original, but each block has changed from one pixel to four after resampling.

3.8

Choosing a Resolution

Table 3.1　Common Image Resolutions

Destination	Line Screen	Scan Resolution
Web/Onscreen	N/A	72–75 ppi
Newspaper	85–150 lpi	125–300 ppi
Magazine	135–175 lpi	200–350 ppi
Art Book	150–200 lpi	225–400 ppi

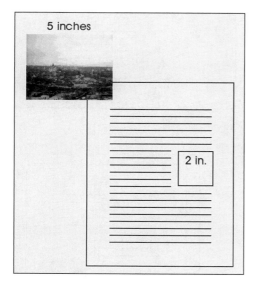

3.9　　　2÷5=0.4

If you are printing, you should determine the line screen, or lines per inch (lpi), of your output device before acquiring your image. You can determine the image resolution (ppi) by doubling the line screen. Because images intended for print can grow quite large, you can use a scale factor that is closer to 1.5 instead of 2 in many cases.

Talk to your service bureau or printer about resolution and sizing suggestions. Some images and jobs may require special techniques or specific resolutions. Table 3.1 lists some common image resolutions.

Knowing the final output resolution enables you to easily determine the scan resolution when the final output and original are the same size. If you want to change the size of a graphic in the output, however, you need to determine the size-change factor.

1. Divide the desired output width by the original width of the image **(3.9)**.

continues

ⓉＩＰ

The 1.5 screen frequency multiplication factor is based on a rounding of the square root of 2, or 1.4142. If image size is critical, you can cheat the value a little lower than 1.5 for many images. In fact, for images that contain little detail, you can use factors as low as 1.2.

Factors above 1.5 can be reserved for images with fine detail, such as hair.

Choosing a Resolution continued

2. Divide the desired output height by the original height of the image (3.10).

The larger of the two values is the size-change factor.

3. Calculate the scan resolution by using this formula (3.11):

```
scan resolution (ppi) =
line screen (lpi) × size
change factor × 2
```

Instead of 2, you can use a value between 1.5 and 2 when appropriate.

ⓣ I P

You should acquire your image at the target resolution whenever possible to avoid resampling and interpolation. It is almost always better to rescan an image than to resample up.

ⓣ I P

Using a precise screen frequency multiplication factor (that is, 1.5 to 2.0) is particularly important when storage space is an issue. Some users choose standard resolution settings (72, 150, and 300 ppi) that are sometimes larger than the 1.5 to 2.0 rule and choose the most appropriate for the image's final output, varying from these standard resolutions only when required by the print or service bureau. You also may need extra image detail (resolution), depending on what you do with the image in Photoshop (compositing, scaling, transformations, and so on).

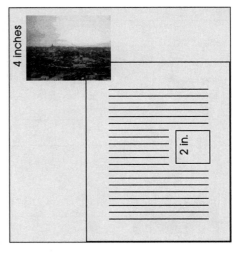

3.10   **2÷4=0.5**

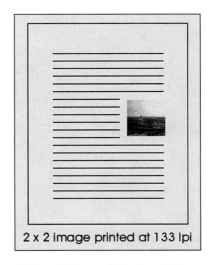

2 x 2 image printed at 133 lpi

3.11   **133 lpi × 0.5 × 2 = 133 lpi**

Changing the Resolution

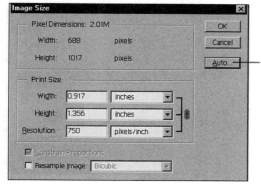

3.12

You can use the Auto button in the Image Size dialog box to calculate the appropriate print resolution (3.13).

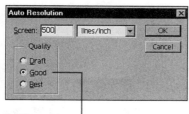

3.13

Draft quality automatically uses 72 ppi. Good quality uses 1.5 times the Screen value. Best quality doubles the Screen value.

You can change the resolution of an image by using the Image Size command. You also can choose whether to resample the image while changing the resolution.

1. Choose Image→Image Size. The Image Size dialog box appears (3.12).

2. If you want to adjust the horizontal and vertical dimensions independently, disable the Constrain Proportions check box.

3. If you do not want to resample the image, clear the Resample Image check box. Constrain Proportions is enabled automatically; the printed width, height, and resolution are constrained to one another, and the pixel dimensions cannot be changed.

4. Choose the units you want to use for the width, height, and resolution.

5. Enter the new horizontal and vertical dimensions and resolution for the image. After you change a value, the other values update automatically because they are constrained.

6. Choose OK when finished or Cancel to disregard the changes. If you press the (Option)[Alt] key, you also can choose Reset to return the values to their original settings.

Changing the Canvas Size

The canvas is the imaginary background on which the image sits. By changing the canvas size, the number of pixels in the image is altered, but the size of the existing image remains unchanged. No resampling occurs when changing the canvas size.

Changing the canvas size often is used to add additional area to an image. You can add area to one side or along the edge of the image.

1. Choose Image→Canvas Size. The Canvas Size dialog box displays the current file size, as well as the current width and height of the image (3.14).

2. Select the units you want to use to change the canvas.

3. Enter the new width and height of the canvas.

4. Select one of the nine anchor positions. The anchor position is where the current image is placed on the new canvas. Choosing the middle box centers the image and adds pixels in the background color around it.

5. Choose OK when finished or Cancel to disregard the changes. If you press the (Option)[Alt] key, you also can choose Reset to return the values to their original settings.

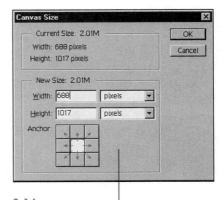

3.14

If the size of the canvas is smaller than the size of the image, Photoshop warns you that clipping will occur. If you decrease the canvas size, image data contained on layers other than the background is preserved, although it is not visible.

3.15

 I P

You can change the units used to measure the image in the Canvas Size dialog box and the units on the rulers by choosing File→Preferences→Units & Rulers.

Cropping an Image

3.16

3.17

The Crop tool provides a powerful method of adjusting the size of an image by selecting only the areas of the image you want. In addition, you can use the Crop tool to rotate the new image and resize the canvas.

1. Select the Crop tool ⬚ from the toolbar. It is under the Marquee tools.

2. Drag a rectangular area in the image (3.16) to select the area that remains after the cropping operation.

3. Resize the crop border by clicking and dragging on any of the eight handles. When dragging a handle, the border snaps to the image boundary.

4. Rotate the crop border by moving the pointer to the outside edge of the crop border and clicking and dragging anywhere outside the crop border. The cursor changes to the rotate cursor (3.17). You can adjust the pivot point of the rotation by clicking and dragging on the pivot-point symbol in the center of the image. If you rotate the border so that some of it lies outside the image, additional canvas is added filled with the background color.

continues

Cropping an Image continued

5. Move the crop border by clicking and dragging inside the crop border. The cursor changes into the move cursor.

6. After you finish changing the crop border, accept the crop by double-clicking inside the crop border or pressing Return or Enter. Cancel the crop by pressing Esc **(3.18)**.

If you have rotated your image before cropping it, Photoshop automatically rotates your cropped selection clockwise to a straight vertical and horizontal position.

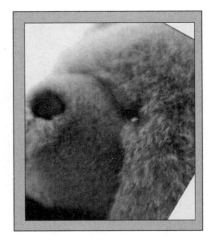

3.18

 I P

To increase the canvas size using the Crop tool, increase the size of the image window so you see the gray background around the image. Use the Crop tool to draw the new canvas size **(3.19)**. *Double-click inside the crop border when finished, and the extra space is added.*

 I P

You also can use Image→Crop to crop to a rectangular selection. To use the Crop command, your selection must be perfectly rectangular, without feathering or any selection modification.

3.19

CHAPTER 4

In this chapter you learn how to...

Convert from RGB to CMYK

Preview Out-of-Gamut Colors

Deal with Out-of-Gamut Colors

Convert to Indexed Color

Convert to Indexed Color using ImageReady

Use RGB for Text and Resampling

Use DitherBox to Control Dithering

Modify a Color Table in ImageReady

Convert to Grayscale

Convert to Duotone

Convert to Bitmap Mode

You can use a variety of image modes in Photoshop. Each mode determines how colors combine using a different process. Color modes are usually specific to particular industries and applications. Indexed Color and RGB modes are commonly seen in electronic publishing. CMYK, Duotone, Bitmap, and Multichannel are often specific to the print industry. You can easily convert between different modes by choosing Image→Mode.

IMAGE MODES

When you convert between image modes, Photoshop may require you to make decisions about how colors should be translated from one mode to the other. Even if Photoshop does not explicitly ask how to handle color changes, you should always be mindful of Photoshop's conversions process with an eye toward the final image. For example, Photoshop does not ask many questions when converting from RGB to CMYK, but this conversion is the most complex and important for anyone creating images that will be printed.

The mode of an image determines which tools and filters are available in the image, the number and names of the channels, and the number of layers allowed. Table 4.1 summarizes some of the features of each image mode.

Grayscale and RGB modes are the most versatile. Before converting to a final image mode, such as CMYK or Indexed Color, you should save a copy of the source image in the original image mode.

Table 4.1   Supported Features of Image Modes

Mode	Layers	Channels	Painting Tools	Filters	Converts From
Bitmap	Background only	One	Some (anti-aliasing unavailable)	None	Grayscale
Indexed	Background only	One	Most (anti-aliasing unavailable)	None	Grayscale
Grayscale,	Unrestricted	Unrestricted	All	Most	All
Duotone	Unrestricted	Unrestricted	All	Most	Grayscale
RGB	Unrestricted	Unrestricted	All	All	All but Bitmap
CMYK	Unrestricted	Unrestricted	All	Most	All but Bitmap
Lab	Unrestricted	Unrestricted	All	Most	All but Bitmap
Multichannel	Background only	Unrestricted (no composite)	All	Most	All but Bitmap

Converting from RGB to CMYK

When you convert from RGB mode to CMYK, Photoshop performs multiple procedures that are transparent to you **(4.1)**. The image is first converted to Lab mode using the settings you specify in RGB Setup. From Lab mode, the image is converted to CMYK using the settings in CMYK Setup. After you make the conversion, changes made to the CMYK Setup may change the appearance of the image on the screen, but they don't change the image. It is only during the conversion process that your CMYK Setup controls the image data.

 I   P

Save in Lab mode if you are sharing an image with a Photoshop 4 user. Lab mode is defined the same in Photoshop 4 and 5, so there won't be a color shift when opening the image in previous versions.

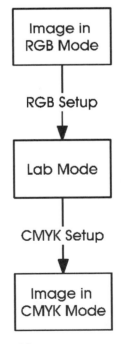

4.1

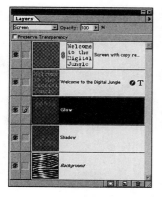

4.2

4.3

1. Choose Image→Mode→ CMYK.

2. If your image contains more than one layer, Photoshop warns you that changing from RGB to CMYK changes layer compositing (4.2). That is, blending modes produce different results in RGB and CMYK modes. Choose Flatten if you used layers with blending modes. Choose Don't Flatten if you didn't use blending modes or if the layering is more important than how the colors blend. Don't forget that layer effects use blending modes (4.3).

For more information about RGB Setup and CMYK Setup, see Chapter 18, "Achieving Consistent Color."

 I P

Before converting from RGB to CMYK, you can preview the effect of changing color models by selecting View→Preview→ CMYK. If you want to view any of the individual CMYK color channels as they would appear after conversion, choose View→Preview and then select Cyan, Magenta, Yellow, or Black. You can also choose CMY to view the combinations of cyan, magenta, and yellow without the black. When you are finished previewing the image, choose View→Preview and deselect the selected preview mode.

Previewing Out-of-Gamut Colors

Because RGB contains a greater range of colors than CMYK, when you convert from RGB to CMYK, some RGB colors may be outside of the CMYK color gamut. Such colors are said to be out-of-gamut. Photoshop determines the colors that are out-of-gamut based on your CMYK setup because different output devices can recreate different ranges of the CMYK gamut.

Many highly saturated colors in RGB cannot be accurately reproduced in CMYK.

If you choose Preview in the CMYK Setup dialog box with the Gamut Warning on, you can preview the gamuts for different devices and CMYK settings. For more information, see "Choosing a CMYK Model and Conversion Method" on page 268 in Chapter 16, "Paper Publishing."

Choose View→Gamut Warning. Photoshop replaces pixels that are out of gamut with the out-of-gamut color selected in Preferences **(4.4)**. (See also **C.1** in the color insert.)

4.4

To change the color used to show out-of-gamut colors, choose File→Preferences→ Transparency & Gamut. Click in the Gamut Warning color swatch and select a color in the Color Picker.

 I P

Save an RGB source version of the file before converting to CMYK so that you can return to it to make changes. Avoid converting between RGB and CMYK repeatedly, if possible. Some image data is lost each time you convert.

Dealing with Out-of-Gamut Colors

4.6

4.5

4.7

The Fuzziness slider is unavailable when you choose Out Of Gamut in the Color Range dialog box because the determination of whether a pixel is in or out of the CMYK gamut is controlled only indirectly by the CMYK setup and the values of the pixel.

You can either allow Photoshop to handle out-of-gamut colors based on your settings in CMYK Setup, or you can attempt to alter the colors manually before conversion depending on the image and how much control you want to have over the process and each color channel, particularly black. For more information about how Photoshop handles out-of-gamut colors, see "Choosing a CMYK Model and Conversion Method" on page 268 in Chapter 16. For more information about replacing colors, see Chapter 13, "Color Correction."

1. Choose Select→Color Range. The Color Range dialog box is displayed (**4.5**).

2. Under Select, choose Out Of Gamut. Choose OK. The out-of-gamut colors throughout the image are selected (**4.6**).

3. Choose View→Hide Edges so that it will be easier to see the color change as you adjust it (**4.7**).

continues

Dealing with Out-of-Gamut Colors continued

4. Choose View→Gamut
Warning to show the colors
that are out-of-gamut with
your gamut warning color
instead of with a selection border.

5. Choose Image→Adjust→
Hue/Saturation. The Hue/
Saturation dialog box appears
(4.8).

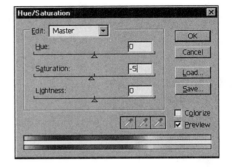

4.8

6. Drag the Saturation slider to
the left to decrease the saturation of your selection. The
Gamut Warning shrinks as you
desaturate the image **(4.9)**.
Choose OK.

You can perform the desaturation in
one step, but those colors that are
only a little out-of-gamut will be
desaturated more than necessary
because colors can be out-of-gamut
to varying degrees. To minimize the
desaturation of colors that are close
to being in the CMYK gamut, move
the slider to the left a small distance
and choose OK. Then repeat steps 1
through 5.

4.9

 I P

*You can also use the Sponge tool (with the
Toning tools in the toolbox) instead of the
Hue/Saturation command to achieve more
control as you desaturate the selected out-of-
gamut colors. Double-click the Sponge tool
to display the Sponge Options palette and
select Desaturate.*

Dealing with Out-of-Gamut Colors with Masks

4.10

4.11

4.12

When selecting out-of-gamut colors, turn on the Gamut Warning to make it easier to see them.

Another way to remove out-of-gamut colors is to save a selection that contains only the out-of-gamut colors and isolate these colors using a layer mask. This technique requires more manipulation of specific areas in the image but also provides additional control. This technique assumes that your image contains only one layer, although it could be repeated for multiple layers.

1. Choose Select→Color Range. The Color Range dialog box appears.

2. Under Select, choose Out Of Gamut **(4.10)**. Choose OK. The out-of-gamut colors throughout the image are selected.

3. Choose Select→Save Selection. This creates an alpha channel that contains all the out-of-gamut colors.

4. Deselect by choosing Select→Deselect.

5. In the Channels palette, select the new alpha channel that you created by clicking its thumbnail **(4.11)**.

6. Choose Filter→Blur→Gaussian Blur **(4.12)**. Choose an amount of blur appropriate to the image size. The blur eases the transition between the colors that are in- and out-of-gamut.

continues

Dealing with Out-of-Gamut Colors with Masks continued

7. In the Layers palette, choose the Background layer and duplicate it. Choose the new layer.

8. Load the blurred out-of-gamut colors as a selection by choosing Select→Load Selection. Choose the alpha channel that you saved and applied the blur to.

4.13

9. Choose Layer→Add Layer Mask→Reveal Selection. Only the out-of-gamut colors are shown on this layer because of the layer mask **(4.13)**.

   When you paint or desaturate on this layer, you change only the out-of-gamut colors.

10. Make sure that the layer, and not the layer mask, is selected. Use the Sponge tool and set to desaturate or any of the other image adjustment tools, such as Hue/Saturation or Levels **(4.14)**.

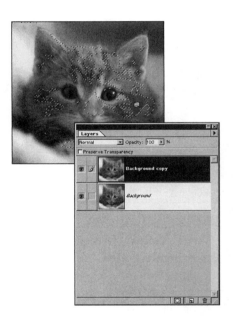

4.14

 I P

Choose View→Gamut Warning to display the out-of-gamut colors and make it easier to see your changes.

Converting to Indexed Color

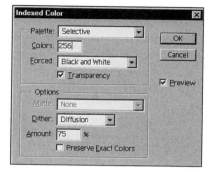

4.16

4.17

When you convert to Indexed Color mode from RGB, Photoshop reduces the number of colors used in the image from a possible 16.7 million to, at most, 256. An image in Indexed Color mode stores its colors in a Color LookUp Table (CLUT) or color table. When you convert from RGB to Indexed Color, you can choose a color table and how RGB colors should be converted to match colors available from the color table.

Although Indexed Color mode is used extensively for the Web, it is also used by interface designers to match the Color palettes available on an operating system; game developers who must use decreased color depths and customized palettes to work with specialized game engines; and professionals in the scientific and industrial imaging fields.

1. Choose Image→Mode→ Indexed Color. If the image contains more than one layer, Photoshop asks if you want to flatten them because Indexed Color images support only one layer. Choose OK. The Indexed Color dialog box appears **(4.16)**.

2. Under Palette, select the color palette that you want to use when converting the image **(4.17)**. See Table 4.2 for options.

continues

Converting to Indexed Color continued

Table 4.2   Indexed Color Palettes

Palette	Description
Exact	Available if your image contains 256 colors or fewer. Especially useful if your image contains large areas of Web-safe colors
Macintosh System	Uses the Mac OS Color palette.
Windows System	Uses the Windows 256 Color palette.
Web	Uses the 216 colors common to both the Windows and Macintosh System palettes.
Perceptual	Derives the color table from the image, favoring colors to which the human eye is sensitive. This palette produces the greatest similarity between the original and converted image.
Selective	Derives the color table from the image, favoring Web-safe colors that appear most often.
Adaptive	Derives the color table from the image based on the colors that appear most often.
Custom	Use Custom to create your own color table or to load a saved color table.

If you choose Custom, the Color Table dialog box appears (4.18). Under Table, select a color table to use as a starting point. Click the individual colors or click and drag through a range of colors to choose new colors from the color picker. Choose Load to load a saved color table.

3. Under Colors, enter the number of colors in the indexed color image. If you chose a Color Table with a fixed set of colors, the number of colors that will be used during the conversion is displayed and cannot be changed.

4. If you specified an Adaptive, Perceptual, or Selective color table, under Forced choose a set of colors that you want to

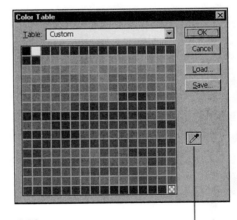

4.18

To specify a color for transparency in the indexed color image, use the eyedropper to select a color swatch.

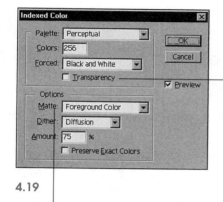

4.19

You can only select a Matte option if the image contains areas of transpar-ency. Select Transparency and choose a Matte color that matches the background that the image will be placed on top of to help blend the image into the background.

If Transparency is turned off, areas of transparency in the original image are filled with the background color. Not all the color tables support transparency. In particular, the Windows and Macintosh System palettes replace areas of transparency with white by default. You can select a Matte color to use instead of white.

be forced or select Custom to specify your own. Forced colors are colors that are included in the color table, whether or not they would naturally occur in the color table.

5. Select Transparency to allow transparency in the Indexed Color image (4.19).

6. Under Matte, select a color to replace areas of transparency in the original image and to use as a replacement for partially transparent pixels in the image.

continues

T I **P**

Because images in Indexed Color mode do not support multiple layers and because image information is discarded when converting to Indexed Color mode, save a master version of the file in RGB mode so that you can return to it if you want to make changes.

You can convert to Indexed Color mode when exporting to GIF89a format, preserving the RGB data and layer information. You can export individual layers as separate GIFs by changing the layer visibility because only visible layers are exported.

You can also use ImageReady to make optimization decisions and save the file from ImageReady before returning to Photoshop.

Converting to Indexed Color continued

7. Under Dither, select a dithering method (see Table 4.3). Dithering replaces colors that are not in the color table with groups of pixels that are. The four types of dithering are shown here **(4.20)**.

If you use a Diffusion dither, you can also select Preserve Exact Colors. Colors from the image that are already in the color table you specify are preserved and not dithered. This is useful to maintain linework and when using specific color tables, such as the Web palette.

8. Choose OK.

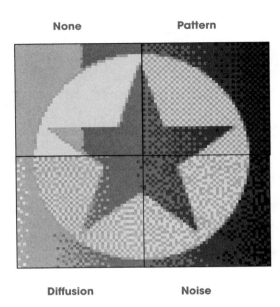

None   **Pattern**

Diffusion   **Noise**

4.20

N O T E

Some color table choices, in particular Selective and Adaptive, can produce images with colors that some browsers are not capable of displaying. You should check your images in all browsers and browser versions that may be used to view your images.

T I P

You can load and save custom color tables. Custom color tables are useful when converting a series of images to indexed color, such as for an animation. You can also use a custom color table to establish a set of colors that can be used throughout a Web site or organization.

Table 4.3   Indexed Dithering Methods

Dither Option	Description
None	Prevents dithering. Distinctions between regions of color are evident and some banding is likely.
Pattern	Uses a square pattern (similar to halftones).
Diffusion	Uses an error diffusion method. Less structured than Pattern, but more structured than Noise.
	Specifies an amount for the dither. Choose 1 to use very little dither. Choose 100 to use the maximum diffusion to reduce banding and retain detail by simulating more colors.
Noise	Uses random noise to generate the maximum dithering effect throughout the image.

Converting to Indexed Color Using ImageReady

4.21

To display and compare how a file appears in a browser or in different operating systems, click a view in 2-Up or 4-Up mode and choose View→Preview. Then select the preview option that you want. It is useful to display the Macintosh and Windows versions together to monitor how the image displays in each platform. Typically, images on Windows systems appear darker because of different Gamma settings.

To base optimization settings on a target file size, choose Optimize to File Size from the fly-out menu.

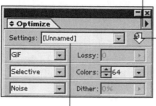

You can also select a preset optimization method, either one of the many that come with ImageReady or one you save yourself.

4.22

You can save your optimization settings in ImageReady by choosing Save Settings from the Optimize palette. If you want to apply the settings to a group of files or include the settings in an action, create a Droplet by clicking the Create Droplet icon in the Optimize palette.

Whenever you optimize an image for the Web, you make a trade-off between image quality and image size. ImageReady enables you to view multiple copies of an image with different optimization settings so that you can compare them and choose the most appropriate level of optimization.

You can also use the Save for Web command directly from Photoshop. The procedure is similar to that outlined here for ImageReady. For more information about saving for the Web, see Chapter 17, "Electronic Publishing."

1. From Photoshop, choose File→Jump To→Adobe ImageReady 2.0. The image is displayed in ImageReady.

2. Choose the 2-Up or 4-Up tab to display multiple versions of the same file with different optimization settings (4.21).

3. Choose Window→Show Optimize to display the Optimize palette (4.22).

4. Select a view in the 2-Up or 4-Up display. The Optimize palette reflects the settings for the selected view. In the Optimize palette, change the file type to either GIF or PNG-8 (both Indexed Color formats). If you select GIF, choose a setting for Lossy

continues

Converting to Indexed Color Using ImageReady continued

compression. The setting for Lossy compression determines how much data can be discarded, decreasing file size. Choose a Lossy compression value that does not noticeably reduce image quality. If you select PNG-8, select Interlace to interlace the image.

5. In the Optimize palette, choose a color palette from the drop-down list to the left of the field that contains the number of colors. (See Table 4.4)

6. In the Optimize palette, choose the number of colors that you want to use. You can select one of the standard presets or enter a custom value between 2 and 256.

7. In the Optimize palette, choose a dithering method (see Table 4.5).

8. Select a different view and Repeat Steps 4 through 7 if you want to compare different optimization settings so that you can select the best image. You can also compare approximate file sizes and download times, displayed under each view in the 2-Up or 4-Up display.

9. Choose File→Save As Optimized. Enter a filename and choose Save.

Note that when you return to Photoshop, the original file is maintained.

Table 4.4   ImageReady Color Palettes

Palette	Description
Macintosh System	Uses the Mac OS Color palette
Windows System	Uses the Windows 256 Color palette
Web	Uses the 216 colors common to both the Windows and Macintosh System palettes
Perceptual	Derives the color table from the image, favoring colors to which the human eye is sensitive. This palette produces the greatest similarity between the original and converted image.
Selective	Derives the color table from the image, favoring Web-safe colors and areas of continuous color.
Adaptive	Derives the color table from the image based on the colors that appear most often.

Table 4.5   ImageReady Dithering Options

Dither Option	Description
No Dither	Prevents dithering. Distinctions between regions of color are evident and some banding is likely.
Pattern	Uses a square pattern (similar to halftones).
Diffusion	Uses an error diffusion method. Less structured than Pattern, but more structured than Noise.
	Specifies an amount for the dither. Choose 1 to use very little dither. Choose 100 to use the maximum diffusion to reduce banding and retain detail by simulating more colors.
Noise	Uses random noise to generate the maximum dithering effect throughout the image. Creates the largest file sizes.

Using RGB Instead of Indexed Color for Text and Resampling

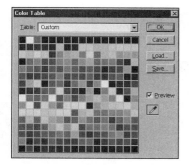

4.23

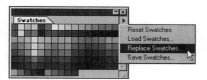

4.24

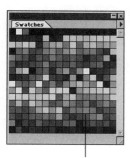

4.25   **Because the swatches are derived from the color table of the indexed color image, if you set the foreground color by picking one of the swatches, the default color will be one of the indexed colors. If you need to use the identical palette when converting to Indexed Color mode, clear the Anti-Aliased check box in the Type tool dialog box and do not convert to RGB before resampling.**

It is often useful to work in RGB mode instead of Indexed Color mode because of the additional layer functionality, especially type layers. Also, you gain better control of the use of intermediate colors in RGB mode because Photoshop is not restricted to a fixed color palette. When adding type, for example, you can control the anti-aliasing. When interpolating, Photoshop can choose from the widest range of colors during resampling.

If you open an image in Indexed Color mode (usually a GIF), you can convert the image to RGB and use only those colors found in the Indexed Color image's color table.

1. Select Image→Mode→Color.

2. In the Color Table dialog box, choose Save (**4.23**). In the Save dialog box, type a name for the saved color table and choose OK.

3. In the Color Table dialog box, choose Cancel.

4. Convert to RGB mode using Image→Mode→RGB.

5. In the Swatches palette, choose Replace Swatches from the Swatches palette menu (**4.24**).

6. In the Replace dialog box, set the Listed File Types to color tables instead of color swatches. Select the saved color table and choose Load (**4.25**).

5.5 Using DitherBox to Control Dithering

When you convert from RGB to Indexed Color mode, you specify a dithering option. You can gain even greater control over how an image dithers by using the DitherBox™ filter.

If you want to expand the size of the dithering pattern, choose a larger grid size.

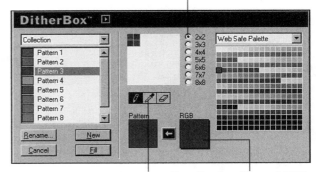

1. Select the area that you want to dither. Using Select→Color Range is useful because DitherBox affects only one RGB value at a time. Choose OK when finished.

2. Choose the Eyedropper tool from the toolbox and select the color in the image that you want to dither. The DitherBox filter uses the foreground color as the basis for the dither.

3. Choose Filter→Other→ DitherBox. The DitherBox dialog box appears (**4.26**).

4. By default, the RGB value that is dithered is based on the current foreground color. You can change the RGB value by clicking the RGB color swatch and choosing a different value in the Color Picker.

5. By default, DitherBox uses the Web Safe palette from which to choose dithering colors. To pick a different palette, choose Load Color Table and select a saved color table (**4.27**).

Use the eyedropper to select a color from the color table. Use the pencil and eraser to edit the pattern in the grid.

To select a different RGB value to dither, click the color swatch and choose a color in the picker.

4.26

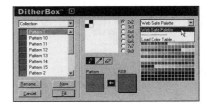

4.27

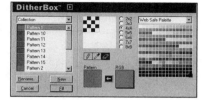

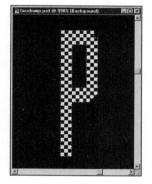

4.28

4.29

6. Click the arrow between the RGB swatch and the Pattern Swatch to select the best 2×2 dither option from the selected color table. The pattern is displayed in the grid **(4.28)** and a named pattern is added to the collection. If you want to use an existing pattern, select it from the pattern collection.

7. When finished, choose Fill to fill the selected area with the dither pattern you created **(4.29)**.

(T) I P

You can create different collections of dither patterns for use in the DitherBox filter. Choose New to save the current collection and start a new collection.

Collections can be used like custom color tables or swatches. You can use DitherBox patterns to simulate flat colors throughout an image (for an image background, for example), or to provide consistency and pre-dictability when converting specific logo colors.

Modifying a Color Table in ImageReady

When you display an optimized image in ImageReady, the Color Table palette displays the color table used for the image. You can edit a color table after you have converted an image to Indexed Color mode by choosing Image→Mode→Color Table and then clicking Save. You can also edit a color table that is created during ImageReady's optimization process or edit a color table that you had previously saved from Photoshop.

1. From Photoshop, choose File→Jump To→Adobe ImageReady 2.0. The current image is displayed in ImageReady.

2. Choose Window→Show Color Table. The Color Table palette appears (4.30). The color table shown is based on the optimization settings for the current view. Different views on the 2-Up or 4-Up tabs may have different color tables. Any changes you make to a color table are reflected in the view that uses the color table.

Web-safe colors are displayed with white diamonds in the color swatch.

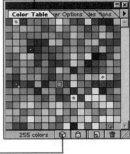

To snap a color to its nearest Web-safe color, click the Snap Selected Colors to Web Palette icon.

4.30

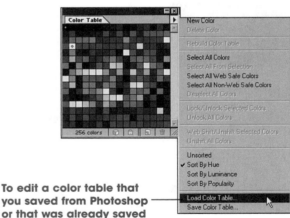

To edit a color table that you saved from Photoshop or that was already saved on your disk, choose Load Color Table from the Color Table palette menu. Select the color table that you want to use and click Open.

4.31

T I P

If an image requires dithering, such as for gradients, or anti-aliasing, such as for smooth text, it might be best to export the image as a JPEG since GIF compression produces larger files in those cases.

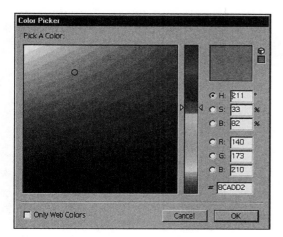

4.32

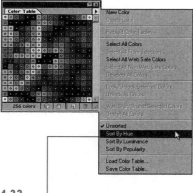

4.33

When using the Color Table palette in ImageReady, you can sort the color swatches by Hue, Luminance, or Popularity. Choose a sort option from the Color Table palette menu. You can load application- and browser-specific formats from color table files, from swatch files, or directly from GIF files.

3. To change a color, double-click a swatch. ImageReady displays its Color Picker (4.32). Choose a new color. To force the new color to be a Web-safe color, select Only Web Colors.

4. Choose OK. The modified color is displayed with a black diamond indicating that it has been shifted. The color is also automatically locked, preventing it from being dropped from the color table. Locked colors are displayed with small white squares in the lower-right corner of the swatch.

5. To clear a shift from a specific color, select the color and choose Unshift Selected Color from the Color Table palette menu (4.33). To clear the shift from all colors, choose Unshift All Colors from the Color Table palette menu.

6. To unlock a color, select the color and choose the Lock/Unlock button.

7. To save the color table for use with Photoshop's GIF89a Export filter or as a custom color table when converting to Indexed Color mode, choose Save Color Table in the Color Table palette menu. In the Save As dialog box, enter a name for the color table and choose Save.

Converting to Grayscale

When you convert from RGB to Grayscale, Photoshop generates the grayscale information by combining the red, green, and blue channels in a 30%, 59%, and 11% mixture. You can determine your own combination of any two of the red, green, and blue channels using the Calculations command. The red channel often contains most of the contrast in the image and the green channel contains much of the detail.

1. Choose Image→Calculations (4.34).

2. Under Source 1, select the Green channel. For Layer, select Background, or if the image contains more than one layer, select Merged.

3. Under Source 2, select the Red channel. For Layer, select Background, or if the image contains more than one layer, select Merged.

4. Set the blending to Normal.

5. The Opacity value determines the percentage of the Source 1 channel that is used. If you specify 80%, for example, the resulting image uses 80% of the information from the green channel and 20% from the red.

6. For Result, choose New Document to save the grayscale conversion as a new file and choose OK.

Turn on the Preview option to display a preview of the results.

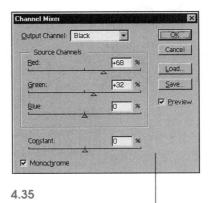

4.34

You can also experiment with different blending modes, for example, Multiply and Screen, to combine the channel information in the Calculations dialog box.

4.35

You can also use Image→ Adjust→Channel Mixer to customize the amount that the red, green, and blue channels contribute to a grayscale image. Choose Monochrome in the Channel Mixer dialog box.

Converting to Duotone

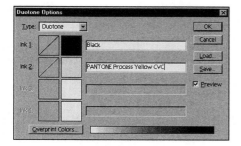

4.36

A duotone is a printing technique using two colored inks in place of tinted grays. In Photoshop, Duotone mode encompasses monotones (one ink), duotones, tritones (three inks), and quadtones (four inks). Each additional ink adds dynamic range to the printed image. When you convert to Duotone, Photoshop uses only one channel to manage the colors. The distribution of the different colors is determined by Duotone Curves.

When you choose colors for a duotone, you usually choose a spot color in addition to black, but you are not limited to these choices. For more information about using spot colors in Photoshop, see "Creating Spot Color Channels" on page 272 in Chapter 16.

1. To convert to Duotone mode, the image must first be in Grayscale mode. If the image is in a mode other than Grayscale, choose Image→Mode→ Grayscale. If your image contains more than one layer, when converting to Grayscale, Photoshop asks if you want to flatten the layers. You should only need to flatten if you have used layer blending modes other than Normal.

2. Choose Image→Mode→ Duotone. The Duotone Options dialog box appears **(4.36)**.

continues

Converting to Duotone continued

3. Choose the Type of Photoshop duotone you want to create.

4. Change a colored ink by clicking the swatch next to the color name. The Custom Colors dialog box appears (4.37).

5. Select an ink manufacturer from the Book drop-down list.

6. Choose a color swatch. You can quickly access a color by typing in its number. Click OK.

7. Change the distribution of an ink over an image (from white to black) by clicking the duotone curve (in the Duotone Options dialog box). The Duotone Curve dialog box appears (4.38). Make the changes and choose OK.

   See C.2, C.3, and C.4 in the color insert for examples of duotones and their curves.

8. When finished, choose OK.

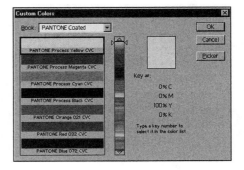

4.37

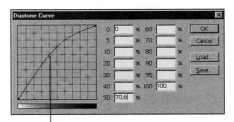

4.38 **Change the curve by clicking and dragging in the curve area or by entering values for the incremental distribution. Control points are added each time you click. To delete control points, click and drag them out of the grid.**

 I P

Photoshop does not display the separate color separations in the channels while in Duotone mode, but you can view the separations by choosing Image→Mode→ Multichannel. Photoshop displays the spot color channels in the Channels palette. If you save as Multichannel, the duotone curve information is lost, so convert a copy of the duotone image.

Converting to Bitmap Mode

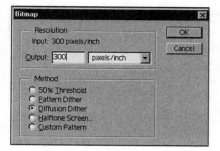

4.39

50% threshold   Pattern dither

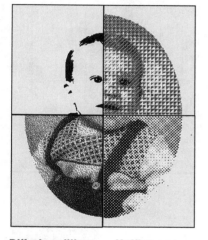

Diffusion dither   Halftone screen

4.40

Bitmap mode contains only two colors: black and white. Photoshop enables you to control how the image is converted to Bitmap mode. Bitmap mode is useful for some special effects and black-and-white printing.

1. You can convert to Bitmap mode only from Grayscale. If your image is in another mode, choose Image→Mode→ Grayscale. All color information is discarded.

2. Choose Image→Mode→ Bitmap. Images in Bitmap mode can contain only one layer, so Photoshop confirms that you want to flatten the layers before converting. The Bitmap dialog box appears (4.39).

3. Choose a resolution. You should choose a resolution that is the same as the final output device. For example, for a 1,200 dpi imagesetter, choose 1,200 ppi, although in reality there is little discernable in-crease in quality after 800 dpi.

4. Under Method, choose the type of dither that you want to use. The first four methods are shown in 4.40.

   Use 50% Threshold to convert all grays lighter than 50% to white and darker than 50% to black. This creates a high-contrast version of the image.

continues

Converting to Bitmap Mode continued

Use Pattern dither to replace gray values with geometric patterns of black and white pixels.

Use Diffusion dither to replace gray values with black and white pixels in a diffusion pattern. The Diffusion dither is less regular than the Pattern dither.

Use Halftone Screen to specify screening options to produce a halftone pattern. When you choose OK, the Halftone Screen dialog box appears **(4.41)**. Choose a frequency, an angle, and a halftone dot shape. Use values appropriate for your output. Check with your printer or service bureau if you aren't sure what values to use.

4.41

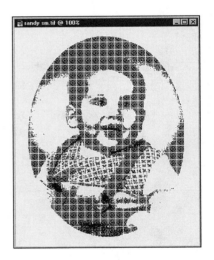

4.42

Use Custom Pattern to replace gray values with a regular pattern **(4.42)**. To use Custom Pattern, you must first select an area and then choose Edit→Define Pattern **(4.43)**.

5. Choose OK.

 I P

You can change the values in an image to black and white using the Image→Adjust→ Threshold command. Threshold is similar to using the 50% Threshold option when converting to Bitmap mode, but you can choose the point at which white changes to black.

4.43

©HAPTER 5

In this chapter you learn how to...

Constrain Selection Sizes

Add, Subtract, and Select Overlapping Areas

Make Color-Based Selections

Make a Selection Based on Contrasting Areas

Transform a Selection Boundary

Expand and Contract a Selection

Make a Border Around a Selection

Fade a Selection

Save and Load Selections

Use Channels to Make Selections

Create a Mask for Objects Without Clearly Defined Edges

Creating a selection is the foundation for most Photoshop processes. The ability to select precisely and efficiently is paramount. An understanding of the various selection tools, commands, and procedures unlocks the power and potential of Photoshop.

When you create a selection, its border is displayed with a dynamic dashed line or "marching ants." Although you can only select whole pixels in Photoshop, the pixels can be selected

SELECTING

at any one of 256 levels. The selection border contains all the pixels that are selected more than 50%. It is possible to make a selection that does not have a selection border if none of the pixels are more than 50% selected. Photoshop warns you if this occurs.

The standard selection tools in ImageReady are identical and work the same as those in Photoshop, though ImageReady also lacks the Magnetic Lasso tool and some of Photoshop's other selection commands. If you want to create a selection using one of these tools or commands, switch to Photoshop and save the selection.

Photoshop 5.5 adds the Extract command. Although not strictly a selection tool (it is located under the Image menu), it is used to isolate foreground objects, particularly those containing hair and other fine detail. The process replaced by the Extract command is usually accomplished through careful and sometimes tedious selection.

Although the creation of selections can often be time-consuming, in general, Photoshop continues to improve and enhance the tools you have available for making complex selections.

Constraining Selection Sizes

When you create a selection, you can constrain the selection to an exact size or define a relationship between the horizontal and vertical sizes. You can use a constrained aspect ratio for any of the marquee tools, including the Elliptical Marquee (to create circles or precisely proportioned ovals) and ImageReady's Rounded Rectangle Marquee.

1. Double-click any of the marquee tools. The Marquee Options palette appears (5.1).

2. In the Marquee Options palette,

   • To set a fixed size for the marquee, select Fixed Size in the Style drop-down list. Enter a horizontal and vertical size.

   • To set a fixed aspect ratio for the marquee, select Fixed Aspect Ratio in the Style drop-down list. Enter a relationship between the width and height.

   • To return the marquee to the normal mode, select Normal in the Style drop-down list (5.2).

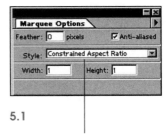

5.1

Constrained aspect ratio is useful when copying and pasting or when cropping an image. Some examples of useful proportions include 8.5 × 11 or other standard page sizes and 640 × 480 or other standard screen resolutions.

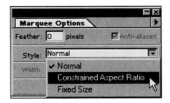

5.2

5.3

3. If you selected Fixed Size, click in the image. The point you pick is used as the upper-left corner of the marquee.

4. If you selected Constrained Aspect Ratio, click and drag in the image. The proportions between the width and height are constrained as you drag (5.3). Hold down (Option)[Alt] as you drag from the center of the marquee.

 I P

When creating buttons, use a fixed size marquee to make all the buttons the same size. You can fill an area with a color on a layer and then apply a layer effect.

Adding, Subtracting, and Selecting Overlapping Areas

After you create a selection, you can add or subtract groups of pixels. You can also create a selection set that includes only overlapping pixels from a current selection and a new selection that you create.

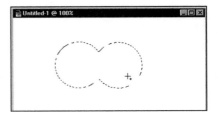

5.4

- To add to a selection hold down Shift while using any of the selection tools **(5.4)**.

- To subtract from a selection, hold down (Option)[Alt] while using any of the selection tools **(5.5)**.

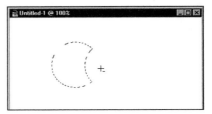

5.5

- To select overlapping areas of a new selection and an existing selection, hold down (Shift-Option)[Shift+Alt] while using any of the selection tools **(5.6)**.

5.6

To constrain a marquee to a circle or square or to select from the center while adding, subtracting, or intersecting, hold down the keys to add, subtract, or intersect and begin the selection. While holding down the mouse button, release the keys and press the keys to constrain or select from center.

Making a Color-Based Selection with the Magic Wand Tool

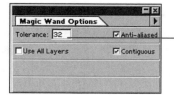

5.7

The Tolerance value set in the Magic Wand Options palette is also used for the Grow and similar commands.

5.8

One of the most useful selection tools is the Magic Wand. It enables you to select a contiguous area that contains similar colors based on a range that you set. You can add or subtract from a selection using the Magic Wand by holding down (Shift and Option)[Shift and Alt], respectively.

1. Double-click the Magic Wand tool to display the Magic Wand Options palette (**5.7**).

2. Choose a Tolerance value, from 1 to 255. The Tolerance value determines the range of colors that Photoshop adds to the selection based on the first pixel that you choose. Smaller values select a smaller range of colors. Larger values select a larger range of colors.

3. Click in the image in an area that contains the color you want to select. A contiguous area is selected (**5.8**).

(T) I P

If you want to select all similar colors in an image, regardless of whether they form a contiguous region, clear the Contiguous option in the Magic Wand Options palette.

Making a Selection Based on Contrasting Areas

If the colors in an image are dissimilar so that the Magic Wand produces unacceptable results, you can use the Magnetic Lasso if there is sufficient contrast along the edge of the selection. The Magnetic Lasso tool lays down fastening points along the contrasting edge as you drag the cursor. After a fastening point is placed, that part of the selection boundary is finalized (although you can delete the most recently added fastening point).

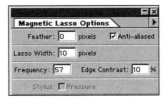

5.9

1. Double-click the Magnetic Lasso tool [image] to display the Magnetic Lasso Options palette (5.9).

2. In the Magnetic Lasso Options palette, enter a value for Feather to fade the selection with the surrounding areas. Values range from 0 to 250 pixels. Setting the Feather value to 0 turns feathering off.

Smaller lasso values mean that you need to select the edge closely.

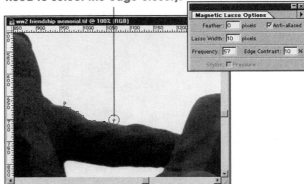

5.10

3. Enter a Lasso Width. The lasso width is the area around the cursor's position (5.10, 5.11) in which Photoshop looks for an edge. The values range from 1 to 40 pixels.

Larger lasso values enable you to be looser in your selection, but may introduce errors.

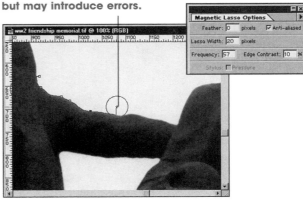

4. Enter a value for the Frequency to determine how quickly fastening points are placed along edges, or how quickly the selection path is finalized. Values range from 0 to 100.

5.11

Higher frequency values place fastening points faster, creating shorter segments.

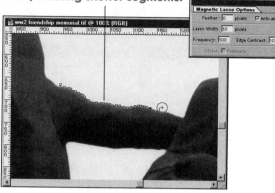

5.12

Choose a lower frequency value to create longer segments.

5.13

5.14

5. Enter a value for the Edge Contrast. The Edge Contrast determines the sensitivity of the Magnetic Lasso tool when finding edges. Values range from 0% to 100% **(5.12, 5.13)**. Higher values require higher contrast between the edges.

6. In the image, click and drag over the edge that you want to trace **(5.14)**. Click to manually insert a fastening point. Press Delete to remove the most recently added fastening point. To switch to the Lasso tool, hold down (Option)[Alt] as you drag with the mouse button depressed. Hold down (Option)[Alt] and pick points to access the Polygon Lasso tool.

7. When finished, double-click to close the selection with a magnetic lasso segment. Hold down (Option)[Alt] and double-click to close the selection with a straight-line segment. If you complete a closed selection circuit, the cursor changes 🔲 and you can close by clicking the start point.

Making a Color-Based Selection with the Color Range Command

Like the Magic Wand tool, the Color Range command makes a selection based on color. The selection is based on the pixels that you select and the fuzziness setting in the Color Range dialog box.

1. Choose Select→Color Range. The Color Range dialog box appears (5.15).

2. In the Select drop-down list, choose the types of colors that you want to select. By default, Color Range uses the sampled colors that you choose in the preview window.

3. Select a color to use as the basis for selection by clicking either in the preview or in the image with the Eyedropper. To add colors to be used for the basis of the selection, use the Add Eyedropper. To subtract color, use the Subtract Eyedropper. If the window in the Color Range dialog box is set to Preview, a preview of the selection is displayed (5.16). Areas shown in white will be selected. Areas shown in black will not be selected. Areas shown in gray are partially selected.

You can save color ranges for use with other images by choosing Save. Choose Load dialog box to retrieve the settings.

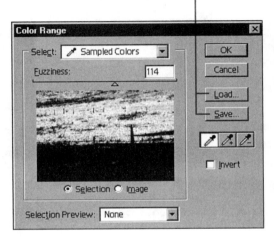

5.15

Add Eyedropper

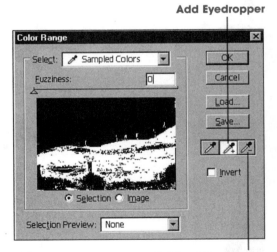

5.16

Subtract Eyedropper

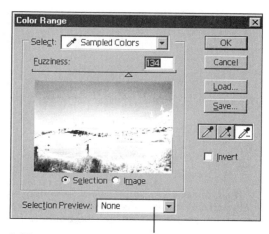

5.17

You can use the entire image window as a preview of the selection, instead of just the window in the Color Range dialog box, by selecting an option under Selection Preview in the Color Range dialog box.

4. To control the range of colors chosen beyond those selected with the eyedropper, adjust the Fuzziness. Values for Fuzziness range from 0 to 200. Similar to Tolerance used for the Magic Wand tool, smaller Fuzziness values select a smaller range of colors. If you set the Fuzziness to 0, only the colors you select with the eye-dropper are selected. Larger values select larger ranges of color (5.17).

5. When finished, choose OK (5.18).

5.18

Color Range works particularly well when combined with other selection tools. For example, you can start with a rectangular selection and use Color Range to select only specified colors within the selection boundary.

You can also combine multiple uses of the Color Range command. For example, you could select all the out-of-gamut colors in an image with Color Range. With that selection active, you could run Color Range again and select all the reds that are out-of-gamut.

Transforming a Selection Boundary

You can transform a selection boundary without altering the selected pixels.

1. With a selection active, choose Select→Transform Selection. A rectangle with handles is placed around the selection (5.19).

2. Drag a color handle to scale the selection boundary. Drag the top, bottom, or side handles to stretch.

3. To rotate the selection, move the cursor to an edge of the rectangle until the cursor changes . When the cursor changes, click and drag.

4. Double-click inside the selection boundary to complete the transformation (5.20) or press Esc to cancel.

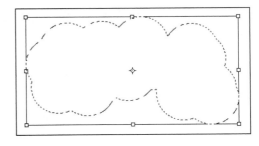

5.19

To move a selection boundary, a Selection tool must be active. If the Move tool is active, the selected area, not the boundary, is moved. Click inside the selection boundary and drag to move the selection.

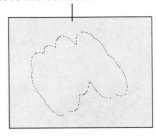

5.20

(T) I P

When you create a selection, you can increase the range of selected colors.

- *To select all the pixels in the image that match the color of the current selection, choose Select→Similar.*

- *To select similarly colored pixels adjacent to the current selection, choose Select→Grow.*

Note that both the Similar and Grow commands base the range of colors on the Tolerance setting in the Magic Wand Options palette.

Expanding and Contracting a Selection

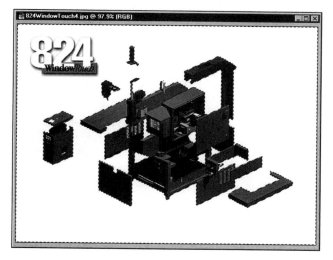

5.21

5.22

You can offset and inset selection boundaries to increase and decrease their size.

1. Create a selection.

2. To increase the size of a selection boundary, choose Select→Modify→Expand.

To decrease the size of a selection boundary, choose Select→Modify→Contract.

3. In the Expand Selection dialog box **(5.21)** or Contract Selection dialog box, enter a value from 1 to 16. If the selection has square corners, they are smoothed when the selection is expanded.

4. Choose OK.

 I P

It is sometimes easier to select a background by selecting an object in an image's foreground and inverting the selection by choosing Select→Inverse. Similarly, it is sometimes easier to select a foreground image by starting with the background **(5.22)**.

The keyboard shortcut to invert a selection is (Shift-Command-I) [Shift+Ctrl+I]. Note that the shortcut to invert the image (making a black-and-white negative out of a black-and-white positive, for example) is (Command-I)[Ctrl+I].

Making a Border Around a Selection

You can create a smoothed and feathered border around a selection by choosing Select→Modify→Border and entering the border width. The resulting selection is useful for halo or glow effects by selecting an object and then creating a border out of the selection.

To create a border around a selection with crisp edges, you can combine the Contract command and a saved selection.

1. Create the outer limits of the border using any selection technique **(5.23)**.

2. Choose Select→Save Selection. The Save Selection dialog box appears **(5.24)**.

3. In the Save Selection dialog box, enter a name for the selection in the Name text box. Choose OK.

4. Choose Select→Modify→ Contract. In the Contract Selection dialog box, enter the width of the border.

5. Choose Select→Inverse.

6. Choose Select→Load Selection. The Load Selection dialog box appears **(5.25)**.

5.23

5.24

5.25

5.26

7. In the Channel drop-down list, choose the selection that you saved in step 3. In the Operation area, choose Intersect with Selection. Choose OK. A crisp border is inset from the original selection (5.26).

5.27

5.28

 I P

If you create a selection that has irregular and jagged edges (5.27), you can use the Smooth command to eliminate the roughness. In particular, when you create color-based selections, small groups of pixels may remain unselected in the middle of a larger selection. The Smooth command eliminates these small pockets of unselected pixels and smoothes the outer edges of the selection (5.28).

Fading a Selection

You can fade the edges of a selection after it is created. For the Marquee and Lasso Selection tools, you can also fade the edges of the selection as it is being created by setting a feather value in the appropriate Options palette. Feathering a selection is useful to create a smooth transition between the selected area and the unselected area. It can be used for shadows, glows, or whenever you want to blend a selection more than the one or two pixels provided by anti-aliasing.

1. With an existing selection **(5.29)**, choose Select→Feather. The Feather Selection dialog box appears **(5.30)**.

2. In the Feather Selection dialog box, enter a value between 0.2 and 250 pixels and choose OK.

   The selection fades by the specified amount **(5.31)**.

 I P

You can use Grow as a replacement for the Magic Wand tool by making an initial selection with any Selection tool and then choosing Select→Grow.

 I P

You can hide a selection border by choosing View→Hide Edges or by pressing (Command-H)[Ctrl+H]. The selection remains active even though the selection border is hidden.

Black-and-white selection channels shown for clarity

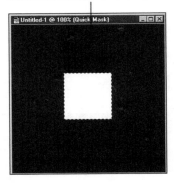

5.29

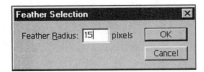

5.30

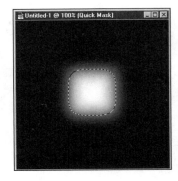

5.31

Saving a Selection

5.32

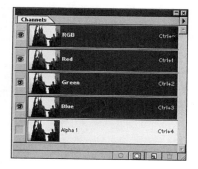

5.33

After you have created a selection, you can save it with the file so that it can be reused. You can also use a saved selection in other open images. Selections are saved as alpha channels. For more information about using alpha channels, see Chapter 11, "Using Channels and Masks."

1. With the selection currently made, choose Select→Save Selection. The Save Selection dialog box appears (5.32).

2. In the Document drop-down list, choose where you want to save the alpha channel. The default is the current image. You can also create a new image with the selection by choosing New.

3. In the Channel drop-down list, select an existing saved selection to overwrite or select New to create a new channel. If you select an existing channel, you can choose how you want the new selection to combine with the existing channel in the Operation area of the dialog box.

4. In the Name text box, enter the name of the selection. If you do not enter a name, it is named Alpha N, where N is the next available number (5.33).

5. Choose OK.

Loading a Saved Selection

After a selection has been saved, it can be loaded and combined with the current selection.

1. Choose Selection→Load Selection. The Load Selection dialog box appears (5.34).

2. In the Document drop-down list, choose the document from which to load the selection. You can choose any open document that contains alpha channels. The default is the current document.

3. In the Channel drop-down list, choose the saved selection that you want to load.

4. If you have an existing selection, choose how you want the saved selection to combine with the current selection in the Operation area of the dialog box.

5. Choose OK.

Control the combination of the selection to be loaded with any existing selections by selecting an operation option.

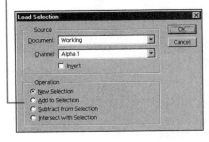

5.34

To create a selection from the non-transparent pixels in a layer, hold down the (Command)[Ctrl] key and click the layer thumbnail in the Layers palette.

Using Channels to Make Selections

5.35

It may be useful to increase the size of the channel thumbnails by choosing **Palette Options** from the Channels palette fly-out menu.

5.36

White areas are completely selected, black areas completely unselected, and gray areas partially selected. Remember that you can invert the selection if the blacks or whites do not appear to be correct for your purposes.

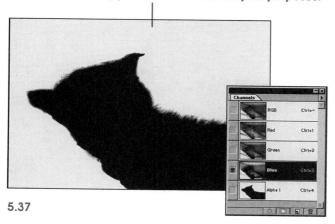

5.37

Because selections are saved as channels, you can use channel information to create selections. When attempting to select specific objects, it may be useful to use a color channel as a starting point for a selection. For more information about using channels and about using painting tools to create selections, see Chapter 11.

1. View each color channel in the Channels palette (5.35) and determine which channel most closely matches the selection that you want to make (5.36). This is often the channel that contains the greatest contrast.

2. Hold down (Command)[Ctrl] and click a layer thumbnail. A selection is created from the channel information (5.37).

    You can continue to refine the selection using Selection tools or by painting in the channel.

 I   P

The selection boundary does not indicate every selected pixel, only pixels that are more than 50% selected.

Because a selection can contain partially selected pixels, pixels outside the selection boundary may be selected. To see how pixels are selected throughout an image, press Q to display the image in Quick Mask mode. To change the color or opacity of the Quick Mask, double-click the Edit in Quick Mask Mode button in the toolbox. Press Q again to exit Quick Mask mode.

Creating a Mask for Objects Without Clearly Defined Edges

You can use the Extract command to create masks for intricate or hard-to-define edges such as hair and fur. The Extract command is new to Photoshop 5.5, and added and improved functionality, such as the capability to save settings or undo, can be expected in future releases.

When you use the extract command the background is eliminated. If you need to preserve the background, duplicate the layer or image from which you are extracting the foreground.

1. Select a layer and choose Image→Extract. The Extract dialog box appears (**5.38**).

2. In the Tool Options area, choose a Brush Size. Choose a size that will easily cover the entire edge of the object you are selecting. The Brush Size is used by the Edge Highlighter tool. Use smaller brushes on well-defined edges and larger brushes on soft edges, such as hair or fur.

3. In the Extraction area, choose a Smooth value from 0 to 100. The Smooth value determines how precisely the background is discarded. Higher values are more precise.

4. Select Force Foreground to specify that the area that you indicate with the Edge Highlighter tool should be

Your edge should be at least 2 pixels wide for the Fill tool to work properly. If your Smooth value is low, you may also want to define a slightly wider edge. However, wide edges tend to produce pixel artifacts, where Photoshop has difficulty determining what to extract. If your image ends up with fill color on both sides of your defined edge, you have at least one gap in your edge and should redefine it.

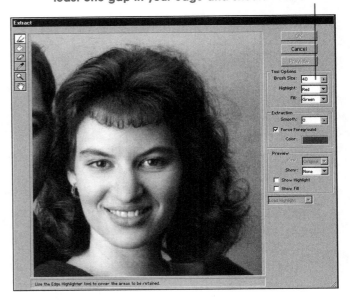

5.38

The highlight should overlap both the foreground and background areas. You don't need to highlight edges that touch the edges of the image.

5.39

5.40   **Use the Fill tool when the object has a well-defined interior area. If the object does not have a well-defined interior area, highlight the entire object and choose Force Foreground.**

retained. Use the Highlighter tool to cover the entire object. This is useful if the object is especially intricate. Click the color swatch to choose a color for the forced foreground or use the Eyedropper to select a color from the image.

5. In the Preview area, select what to preview in the View list. You can preview the original image or the extracted image. In the Show list, select how the transparent areas should be displayed. The default, None, displays the Photoshop transparency checkerboard.

6. Choose the Edge Highlighter tool from the toolbox. Highlight the edges of the foreground object (the areas that you want to retain) (5.39). Use the Eraser tool to remove highlighted areas.

7. Choose the Fill tool 🖌 from the toolbox. Click in the area that you want to retain (5.40). The area should be bounded by the highlighted edges. Note that you cannot select the Fill tool if Force Foreground is selected.

8. Choose Preview to display a preview of the foreground extraction **(5.41)**.

9. If the preview looks correct, choose OK. If not, change the settings and highlight until you achieve the desired results.

After making the extraction, you may need to further refine the foreground and background by using the Background Eraser or History Brush **(5.42)**.

5.41

 T I P

You can base the highlight in the Extract dialog box on an existing saved selection by choosing an alpha channel from the Load Highlight menu. The alpha channel should be based on a selection of the edge boundary.

 T I P

The Extract command isolates the foreground of an image, similar to floating a selection in previous versions. You can float a selection onto its own layer by choosing Layer→New→layer via Copy or (Command-J)[Ctrl+J].

In images that do not support multiple layers (such as indexed color), or when editing individual channels, you can use the Filter→Fade command to change the opacity and blending mode of a floating selection.

5.42

CHAPTER 6

In this chapter you learn how to...

Measure Distances and Angles

Add Perspective

Straighten an Image

Remove Keystoning

**Specify Numeric Values
for a Transformation**

Photoshop provides a variety of Transformation tools that can be applied to selections or layers. In addition to Transformation tools, Photoshop's Measure tool enables you to easily measure distances and angles in your image. Photoshop remembers the measurements and assumes values when transforming numerically.

TRANSFORMING SELECTED AREAS

Photoshop's basic transformation tools include the Move, Rotate, Scale Distort, Skew, and Perspective tools. Use the Rotate command to straighten images that were not scanned squarely. Use the Perspective command to match perspective between objects. Use the Distort command to add or remove keystoning in an image.

Photoshop's Free Transform command, (Command-T)[Ctrl+T], combines the capabilities of the Move, Rotate, Scale, and Distort commands into a convenient and easily remembered command.

Whenever you transform pixels, Photoshop must resample the area of the image. You can combine multiple transformations to limit the number of times that Photoshop interpolates image data.

While transforming, Photoshop displays handles around the selected area. You can drag the handles to scale, skew, or distort. Move the cursor to the edge of the boundary, and you can rotate the area after the cursor changes. Double-click in the area or press Enter to "hammer down" the transformation. Press Esc or (Command-.)[Ctrl+.] to cancel the transformation. You can undo any single transformation step. Individual transformation steps are not recorded in the History palette—only the completed transformations are recorded.

Measuring Distances and Angles

The Measure tool enables you to measure distances and angles. The information is displayed in the Info palette.

To measure a distance, select the Measure tool and click and drag two points **(6.1)**. The Info palette displays the measured distance, the horizontal and vertical components, and the angle (using East as 0 degrees).

To measure an arbitrary angle, you can use the Measure tool as a protractor. Click and drag the first leg of the angle **(6.2)**. Press (Option) [Alt], click an endpoint, and drag the second leg of the angle **(6.3)**. You can change the position of the legs by clicking and dragging them.

 I P

The units used to display the measurements in the Info palette are based on your preferences. To change the units, choose File→Preferences→Units & Rulers.

 I P

When comparing units acquired using the Measure tool, compare them to objects that have a known size. If you take a photograph of a house and know that the front door is 80 inches, for example, you can determine the approximate sizes of other objects on the house by using the Measure tool and calculating the ratios.

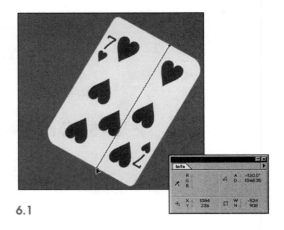

6.1

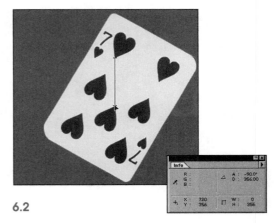

6.2

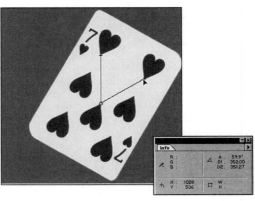

6.3

Adding Perspective

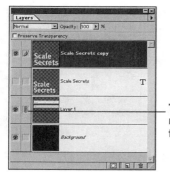

6.4

To add perspective to
multiple layers, link
them first.

6.5

6.6

Perspective is one of several visual cues that give the appearance of distance. (Some others are color, blur, and shadows.) You can add perspective to objects and areas to match the perspective elsewhere in an image. You can add text to a building's wall or fascia, for example, and match the perspective to create a sign or graffiti. Adding perspective is particularly effective when combined with other techniques, such as blurring and creating shadows.

1. Select the area to which you want to add perspective, or select a layer (**6.4**). To add perspective to more than one layer at a time, link the layers. You cannot add perspective to a type layer; you must render it first.

2. Choose Edit→Transform→ Perspective. A box with transform handles appears around your selection (**6.5**).

   Depending on the image, you also may need to combine the Perspective command with the Rotate, Skew, or Distort command to create a proper perspective, especially when matching perspective in an image.

3. Drag a corner handle to change the vanishing point (**6.6**). Drag a top, bottom, or side handle to change the horizontal or vertical skew.

continues

Adding Perspective continued

4. Double-click in the transformation area when finished adding perspective.

5. To make the objects fade as they recede into the distance, add a layer mask and fill it with a gradient (6.7).

6. To blur the objects as they recede into the distance, create a selection that increases in intensity as the objects fade. Press (Command-Option) [Ctrl+Alt] and click on the layer mask created in the previous step to select an inverted selection from the mask. Then choose Filter→Blur→Gaussian Blur. Choose a radius that looks appropriate for your image and choose OK (6.8).

To add an identical layer mask to a second layer, press (Command)(Ctrl) and click on the mask thumbnail in the Layers palette. Select the second layer and choose the Add Layer Mask button in the Layers palette.

6.7

To create a selection that varies in intensity, create an alpha channel and paint with white where you want 100 percent selection and black where you want 0 percent selection. Paint with gray to vary the selection intensity elsewhere. Choose Select→Load Selection to create a selection from the alpha channel. For more information about channels and masks, see Chapter 11, "Using Channels and Masks."

6.8

T I **P**

If you are matching the perspective in an image, you can create visual guides for the vanishing point using the Pen tool. Click and drag with the Pen tool to create paths that match the boundary of your perspective. The Pen tool works particularly well because you can create paths that extend out of the image area. After you create the paths, create a new layer and use the Stroke Subpath command, because you need to deselect the path in the Paths palette before transforming the image.

Straightening an Image

6.9

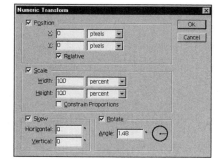

6.10

6.11

If an object is rotated, either in the original acquisition or when scanning, you can straighten it using the Measure tool and the Rotate commands.

1. Use the Measure tool to select two points that should be horizontal or vertical in the image (6.9). The longer the line that determines the angle, the more precise the rotation will be. You can adjust the endpoints by clicking on them and dragging.

2. To rotate the entire image, choose Image→Rotate Canvas→Arbitrary. The Rotate Canvas dialog box appears (6.10). The angle and direction used by default is based on the angle determined by the Measure tool.

   To rotate a selection or layer, choose Edit→Transform→ Numeric. The Numeric Transform dialog box appears (6.11). The angle and direction used by default is based on the angle determined by the Measure tool.

continues

(T) I P

Select Auto Select Layer in the Move Options palette to force Photoshop to select the layer under the cursor when you click with the Move tool.

Straightening an Image continued

3. Choose OK. The canvas or
selection is rotated **(6.12)**. If
you rotate the canvas, extra
pixels are added to the edges
in the background color.

To eliminate the extra pixels,
use the Crop tool.

6.12

*You can make a selection after measuring
because Photoshop remembers the last meas-
urement. To use the measured angle for the
defaults in the Numeric Transform and
Rotate Canvas dialog boxes, choose the
Measure tool from the toolbox.*

*Every time you make a transformation, some
image data is lost. Use Free Transform to
combine several transformations into one so
that Photoshop resamples and degrades
image data only once.*

Removing Keystoning

6.13

6.14

6.15

Keystoning occurs any time objects are not uniformly perpendicular to the camera lens. When photographing a building from the ground, for example, the sides appear to lean in slightly as the distance and angle from the ground increase. In some situations, you will want to leave this effect or even accentuate it. You can use this technique to remove or exaggerate keystoning.

1. Choose View→Show Rulers to display the rulers.

2. Create guidelines to indicate the horizontal or vertical edges you want to match (6.13).

3. Select the area you want to correct. For regular geometric objects, the polygon lasso works well. It also may be appropriate to select the entire image.

4. Choose Edit→Transform→ Distort. Drag the corner handles until the sides of the object match the guidelines (6.14). Press Shift to constrain the movement horizontally or vertically. Press (Shift-Option) [Shift+Alt] to drag parallel handles in opposite directions.

   If you want to exaggerate the keystoning effect, drag in the handles (6.15).

5. Double-click in the selection area to finalize the distortion.

Specifying Numeric Values for a Transformation

The Numeric Transform command
enables you to enter precise values
for movement, scaling, skewing, and
rotation. By using Numeric
Transform and noting the values,
you can repeat the transformation
on other selections and in other
images. Numeric Transform is useful when you know the amount of
change you want to make ahead of
time. You can skew an area of an
image to match text that is italicized
12 degrees, for example.

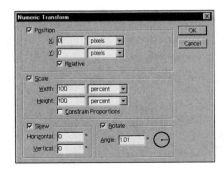

6.16

1. Select the area, layer, or path
   that you want to transform. If
   you want to transform a selection boundary, choose
   Select→Transform Selection.

2. Choose Edit→Transform→
   Numeric (6.16).

3. Clear any transformations that
   you don't want to make.

4. In the Position section, enter
   horizontal and vertical values
   for the movement. By default,
   the movement is relative to the
   current location of the selection. If you clear the Relative
   check box, the movement is
   based on the upper-left corner
   of the image.

5. In the Scale section, enter
   width and height values.

6. In the Skew section, enter horizontal and vertical values.

6.17

6.18

7. In the Rotate section, enter an angle or drag the indicator inside the circle.

If you choose Edit→Transform→ Numeric Transform again, Photoshop remembers the last values you entered.

 I P

Press (Option)[Alt] while choosing Edit→Free Transform (or press (Command-T)[Ctrl+T]) to transform a copy of the selected area or layer instead of the original (6.17).

Press (Command-Shift-T)[Ctrl+Shift+T] to repeat the last transformation.

Press (Command-Option-T) [Ctrl+Alt+Shift+T] to repeat the last transformation on a copy. This action duplicates both the object and the transformation (6.18).

 I P

You can use Numeric Transform with other Transform tools. You can start a free transform, do a numeric transform, and then return to the free transform, for example.

 I P

Because numeric transformations are repeatable, they work especially well with actions that involve batch processing images.

CHAPTER 7

In this chapter you learn how to...

Choose How Paint Should Blend

Edit an Existing Brush

Make a New Brush Shape

Save and Load Brush Sets

Smudge and Finger Paint

Erase Areas of a Layer to Transparency
Fill an Area with a Pattern

Paint with the Pattern Stamp

Create Geometric Shapes

Paint with Previous Versions of an Image

Create Artistic Effects with Previous
Versions of an Image

Create Shaped Gradients

Customize Gradients

P ainting techniques are used to apply color to areas of an image using tools that mimic those used in traditional graphic design, such as the Airbrush and Paintbrush tools. Like their predecessors, you can control the pressure and amount of paint applied at each point on the canvas. In the digital imaging world of Photoshop, however, you can control not only where the color is applied, but also how the color interacts with the colors underneath the painting tool.

PAINTING

You can precisely control the size, opacity, and blending mode of each tool. In addition, you can paint with any shape or pattern that you can create. All of the brush tools use the Brushes palette and their Options palette to control how color applies throughout the image. Photoshop 5.5 adds the Background Eraser and Art History Brush tools. The Background Eraser enables you to erase areas on a layer to transparency. The Art History Brush, an advancement from the Impressionist option for the History Brush in Photoshop 5.0, enables you to control how paint is applied from the history to create a variety of artistic effects.

ImageReady contains many of the same tools as Photoshop and generally they work the same way. ImageReady also adds a Rectangle, Rectangle with Rounded Corners, and Ellipse tool. These tools can be used to create buttons and other useful shapes that, in Photoshop, are created by filling selections.

This chapter covers painting tools. For more information about the toning and blur/sharpen tools, see Chapter 12, "Image Adjustments and Corrections."

Choosing How Paint Should Blend

Blending modes determine how pixels combine with those immediately below it on the active layer. For example, Lighten compares each painted pixel to the one immediately under it and uses the lighter of the two.

You can use blending modes to produce a range of effects. In the tool's Options palette, select a blending mode from the list (7.1).

7.1

Table 7.1   Paint Blending Modes

Blending Mode	What It Does	Uses
Normal	Replaces the pixels in the underlying layer with those on the Normal layer	This is the default mode and should be used for most straight painting
Dissolve	Randomly removes pixels from the Dissolve layer based on the layer's opacity	Special effects
Behind	Paints on only the transparent areas of a layer	Drop shadows, glows
Clear	Makes pixels transparent (only available for the Line tool, the Paint Bucket tool, and the Fill and Stroke commands); Preserve Transparency must be off	Create transparent areas in a layer
Multiply	Multiplies the color of each painted pixel with the one under it to create a darker complementary color; multiplying with black yields black; multiplying with white yields no change	Creating shadows; darkening areas of an image
Screen	Blends the color of each painted pixel with underlying pixels to create a lighter color; screening with white yields white; screening with black yields no change	Highlights and glows Lightening areas of an image
Overlay	Multiplies or Screens, depending on the underlying color, to preserve the highlight and shadows of the underlying pixels; 50% gray in the underlying pixels yields no change	Create texture and pattern effects
Soft Light	Darkens or Lightens each underlying pixel based on the light and dark values of the pixel above it; painting with 50% gray yields no change	Paint with black or white to dodge or burn

Blending Mode	What It Does	Uses
Hard Light	Multiplies or Screens, depending on the painted color	Increase contrast and color density (adjust opacity as needed)
Color Dodge	Lightens and saturates the underlying pixels to match the painted pixels	Lightening an image
Color Burn	Darkens and desaturates the underlying pixels to match the painted pixels	Darkening an image
Darken	Compares the underlying and painted pixels and uses the darker of the two	Special effects
Lighten	Compares the underlying and painted pixels and uses the lighter of the two	Special effects
Difference	Subtracts color values of each pixel; identical pixels yield black (0); a black and a white pixel yield white	Special effects
Exclusion	Similar to Difference, but a softer effect; white pixels invert the underlying pixels; black yields no change	Special effects
Hue	Changes the hue of the underlying pixels to match those painted, while leaving brightness and saturation alone	Tinting
Saturation	Changes the saturation of the underlying pixels to match those painted, while leaving the brightness and hue alone	Controlling saturation throughout an image
Color	Preserves the gray levels in the underlying pixels, while replacing the hue and saturation of the underlying pixels with those painted	Tinting
Luminosity	Changes the luminosity (brightness) of the underlying pixels to match those painted, while leaving the hue and saturation alone	Special effects

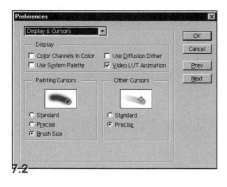

7-2

 I P

By default, when you paint with any of the brush tools, Photoshop displays the tool icon as you paint. You can change the cursor to display a precise target instead of the tool icon by pressing Caps Lock. You can also set the tool to always display the precise target or the brush size in Preferences→Display & Cursors (7.2). When you choose the Precise or Brush Size option, pressing Caps Lock toggles between the other option.

Editing an Existing Brush

Photoshop starts with six hard-edged brushes ranging in size from 1 pixel to 19 pixels and ten soft-edged brushes that range from 5 to 100 pixels. You can edit the diameter, hardness, spacing, angle, and roundness of these standard brushes or create your own brushes.

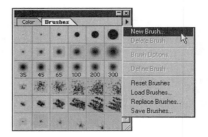

7.3

1. To edit an existing brush, double-click the brush that you want to edit in the Brushes palette. To create a brush, choose New Brush from the Brushes palette menu (7.3). The Brush Options dialog box displays (7.4).

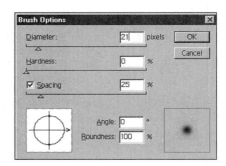

7.4

2. Set the Diameter, or size of the brush, measured in pixels. Brush sizes range from 1 to 999 pixels.

3. Choose a Hardness or the sharpness of the edge. A hardness of 100% creates a very crisp edge; 0%, a very fuzzy one.

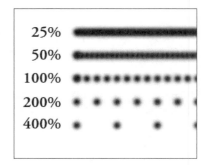

7.5

4. Set a value for the Spacing. Spacing is the distance between brush marks as you paint, measured as a percentage of the brush diameter. Larger values create skips as you paint (7.5). You can turn the spacing off.

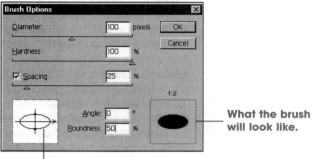

What the brush will look like.

You can change the Roundness and Angle values dynamically by dragging the control points and axis in the left preview box.

7.6

7.7

5. Set the Roundness. Changing the Roundness creates an ellipse based on a percentage. For example, if you set the Roundness to 50%, the minor axis of the ellipse is 50% of the major axis (7.6). Choose an Angle if the Roundness is set to something other than 100%. The Angle determines the rotation of the major axis of the ellipse. You can set the Angle if the Roundness is set to 100%, but painting with a circular brush is the same at any angle. Changing the Roundness and Angle enable you to paint with calligraphic effects (7.7).

6. Choose OK when finished.

I   P

If you make changes to the brushes and want to return to the defaults, choose Reset Brushes from the Brushes palette menu.

Making a New Brush Shape

You can create a custom brush from any shape or area that you can select. You can use custom brush shapes as stamps, or to create a variety of texture variations throughout an image.

1. Create a selection (using any selection technique). The selection must be smaller than 1000×1000 pixels. The opacity throughout the brush is based on the color under the selection sampled through all visible layers. If the area under a selection is completely black, the created brush is completely opaque. Where the area under the brush contains transparency or white, the brush is transparent (7.8).

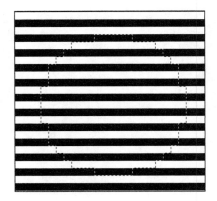

7.8

2. Choose Define Brush from the Brushes palette menu. A preview of the new brush is displayed in the Brushes palette (7.9).

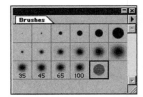

7.9

3. Set the brush options by double-clicking the new brush in the Brushes palette. In the Brush Options dialog box, set a value for the spacing (7.10). If the brush is small, you can also turn on anti-aliasing for the brush.

7.10

After you have created a new brush, you can select it in the Brushes palette and use it with any of the painting tools (7.11).

7.11

Saving and Loading a Brush Set

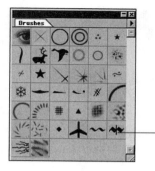

7.12

If you want to save brushes that you create, clear the brushes you don't want saved in the Brushes palette first. Select a brush and choose Delete Brush from the Brushes palette menu. You need to delete each brush separately. Then choose Save Brushes from the Brushes palette menu.

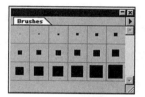

7.13

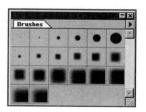

7.14

If you create custom brushes and define custom brush shapes, you can save them as brush sets that can be reloaded and distributed. Photoshop also comes with three extra sets of brushes in the Goodies folder:

- Assorted Brushes. An array of brush shapes ranging from stamps and symbols to textures (7.12).

- Square Brushes. Square brushes ranging in size from 1 pixel to 24 pixels (7.13).

- Drop Shadows Brushes. Round and square brushes with soft edges in a variety of sizes designed specifically for creating drop shadows behind objects (7.14). You can use these brushes on layers that contain transparency when painting in Behind mode.

1. To load a set of brushes, choose Load Brushes from the Brushes palette menu.

2. In the Load dialog box, choose the brush set that you want to load. If you want to load one of the standard brush sets provided with Photoshop, look in the Goodies folder.

 I P

You can define custom brush shapes with large spacing values to use the painting tools as stamps. You can use any type symbol or dingbat by defining a selection using the Type Mask tool.

Smudging and Finger Painting

Use the Smudge tool to pull color from one area of an image to another. The tool behaves like a finger dragged through wet paint. The Smudge tool is useful when retouching images with soft, smooth features such as faces and clouds.

1. Select the Smudge tool from the toolbox.

2. Double-click the tool to display the Smudge tool options (7.15).

3. Select a blending mode and pressure for the Smudge tool in the Smudge Options palette. Select Use All Layers if you want to pull colors across all visible layers.

4. Drag in the image to smudge (7.16). Note that the Smudge tool is one of the more resource-intensive painting tools, and there may be delays depending on the image and your configuration.

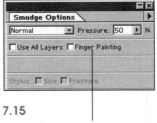

7.15

By default, the Smudge tool uses the color under the tool when you start dragging. Select Finger Painting if you want to start smudging with the foreground color.

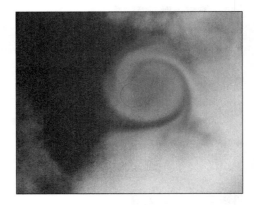

7.16

5.5 Erasing Areas of a Layer to Transparency

7.17

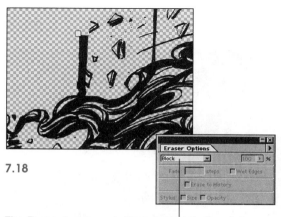

7.18

The Background Eraser replaces pixels with transparency based on its Tolerance setting.

The Eraser is a special brush tool that paints with the background color on the Background layer or with transparency on any other layer. You can set the Eraser to behave like other brush tools; specifically, the Airbrush, Paintbrush, and Pencil. The Eraser also has a special Block option in which the Eraser is a hard-edged square the size of which is based on the zoom magnification.

7.19

Discontiguous erases the sampled color wherever it occurs in the layer. Contiguous erases connected areas that contain the sampled color. Find Edges erases connected areas containing the sampled color, and attempts to maintain edge detail.

Photoshop 5.5 adds the Background Eraser tool to erase areas on a layer to transparency (7.17). This tool can be used to isolate objects with clearly defined edges or, for objects without clearly defined edges (such as hair or fur), it can be used after making an initial extraction of foreground objects with the Extract command. For more information on the Extract command, see "Creating a Mask for Objects without Clearly Defined Edges" on page 96 in Chapter 5, "Selecting."

1. In the Layers palette, select the layer containing the areas you want to erase.

2. Double-click the Background Eraser tool 🖉 to select the tool and display its Options palette. You can toggle quickly between the Eraser and Background Eraser tools in the toolbox by holding down (Option)[Alt] and clicking the tool.

3. In the Background Eraser Options palette (7.19), choose a method for erasing the sampled color.

4. Enter a value for the Tolerance. Lower values erase only colors very similar to the sampled color. Higher values erase a wider range of colors.

continues

Erasing Areas of a Layer to Transparency continued

5. Choose a Sampling option (7.20).

6. To prevent erasing areas that match the foreground color, select Protect Foreground Color.

7. Choose a brush in the Brushes palette.

8. Drag in the image to erase areas of the active layer to transparency (7.21).

The Background Eraser tool cursor appears as a brush shape with a crosshair indicating the tool's hot spot.

To continuously sample colors as you drag the cursor, choose Continuous. Use Continuous to erase adjacent areas that differ in color. To erase areas based on the color where you first click, choose Once. Use Once to erase areas of solid color. To erase areas based on the current background color, choose Background Swatch.

7.20

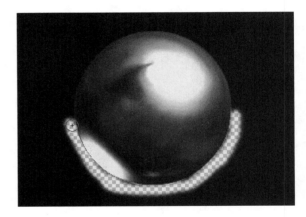

7.21

 I P

Filling with a solid color can be especially useful when attempting to apply a filter because you cannot apply a filter to an empty layer.

 I P

Like the Background Eraser, the Magic Eraser erases areas of a layer to transparency. The Magic Eraser selects contiguous areas based on a tolerance setting (like the Magic Wand), and makes the selected areas transparent. You can also set the Magic Eraser to select noncontiguous areas, in which case it selects all similar colors on a layer. To switch between the Eraser, Magic Eraser, and Background Eraser, press Shift+E.

Filling an Area with a Pattern

7.22

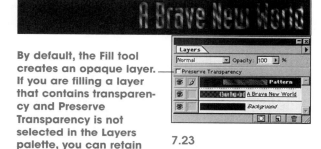

By default, the Fill tool creates an opaque layer. If you are filling a layer that contains transparency and Preserve Transparency is not selected in the Layers palette, you can retain the transparency after filling that layer with your pattern by choosing Preserve Transparency in the Fill dialog box.

7.23

If you define a pattern, you can use that as a fill option. Before filling with a pattern, you must first define a pattern. If you start the Fill command without first defining a pattern, the Pattern option is dimmed.

1. Select an area of any open image to use as a pattern (7.22), and then choose Edit→Define Pattern.

2. Choose Edit→Fill.

3. Select Pattern under Use.

4. Select a blending mode and opacity for the fill.

5. Choose OK when finished. The selection or layer fills with the defined pattern (7.23).

Table 7.1   Fill Keyboard Shortcuts

To	Command
Fill with the Foreground Color	(Option-Backspace) (Alt+Backspace)
Fill with the Background Color	(Command-Backspace) (Ctrl+Backspace)
Fill with the current History State	(Command-Option-Backspace) (Ctrl+Alt+Backspace)
Display the Fill dialog box	Shift+Backspace

 I P

You can clear the Photoshop's pattern buffer to free up resources by choosing Edit→Purge→Pattern.

 I P

When filling with a pattern, if you want the pattern to tile seamlessly, make sure that the top and bottom pixels match and that the left and right side pixels match.

Painting with the Pattern Stamp

The Pattern Stamp tool enables you to paint with a defined pattern. Before painting with the Pattern Stamp, you must first define a pattern. If you attempt to use the Pattern Stamp before defining a pattern, Photoshop warns you that you must define a pattern.

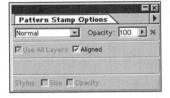

7.24

1. Select an area of any open image to use as a pattern. Once selected, choose Edit→Define Pattern. The pattern is saved in the pattern buffer.

2. Select the Pattern Stamp from the toolbox. Click and hold down on the Stamp icon for the flyout, which contains the Pattern Stamp. You can toggle quickly between the two tools in the toolbox by holding down (Option)[Alt] and clicking the tool.

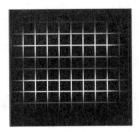

7.25

3. Double-click the Pattern Stamp in the toolbox to display the Pattern Stamp Options palette if it is closed (7.24). Select a blending mode and Opacity for the pattern stamp.

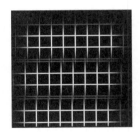

7.26

4. The default is to use an aligned pattern throughout the image (7.25). Clear the Aligned option if you do not you want the pattern to align on consecutive strokes of the tool (7.26).

5. Choose a brush from the Brushes palette.

6. Drag in the image to apply the pattern (7.27).

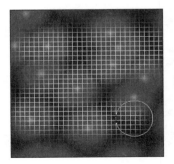

7.27

Creating Geometric Shapes

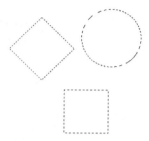

7.28

7.29

If you are stroking a selection on a layer that contains transparency and Preserve Transparency is not selected in the Layers palette, you can choose Preserve Transparency in the Fill dialog box.

If you want to create a circle, square, or rectangle in Photoshop, the simplest method is to use a Selection tool to create the shape and stroke the selection. ImageReady also has special tools to create these filled shapes, although this method works there as well.

1. Create a selection using the Elliptical and Rectangular Marquee tools **(7.28)**. Hold down (Option)[Alt] to create the rectangle or ellipse from the center.

2. Choose Edit→Stroke **(7.29)**.

3. Choose a thickness for the stroke, in pixels, ranging from 1 to 16.

4. Select the position of the stroke, Inside, Outside or Center.

5. Select an Opacity and Blending Mode for the stroke.

6. Choose OK when finished. The selection is stroked **(7.30)**.

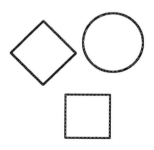

7.30

You may want to use an illustration program or Photoshop's path tools to create more sophisticated geometric shapes. In addition to having editing control over these shapes, you can also control their anti-aliasing or aliasing at a variety of sizes.

 I P

You can also create geometric shapes with path. For more information about stroking paths and subpaths, see "Stroking a Path" on page 242 in Chapter 14, "Working with Paths."

Painting with Previous Versions of an Image

The History Brush applies paint from a previous version of your file. You can use a snapshot or a history state as the source for the History Brush.

Using the History Brush, you can paint with the effects of a filter over an image. This gives you significant control of the area of a filter's effect (7.31). (See also Figure C.5 in the color insert.) You can make a snapshot of a change to the image made with an adjustment or filter. Use the History Brush to apply the change selectively to areas of the image after undoing the change to the image. Be sure to create a merged snapshot, or the History Brush paints from a layer in the snapshot to the same layer in the image. For more information about creating snapshots and using the History palette, see Chapter 2.

1. In the History palette, select the source for the History Brush by clicking in the box next to the snapshot or history state (7.32).

7.31

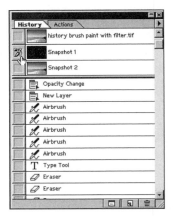

7.32

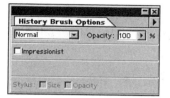

7.33

7.34

7.35

2. Choose the History Brush from the toolbox. Double-click the History Brush in the toolbox to set its options (7.33). You can select Impressionist to paint from the History State or snapshot with a copy of the history in an Impressionistic style (7.34). For greater control of the pattern used for artistic effects with the History Brush, use the Art History Brush.

3. Select a brush size.

4. Paint in the image. Wherever you paint, the selected History State or snapshot is applied (7.35).

(T) I P

When using the Eraser, hold down (Option)[Alt] while erasing to paint with the active History State. For more information about the History Brush, see "Painting with Previous Versions of the File with the History Brush " on page XX in Chapter 2, "Using the History Palette."

5.5 Creating Artistic Effects with Previous Versions of an Image

The Art History Brush in Photoshop 5.5 enables you to customize the way that the selected History State is applied to the image. Like the Impressionist option in the History Brush, the Art History Brush scatters image data from the History State randomly as you drag. However, you have greater control of the amount of scattering, the shape of the stroke, and the amount that the color is permitted to change.

By experimenting with the settings in the Art History Brush Options palette, an array of artistic effects and styles can be achieved.

1. In the History palette, select a state or snapshot to use as the source for the Art History Brush.

2. Double-click the Art History Brush 🖌 to display its Options palette (7.36). The Art History Brush is grouped with the History Brush in the toolbox.

3. Choose a blending mode and opacity.

4. Choose an option from the Paint Style menu, located below the blending mode menu in the Art History Brush Options palette. This controls the shape of the paint stroke. Available shapes range from small dabs (7.37) to long curls (7.38).

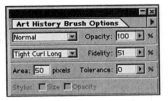

7.36

7.37

7.38

7.39

7.40

7.41

A low tolerance enables you to paint unlimited strokes anywhere in the image. A high tolerance enables you to paint only in areas that differ considerably from the color in the history source.

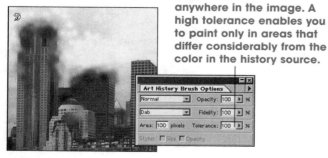

7.42

5. To control how much the paint color deviates from the color in the history source, enter a value for Fidelity. The lower the fidelity, the more the color varies from the source.

6. To specify the area covered by the paint strokes, enter a value for Area. The greater the size, the larger the covered area and more numerous the strokes (**7.39** and **7.40**).

7. To limit the regions where paint strokes may be applied, enter a value for the Tolerance (**7.41** and **7.42**).

8. Select a brush in the Brushes palette. The size of the brush determines the size of the strokes. The Area setting controls the actual area of effect.

9. Drag in the image to paint. As you hold down the mouse button, brush strokes are randomly placed, based on the settings in the Art History Brush Options palette.

Creating Shaped Gradients

You can use Photoshop to create blends between colors in a variety of shapes beyond a linear gradient. Photoshop's gradient tools provide an endless variety of possible blends. Photoshop comes with 15 preset gradients in a variety of colors, all of which can be used with any gradient type. Gradients can be used as backgrounds, as special fills (such as the Chrome or Copper gradients), or as layer masks when compositing layers.

1. Select one of the gradient tools from the toolbox: radial **(7.43)**, angle **(7.44)**, reflected **(7.45)**, or diamond **(7.46)**

  I P

Use Shift+G to quickly move through the gradient tools in the toolbox. You can also move through the gradient tools by holding down (Option)[Alt] and clicking the tool in the toolbox.

 **O T E**

ImageReady does not have a Gradient tool like Photoshop. Instead, use the Gradient/Pattern layer effect and modify the settings in the Gradient/Pattern palette. In addition, ImageReady can only produce linear and radial gradients. For complete gradient options, create the effect in Photoshop and then open the document in ImageReady.

Radial gradients blend in a circle from the first point to the second point. The first color is at 100% in the center of the circle and blends to the final color at the edge of the color. Areas outside the circle are filled with the final color.

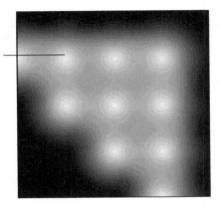

7.43

Angle gradients sweep counter-clockwise around the first point.

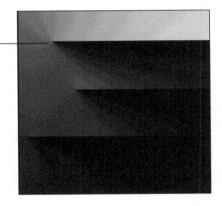

7.44

Reflected gradients create a symmetrical blend about the line you drag. The middle of blend contains 100% of the first color and fades in both directions to the final color using the angle and distance of the dragged line.

7.45

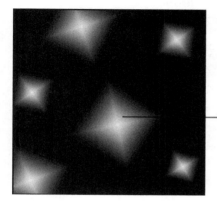

Diamond gradients blend from the first point to the second point in a square pattern. The first point is at the center of the square while the second point is on one corner of the square. In the center of the square, 100% of the first color is used and at the edges of the square, 100% of the final color.

7.46

7.47

2. Double-click the Gradient tool to display the Gradient Options palette if it is not visible (7.47).

3. Choose a Blending Mode and Opacity for the gradient.

4. Choose a Gradient type from the list. The default is Foreground to Background.

5. If the gradient contains transparency, you can disable the transparency mask by clearing the Transparency check box. Clear the Dither option to disable dithering. Without dithering, the gradient may contain noticeable banding. To reverse the order of colors in the gradient, select Reverse.

6. Click and drag in the image to create the gradient.

T I **P**

Clear the Dither option to disable dithering. If your gradient contains noticeable banding, be sure that the Dither option is selected in the Gradient Options palette.

Customizing Gradients

In addition to the many standard gradient types provided with Photoshop, you can create and edit your own gradients. A gradient has two components—a color scheme and a transparency mask. The transparency mask determines where the gradient is opaque and where it is transparent. Change the transparency mask when you want the gradient to have gaps between the color fill areas or when you want it to fade to or from transparency.

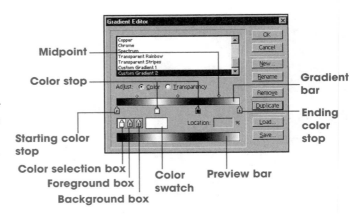

7.48

1. In the Gradient Options palette, choose Edit **(7.48)**.

2. Select a gradient from the list to edit it or choose New to create a new gradient. If you choose New, enter a name in the Gradient Name dialog box.

3. Change the start color of the gradient by clicking the starting color stop and then accessing the Color Picker by clicking on the color swatch. You can also choose a color in the image with the Eyedropper tool. If you want to use the foreground or background color as the gradient's start color, click the starting color stop and then pick either the foreground box or background box.

4. Repeat the same process to change the end color of the gradient by clicking the ending color stop.

7.49

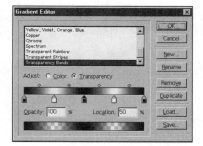

7.50

5. Change the midpoint of the gradient, drag the midpoint above the gradient bar. You can also select the midpoint and enter a percentage in the Location box.

6. To add color stops to the gradient, click below the gradient bar. You can change the location of the color stops by dragging them or by entering a location. Each pair of color stops has a midpoint that can be adjusted. To delete a color stop, select the color stop and drag it off the gradient bar. To duplicate a color stop, hold down (Option)[Alt] and click a color stop.

7. To alter the transparency mask of a gradient, choose Transparency. You alter the transparency stops the same way you change color stops. Click a transparency stop to select it. You can change the opacity and location of a transparency stop. If you change the opacity, the color of the stop changes. Black represents opaque and white represents transparent. Gray values are used for transparency stops that are not completely opaque or transparent **(7.49)** and **(7.50)**.

8. When finished, choose OK.

If you want to save your gradients, choose Save in the Gradient Editor dialog box. Use Remove to delete any gradients that you do not want to save. Once you save a set of gradients, they can be loaded by choosing Load in the Gradient Editor dialog box.

Saving your gradients also enables you to share your gradients with others.

CHAPTER 8

In this chapter you learn how to...

Change a Layer's Properties

Link Layers

Align Layers

Merge and Flatten Layers

Choose a Layer Blend Mode

Preserve Transparency

Create Shadows for Objects

Select Nontransparent Pixels on a Layer

Copy Layers from One Image to Another

Control a Layer's Blend If Options for Compositing

Remove Halos from Layers

Photoshop's layers provide a powerful method of organizing images and objects. You can think of layers as sheets of acetate on which artwork can be placed, moved, and edited. Further, you can control the way that pixel information on different layers combines using one of the many layer blending modes. You also can control the visibility of layers. Turning off layers not only enables you to work with selected parts of the image, but also to selectively save using the Save a Copy command.

USING LAYERS

By default, images begin with one layer called the background. Additional layers are added above the background layer. Each layer can be either independent or linked with other layers. If linked, the layers move and transform together. In addition, linked layers can be aligned and distributed. You can also apply copied-layer effects to a group of linked layers.

Layers in ImageReady rely on the same model as Photoshop and generally work identically. ImageReady supports all the same layer effects and features, such as clipping groups and layer masks. In addition, though, ImageReady adds the ability to use layers as image maps and to construct animations using each layer as a frame. Because of its animation ability, ImageReady is not limited to 100 layers like Photoshop. If you create an ImageReady document that contains more than 100 layers, Photoshop cannot open it.

Changing Layer Properties

Layers in Photoshop have four properties that you can change as listed in Table 8.1

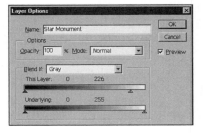

Additionally, in ImageReady, choose whether you want to use the layer as an ImageMap. Then choose the shape of the map and the URL associated with the layer.

8.1

To change any of these properties, double-click the layer thumbnail in the Layers palette. The Layers Options dialog box is displayed (8.1).

 I P

Many file formats do not support Photoshop layers. If you change the background layer into a normal layer, you cannot save in any format other than the Photoshop native format. Either flatten the image or use the Save a Copy command to save the file in another format.

 I P

By default the name of a type layer is based on the text in that layer. When you copy a type layer, though, the layer name remains the same with the word copy appended to the end of it. After making a copy of a type layer, change the name to make it easier to keep track of.

Table 8.1   Editable Layer Properties

Property	Description
Name	Although layer names can contain up to 255 characters, keeping them less than 30 characters reduces the odds that the names will be truncated in the Layers palette.
Transparency	Change the transparency in Layer Options by dragging the slider in the Layers palette or by typing a number when you have one of the selection tools selected.
Mode	You can change the mode in Layer Options by selecting a mode from the list or by using one of the keyboard combinations when you have one of the selection tools selected. The most common ones are: Normal: (Shift-Option-n) (Shift+Alt+n) Multiply: (Shift-Option-m) (Shift+Alt+m) Screen: (Shift-Option-s) (Shift+Alt+s)
Blend If	Control how pixels on a layer interact with the pixels on layers below it. This feature is not available in ImageReady.

Linking Layers

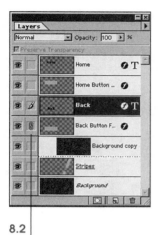

8.2

Indicates that the layer is linked to the active layer.

Depending on the image you are editing, you may want to change the transparency color and the size of the transparency pattern. You can choose colors that do not appear in the image so that the areas of transparency are more apparent. Change these settings by selecting File→ Preferences→Transparency and Gamut.

By linking layers together, when one layer moves, the other moves with it. This is useful not only for maintaining spatial relationships between layers, but also for aligning layers, selectively merging layers, and pasting copied effects.

1. Select the layer to which you want to link by clicking the layer thumbnail in the Layers palette.

2. Click in the link box next to each layer that you want to link in the Layers palette. Photoshop displays the link icon for the group of linked layers whenever one of them is made active (8.2).

You can clear the layer link by clicking in the same box.

 I   P

To drag and drop multiple layers from one file into another, link the layers together, select the Move tool and starting in the Photoshop image window (not the Layers palette), drag and drop into another document.

Aligning Layers

When two or more layers are linked
together (8.3), you can align the layers to one another. Aligning layers
uses the pixel information on the
currently selected layer to determine
the top, bottom, center, and sides for
alignment.

1. Begin by linking any layers
   that you want to align.

2. Select the layer in the Layers
   palette that you want to
   align to.

3. Select Align Linked from the
   Layer menu and then select the
   alignment option that you
   want (8.4).

In this image, the text box was centered on the buttons by selecting the
button layer and then using
Horizontal Center and Vertical
Center. Then the buttons were
aligned along their horizontal centers (8.5).

8.3

8.4

8.5

*You can also use the keyboard shortcuts to
move a layer up or down. To move the layer
one step at a time, use (Command-])[Ctrl+]]
(right bracket) to move up and (Command-[)
[Ctrl+[] (left bracket) to move down. Hold
down the Shift key with either of these shortcuts to move the layer all the way to the top
or bottom.*

Merging and Flattening Layers

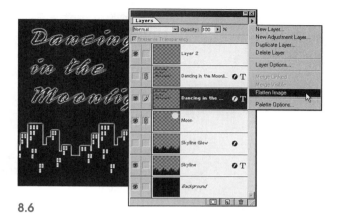

8.6

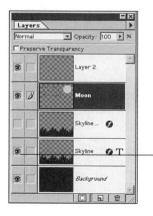

8.7

Photoshop must store information for every pixel on every layer. To reduce the amount of space that an image requires, you can merge together layer information or merge together all the layers in a document by flattening. Flattening is also necessary to save a file in a format other than the Photoshop native format.

To flatten all the layers in a Photoshop image, choose Flatten Image **(8.6)** from the Layers palette menu or from the Layer menu.

Merging layers together combines the information on selected layers as it appears in the image **(8.6)**, **(8.7)** without changing the image.

1. Select one of the layers that you want to merge. The layer must be active and visible.

2. Choose one of the merge commands from the Layer menu.

If layers are linked together, you can use the Merge Linked command to merge just those layers. One of the layers must be active. You can also turn off layers that you don't want to merge and use the Merge Visible command.

8.8

 I P

If you think you may need to make changes to the image, save a layered version of the file in the Photoshop native format and then use the Save a Copy command to save a flattened version of the file. Just click the Flatten Image option in the dialog box.

Choosing a Layer Blend Mode

Photoshop provides 17 different methods to mix the contents of a layer with those under it. The most commonly used are Normal (the default mode), Multiply, and Screen. To understand what each mode does, it is helpful to examine the effect at the pixel level.

1. In the Layers palette, select the layer in which you want to change the blending mode (8.9).

2. Select a blending mode from the list in the Layer's palette.

8.9

Choose a blending mode appropriate to your task.

Blending Mode	What It Does	Uses
Normal	Replaces the pixels in the underlying layer with those on the Normal layer	This is the default mode and should be used for most straight compositing
Dissolve	Randomly removes pixels from the Dissolve layer based on the layer's opacity	Special effects
Multiply	Multiplies the color of each pixel in the top layer with the one under it to create a darker complementary color; multiplying with black yields black; multiplying with white yields no change	Creating shadows; darkening an image; multiply a layer by a duplicate to restore tonal density to an overexposed image (adjust opacity as needed)
Screen	Blends the color of each pixel in the Screen layer with underlying pixels to create a lighter color; screening with white yields white; screening with black yields no change	Highlights and glows; lightening an image; screen a layer with a duplicate to lighten an underexposed image (adjust opacity as needed)
Overlay	Multiplies or Screens, depending on the underlying color, to preserve the highlight and shadows of the underlying layer; 50% gray in the underlying layer yields no change	Create texture and pattern effects; overlay a layer with a duplicate to increase contrast and color density (adjust opacity as needed)

Blending Mode	What It Does	Uses
Soft Light	Darkens or lightens each underlying pixel based on the light and dark values of the pixel above it; 50% gray in the Soft Light layer yields no change	Paint with black or white to dodge or burn
Hard Light	Multiplies or Screens, depending on the color in the Hard Light layer	Apply Hard Light to a duplicate layer to increase contrast and color density (adjust opacity as needed)
Color Dodge	Lightens and saturates the underlying pixels to match the Color Dodge layer	Lightening an image
Color Burn	Darkens and desaturates the underlying pixels to match the Color Burn layer	Darkening an image
Darken	Compares each pixel on the underlying and Darken layer and uses the darker of the two	Special effects
Lighten	Compares each pixel on the underlying and Lighten layer and uses the lighter of the two	Special effects
Difference	Subtracts color values of each pixel; identica pixels on the two layers yield black (0); a black and a white pixel yield white	Special effects
Exclusion	Similar to Difference, but a softer effect; white pixels on the Exclusion layer invert the pixels in the underlying layer; black yields no change	Special effects
Hue	Changes the hue of the underlying layer's pixels to match those in the Hue layer while leaving brightness and saturation alone	Tinting
Saturation	Changes the saturation of the underlying layer's pixels to match those in the Saturation layer while leaving the brightness and hue alone	Controlling saturation throughout an image. Note that a Hue/Saturation adjustment layer may be easier to work with. See "Creating an Adjustment Layer" on page 228 in Chapter 13, "Color Correction."
Color	Preserves the gray levels in the underlying layer while replacing the hue and saturation of the underlying layer with those in the Color layer	Tinting
Luminosity	Changes the luminosity (brightness) of the underlying layer's pixels to match those in the Luminosity layer while leaving the hue and saturation alone	Special effects

Preserving Transparency

When you paint or fill a layer, the transparent pixels are changed along with the nontransparent pixels (8.10). When a layer's transparency is preserved, the transparent pixels on the layer are not affected by any painting or editing. (8.11). This is especially useful when working with layers that contain objects or text because you can fill the layer with a color or pattern and only the object or text will be filled.

1. Select the layer in the Layers palette.

2. Select Preserve Transparency in the Layers palette (8.12).

Preserve Transparency turned off

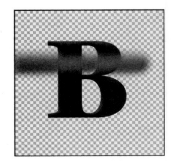

8.10

Preserve Transparency turned on

8.11

8.12

I P

The transparency of type layers is preserved by default. After you render the layer, however, the Preserve Transparency option is cleared. Be sure to select Preserve Transparency if you want to protect the transparent areas from change.

Creating Shadows for Objects

Set the layer mode for the new layer to Multiply so that the shadow darkens all layers beneath it.

8.13

8.14

Shadows provide important visual cues to determine an object's size and distance both from other objects and from the page. You can create drop shadows and cast shadows for text as well as for objects. The following procedure requires that you pay special attention to the Preserve Transparency option in the Layers palette. Turn Preserve Transparency on when filling the layer to change only the pixels of the object or text. Turn Preserve Transparency off when using blur filters.

1. Select the layer with the object or text.

2. Duplicate the layer by dragging the layer thumbnail onto the Create New Layer button in the Layers palette (8.13). Make sure that Preserve Transparency is selected for the new layer. If Preserve Transparency is selected for the original, the copy will inherit this setting.

3. Drag the layer so that it is under the object for which you are creating a shadow. This creates a duplicate that will be used for the shadow behind the object (8.14).

continues

Creating Shadows for Objects continued

4. Choose Edit → Fill. In the Fill dialog box, select Black from the list of colors **(8.15)**.

In Photoshop 5.5 and ImageReady, you can also use the Color Fill layer effect. Choose black as the fill color.

8.15

5. To create a drop shadow, move the shadow layer away from the object. The further you move the shadow, the higher the object appears to float above the page.

To create a cast shadow, choose Edit → Transform → Distort and modify the shape of the shadow. In most cases, you should drag the top handles so that the base of the object and the base of the shadow are the same **(8.16)**. The exact distortion varies based on your imaginary light source.

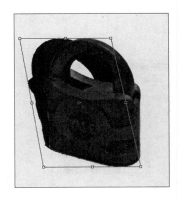

8.16

6. Clear the Preserve Transparency check box on the shadow layer so that when you use the blur filter the pixels can spread into transparent areas of the layer.

7. Use Filter → Blur → Gaussian Blur to blur the shadow **(8.17)**. The Gaussian Blur filter provides a preview, so you can choose a radius value appropriate for your image.

Note that when creating a cast shadow for some objects, the blur creates extra shadow at the base of the image. Use the eraser to eliminate any unwanted shadow. If you are working in a display mode higher than 8-bit (256 colors), the unwanted shadow may be difficult to see. Switch your operating system display settings to 8-bit to see unwanted dithering.

8.17

8.18

8.19

8. For a cast shadow, choose the Add layer mask button in the Layers palette. Use a black-and-white-linear gradient to create the appearance that the shadow is fading as the distance from the object and the background increases (8.18).

You can also paint with black on the layer mask to make any unwanted shadow areas transparent (8.19).

Depending on the background, you may want to change the opacity of the shadow layer.

You can also create drop shadows for objects and text using a layer effect. (See "Creating a Drop Shadow," page 158 in Chapter 9, "Layer Effects and Techniques.")

 T I P

To duplicate a layer, drag the layer's thumb-nail to the Create New Layer button in the Layers palette. If you want to enter a new name for the layer, hold down the (Option)[Alt] key while dragging so that the Duplicate Layer dialog box displays.

 T I P

If you want to create a background layer in an image, choose Layer → New → Background. A background layer filled with the current background color is created. This command is available only if you don't already have a background layer.

Selecting Nontransparent Pixels on a Layer

The Preserve Transparency setting eliminates much of the need to isolate nontransparent pixels on a layer when painting and running filters. However, you may need to create selections of all the nontransparent pixels for layer masks, clipping paths, and other effects.

1. Select the layer that contains the nontransparent pixels you want to select in the Layers palette.

2. Choose Select → Load Selection (**8.20**).

3. In the Load Selection dialog box, the transparency for the selected layer should already be selected in the list of channels (**8.21**). Choose OK. If you want to select the transparent areas of a layer, select Invert in the Load Selection dialog box.

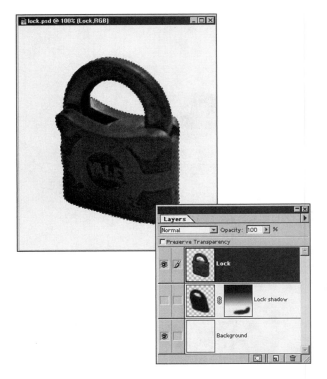

8.20

8.21

You can select the contents of a layer by holding down the (Command)[Ctrl] key and clicking on the layer thumbnail in the Layers palette.

Copying Layers from One Image to Another

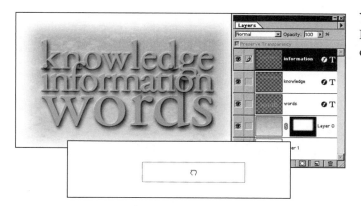

8.22

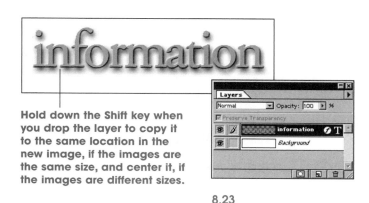

Hold down the Shift key when you drop the layer to copy it to the same location in the new image, if the images are the same size, and center it, if the images are different sizes.

8.23

You can copy layers from one open Photoshop document to another by dragging and dropping.

1. Open both the image that contains the source layers and the destination image.

2. Make sure that the image that contains the source layers is the active document so that its layers are visible in the Layers palette.

3. To copy a single layer, drag the layer thumbnail from the Layer palette (8.22) and drop it anywhere in the destination image (8.23).

4. To copy multiple layers, make one of the layers you want to copy active. Link any other layers you want to copy to the active layer and using the move tool, click and drag from the source image window to another image.

 I P

You can also use Layer → Duplicate Layer to copy a layer between open images or to create a new file from a layer. Using Duplicate Layer to copy a layer into an open image centers the copied layer. In addition, using Duplicate Layer does not store any information on the clipboard.

Controlling a Layer's Blend If Options for Compositing

The Blend If sliders in the Layer Options dialog box enable you to control how pixels on a layer interact with the pixels on layers below it. For example, you can drop out all the black pixels or all the white pixels on a layer so that underlying layers show through.

1. Select the layer that contains the Blend If option you want to change (8.24).

2. Choose Layer → Layer Options (8.25).

3. In the list of color choices, select a color to blend. Choosing Gray blends all the color channels.

4. In the Layer Options dialog box, use the This Layer slider to drop out selected colors or grayscale equivalents from the layer and show through to the underlying layers. When blending gray, moving the black and white sliders sets the darkest black and brightest white that appears in the layer. If you move the white slider to the left, bright whites drop out (8.26).

In the original image, the sky is a light gray.

8.24

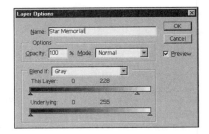

8.25

8.26

The underlying landscape contains the clouds that show through.

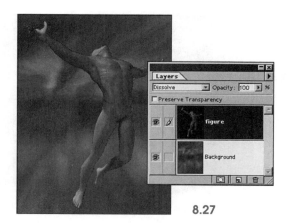

8.27

If you move the black slider to the right, black drops out **(8.27)**.

5. Change the values on the Underlying slider to force colors on the underlying layers through the layer. Moving the black slider to the right forces dark colors through. Moving the white slider to the left forces the light colors through.

8.28

I P

You can set a range to blend for the white and black sliders by holding down the (Option)[Alt] key while dragging the sliders. This creates a smooth transition between the points where the blending between the layers starts and stops.

*In the figure, there is a gradient running from black to 50% gray in the background **(8.28)**. Setting the left half of the black slider to 10 forces anything darker than 96% gray (including black) to completely drop out. The colors between 10 and 192 blend smoothly with the underlying layer. The blend begins to fade at 10, until at 192, there is no blend. Setting the right half of the black slider to 192 causes only the colors lighter than 25% gray to remain completely opaque **(8.29)**. (See also Figure **C.6** in the color insert.)*

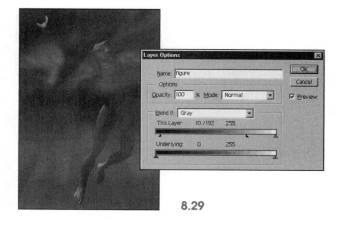

8.29

Removing Halos from Layers

When you create a selection that uses anti-aliasing (using the Magic Wand, for example), a thin halo of pixels is picked up from the background **(8.30)**. You can eliminate this halo by using the Defringe command. The Defringe command replaces pixels along the outside edge of the nontransparent pixels in a layer with pixels that do not contain any background color **(8.31)**.

8.30

1. Select the layer that you want to defringe in the Layers palette.

2. Choose Layer → Matting → Defringe **(8.32)**.

3. In the Defringe dialog box, choose the number of pixels to defringe. Usually a setting of one or two is sufficient. You can often count the number of pixels along the border that need to be defringed by zooming in.

8.31

If the selection was made against a white or black background, you can use the Layer → Matting → Remove White Matte or Remove Black Matte.

8.32

 I   P

You can also set the layer's Blend If values in the Layer Options dialog box to remove a black or white fringe.

CHAPTER 9

In this chapter you learn how to...

Fill Text or an Object with an Image

Create a Layer Mask with a Selection

Create and Edit a Layer Mask by Painting

Move a Layer Mask

Remove or Disable a Layer Mask

Create a Drop-Shadow or a Cut-Out Effect

Create a Glow

Create a Bevel and Emboss Effect

Apply a Solid Color Fill to a Layer

Apply a Gradient or Pattern to a Layer

Apply a Preset Layer-Effect Style
to a Layer

Copy Layer Effects to Other Layers

Break Layer Effects into Their Component
Layers

After you have created layers in a Photoshop image, you can use those layers to create a range of effects. You can use layers to clip information in other layers by grouping them together, precisely control areas of opacity and transparency using masks, and use a variety of elegant layer effects to enhance the appearance of a layer.

LAYER EFFECTS AND TECHNIQUES

Many of the most commonly used graphic techniques, such as drop shadows, glows, bevels, and embosses, can be easily attained through the use of Photoshop's Layer Effects. These straightforward tools provide you with powerful control over objects in a layer. Layer effects work best with layers that contain objects surrounded by or containing areas of transparency. They work especially well with type layers. Layer effects have quickly become a favorite production tool, particularly among Web designers. Photoshop 5.5 adds a solid color layer effect to those available in Photoshop 5.0. ImageReady contains all the same layer effects as Photoshop 5.5 and adds a gradient and pattern fill.

Whether you are creating buttons and other Web page graphics or compositing images for a printed work, you can combine layers, masks, and effects to further your design's communication. Looking at the advertisements in any major magazine or browsing the Web, you will see countless examples of these techniques being used alone and in combination.

ImageReady's layer capabilities mirror Photoshop's. ImageReady's layer effects can be put to excellent use when creating rollovers or animations.

Filling Text or an Object with an Image

Clipping groups use a base layer—the bottom-most layer in the group's stack—as a mask for all the layers grouped with it. The layers grouped with the base layer inherit the opacity of the base layer. Wherever the base layer is opaque, the layers grouped with it show. Wherever the base layer is transparent, the layers grouped with it are also transparent.

This particular technique works with any layer that contains areas of opacity and transparency. In particular, it works quite well with text.

1. Open an image that you want to use to fill the text **(9.1)**.

2. If the image is on the background layer, double-click the layer thumbnail. When the Make Layer dialog box appears, type the name for the layer. The layer that you use for the clipping group cannot be the background layer.

3. Use the type tool to place text in the image **(9.2)**. The color of the text is unimportant. A clipping group uses the opacity and transparency to determine what should show through.

4. Reorder the layers if necessary. Rearrange the layers if necessary, so that the type layer is under the image layer that is to be masked with the text. The text acts as the base layer and mask for the image after the

9.1

9.2

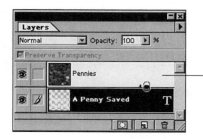

9.3

You also can select the image layer and choose Layer→Group with Previous to create a layer mask.

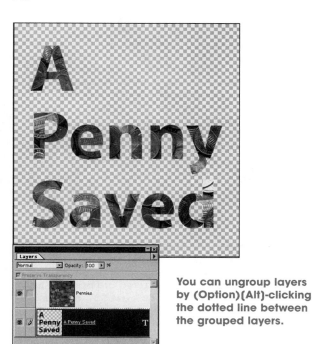

You can ungroup layers by (Option)(Alt)-clicking the dotted line between the grouped layers.

9.4

layers are grouped. Note that the text may be temporarily hidden.

5. Hold down the (Option)[Alt] key and move the cursor to the line between the two layers until the cursor changes to the group icon **(9.3)**.

The image will be visible only through the text, and the layer palette indicates that the layers are grouped by showing a dotted line between the layers and by indenting the layer that is clipped **(9.4)**.

 I P

The keyboard shortcut for grouping layers is (Command-G)[Ctrl+G]. The keyboard shortcut for ungrouping layers is (Shift-Command-G)[Shift+Ctrl+G].

 I P

Layer groups can contain more than one type of layer. For example, a layer group might use a type layer as the base to clip an image, but the image could be grouped with an adjustment layer.

You can rearrange layers in a group at any time by dragging them in the Layers palette. If you move a grouped layer in front of or behind a nongrouped layer, it will be ungrouped. If you move a layer under a layer in a group, it will automatically join the group.

Creating a Layer Mask with a Selection

A layer mask is a simple but powerful method of creating variable levels of transparency on a layer. Layer masks are generally used for compositing layers. For example, you can select a person or object and create a mask so that they appear against a new background. You also can use Photoshop 5.5's Extract command to isolate a person or object without clearly defined edges. For more information about using the Extract command, see "Creating a Mask for Objects without Clearly Defined Edges" on page 96 in Chapter 5, "Selecting."

9.5

A layer mask must be added to a layer other than the background. Because a mask is another name for a selection, one way to create a layer mask is to start with a selection.

1. To create a layer mask from a selection, begin by stacking the layers in the correct order. The image that will show through the transparent areas created by the mask should be beneath the layer that will have the mask applied to it. Also, be sure that the layer to which the mask is applied is active and visible **(9.5)**.

2. Create a selection using any method. In this example, the overall shape of the eyes was traced with paths and converted into a selection, which was intersected with circles created with the elliptical marquee. Finally, the highlights were subtracted from the selection with the magic wand and the resulting selection was feathered **(9.6)**.

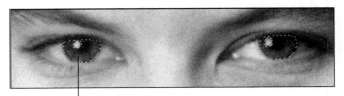

9.6 **When creating a layer mask from a selection, selected areas remain opaque while unselected areas show through to the layer underneath. Any pixels that are partially selected are partially transparent. Pixels selected at 50% are 50% opaque.**

Because the mask is an 8-bit grayscale channel, you can paint on the mask to change the areas of transparency and opacity.

Painting with black creates areas of transparency, while painting with white creates areas of opacity on the masked layer. Shades of gray create levels of transparency based on the distance from black or white (so 50% gray creates 50% opacity).

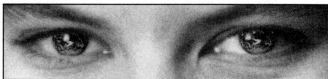

9.7

When a layer mask is created from a selection, selected areas remain opaque, so the selection was then inverted. (The selection didn't need to be inverted in this step. Photoshop provides several methods of inverting the mask during or after its application.)

3. With the selection active, choose the Add Layer Mask button at the bottom of the Layers palette.

The mask's thumbnail appears next to the layer thumbnail. Click the mask in the Layers palette to paint on it instead of the layer. It is 8-bit grayscale, is white where the pixels are selected, and black where deselected **(9.7)**. Where the layer mask is white, the selected layer remains opaque. Where the layer mask is black, the layer becomes transparent

 I P

If you want to choose between hiding and revealing the selection through the mask, you can use choose Layer→Layer Mask and select the appropriate option.

T I P

You can duplicate a mask for use with other layers or in case you delete the original by selecting it in the Channels palette and choosing Duplicate Channel in the Channels palette menu.

Creating and Editing a Layer Mask by Painting

You do not always need to start a layer mask with a selection. If you select a layer and add a layer mask, you can immediately begin painting to alter the transparency and opacity of a layer. When you add a layer mask, the foreground and background colors change to levels of gray because the mask is grayscale.

1. Create a layer mask by choosing the Add Layer Mask button in the Layers palette.

2. Wherever you want the layer to be transparent, paint with black. Wherever you want the layer to be opaque, paint with white (9.8).

3. To edit the layer instead of the mask, click the layer thumbnail. The icon next to the layer will change to a paintbrush when you are editing the layer and to a mask icon when editing the mask.

Gradients that fade from black to white are an easy and effective way to make a transition from one layer to another (9.9).

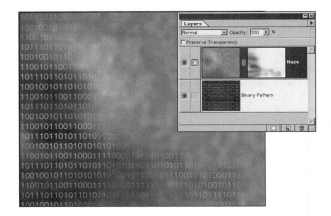

9.8

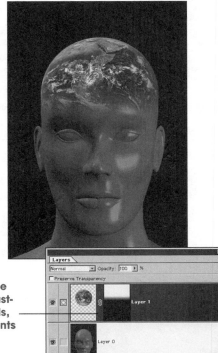

You also can use any image adjustment commands, filters, or gradients to alter a layer mask.

9.9

(T) I P

If you start a layer mask with a selection and have black where white should be, you can use the Image→Adjus→Invert command to reverse the effect of the layer mask.

Moving a Layer Mask

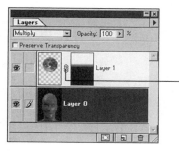

9.10

Layer and mask are linked and move together.

By default, Photoshop links the layer mask to the layer (9.10).

The links indicate that when the layer moves, the mask moves with it.

You can detach the layer and mask by clicking the link symbol (9.11).

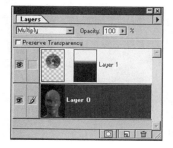

9.11

When there aren't any links between the layer thumbnail and the mask thumbnail, the mask and the layer move independently. You can move the layer mask to crop different areas of a layer or, if you are using a gradient, to change the areas of transition from one layer to another.

Removing or Disabling a Layer Mask

9.12

You can temporarily turn off a layer mask by choosing Disable Layer Mask from the Layer menu or the shortcut menu. When a mask is disabled, it still exists but is not applied. Photoshop indicates that the layer is disabled by placing a red X through the mask's thumbnail.

Remove a layer mask by choosing Remove Layer Mask from the Layer menu or the shortcut menu. Regardless of what method you use, Photoshop asks you whether you want to apply the layer mask or discard it. Discarding it returns your image to its original state, while applying it changes your image permanently. Flattening and merging automatically apply the layer mask.

Creating a Drop-Shadow or a Cut-Out Effect

Drop shadows are one of the most common effects created in Photoshop, used to increase text's readability against light backgrounds. Drop shadows also enable you to place light or white text against a similarly colored background **(9.13)**.

You can bring elements in an image forward by adding a drop shadow. When creating a selection to isolate an element, anti-aliasing often causes a white halo effect around the selection, which is made more obvious by the drop shadow. Use defringing to eliminate the halo. See "Removing Halos from Layers," page 148 in Chapter 8, "Using Layers," for more information about defringing a layer.

Like drop shadows, inner shadows help when light text is placed against a light background **(9.14)**.

Inner shadows make objects and shapes appear cut into a background. In **(9.15)**, the background layer was copied, lightened with an adjustment layer, and grouped with the pattern layer .

 I P

When applying an inner shadow to text that is the same color as the background, thinner-stroked fonts are easier to read because it is easier to identify the letter form. Further, fonts with serifs and script fonts work better than san serif fonts.

9.13

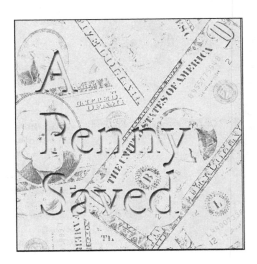

9.14

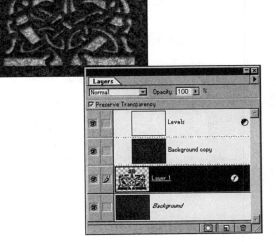

9.15

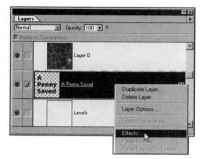

9.16

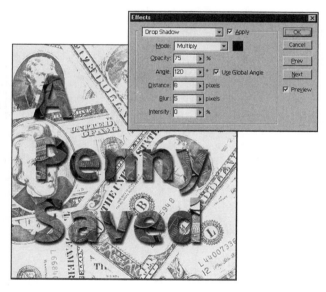

9.17

The options for the inner-shadow and drop-shadow effects are similar. Both shadow types use the Multiply Blending mode by default, so the shadows always darken the pixels beneath the shadows.

1. Begin by selecting the layer to which you want to apply the shadow in the Layers palette.

2. Select Layer→Effects and either Drop Shadow or Inner Shadow. You also can use the contextual menu (Ctrl-click) [right-click] and choose Effects **(9.16)**.

   If you choose Effects from the shortcut menu, a drop shadow is automatically selected and applied. If you want to apply an inner shadow, turn off the drop shadow by unchecking the Apply check box and select Inner Shadow from the list of effects.

3. The Layer Effects dialog box enables you to select between the different effects and the effect options. A preview of the effect is displayed immediately in the image **(9.17)**. Choose the options that you want for your shadow.

continues

Creating a Drop-Shadow or a Cut-Out Effect continued

4. You can set the distance and angle of the drop shadow dynamically by dragging in the image. The values update automatically in the dialog box.

Table 9.1   Layer Effects Settings

Option	Description
Mode and color	Determines the color and blend mode of the effect. The default mode, Multiply, darkens the image with the default color, black. Click the color box to change the color.
Angle	Changes the apparent direction of the light source **(9.18)**. Select the Use Global Angle option to apply the same lighting direction to all effects.
Distance	Changes the apparent height of the object or text from the page **(9.19)**.
Blur	Softens the shadow **(9.20)**.
Intensity	Strengthens shadows and glows by increasing the amount of the effect's area that is filled with the shadow or glow color. Very high values may produce unacceptable results.

 I P

For the most accurate preview of your effect, view the image at 100% magnification. Other magnifications may make the effect look darker than it actually is.

 I P

You also can adjust the location and angle of layer effects by clicking and dragging the effect in the image while the dialog box is open.

9.18

9.19

9.20

Creating a Glow

9.21

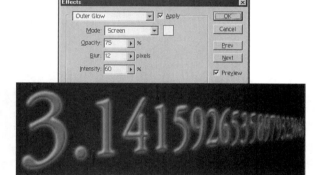

9.22

9.23   **An inner glow that forms from the center can be used as a very soft bevel or to create additional texture to a bevel or emboss effect.**

Glows are often used with dark objects against dark backgrounds. A halo is added evenly around the object in the case of the outer glow effect and inside the object in the case of the inner glow.

By default, glows use the screen-blending mode, so they always produce a lighter color.

To create directional glow effects, use the drop shadow and inner shadow with a light color and screen mode selected **(9.21)**.

1. Begin by selecting the layer on which the objects will glow and select either an outer-glow or inner-glow layer effect from either the Layer menu or from the list of effects in the Layer Effects dialog box.

2. Select the options that you want in the dialog box. You may often need to adjust the intensity of the glow to get the desired effect **(9.22)**.

3. Change the color of the glow by picking on the color swatch. The default color is a pale yellow.

4. If you are creating an inner glow, select whether you want the glow to form at the edge of the objects or from the center.

Creating a Bevel and Emboss Effect

The bevel and emboss layer effects streamline a process that involves the creation of several layers and selection techniques. All the bevels and embosses use a highlight color and a shadow color. Like the shadow and glow effects, the shadows use Multiply mode by default and the highlights use Screen mode.

You can reverse the direction of the bevel or emboss by selecting the Down option button instead of the Up button.

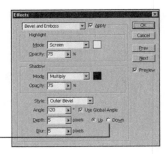

9.24

1. In the Layers palette, select the layer on which you want to bevel or emboss objects and choose Layer→Effects→Bevel and Emboss **(9.24)**.

2. Select a Highlight color and mode and a Shadow color and mode.

3. Select a Style.

    ● Outer Bevel. The objects in the layer bevel along the outside edges **(9.25)**.

    ● Inner Bevel. The objects in the layer bevel along the inside edges **(9.26)**.

    ● Emboss. The objects in the layer are embossed against the underlying layers **(9.27)**.

9.25

9.26

 I P

If you are having difficulty getting drop shadows dark enough, break the effect into its components and duplicate the shadow layer as many times as you need to achieve the desired intensity. Adjust the opacity of the duplicated layers to further refine the shadow's intensity.

9.27

9.28

9.29

9.30

- Pillow Emboss. The edges of the layer are stamped into the underlying layers **(9.28)**.

In each of the sample images, the layer with the objects was grouped with a layer containing a pattern. In the example showing the emboss effect, the grouped layer and the background are the same **(9.29)**.

4. Set an angle for the highlight and shadow. Set a depth for the bevel or emboss to control how much the objects in the layer come forward or recede.

 I P

*Mutiple layer effects can be combined to create increasingly sophisticated results **(9.30)**. You can use as many layer effects as you want on a single layer or in an image. In this image, a drop shadow and inner shadow are used on the white type. A pillow emboss is used on the black type and an inner bevel and drop shadow are used on the ampersand.*

5.5 Applying a Solid Color Fill to a Layer

Photoshop 5.5 adds the capability to fill all the opaque pixels on a layer with a solid color while still maintaining the original colors of the layer's contents. You can use this layer effect to quickly change the color of an entire layer. This layer effect is also available in ImageReady and can be used with rollovers to change the color of buttons and text.

9.31

1. Select a layer in the Layers palette. In this example, the layer contains areas of transparency around the figure, showing through to the white background (9.31).

2. Choose Layer→Effects→Color Fill (9.32).

3. In the dialog box, click the color swatch and choose a color from the Color Picker.

9.32

4. Choose a Blending mode and Opacity for the color fill.

5. Choose OK.

The entire layer is filled with a solid color (9.33).

9.33

Applying a Gradient or Pattern to a Layer

9.34

9.35

ImageReady enables you to apply a gradient or pattern fill to a layer, including an unrendered type layer. You can use this to apply textures and color blends to all the objects on a layer while preserving the layer's contents. In particular, you can dramatically alter the appearance of a type layer while maintaining the ability to edit the type.

1. Select a layer in the Layers palette.

2. Choose Layer→Effects→ Gradient/Pattern.

3. To apply a gradient, select Gradient in the Gradient/ Pattern palette **(9.34)**. Select a type of gradient—linear or radial **(9.35)**. Enter an angle for a linear gradient. Click the down-arrow button and select a gradient style. You can edit the gradient style by editing the gradient preview similar to Photoshop with a few exceptions, such as the inability to select gradient colors from the image with the eyedropper. See "Customizing Gradients" on page 130 in Chapter 7, "Painting," for more details.

continues

Applying a Gradient or Pattern to a Layer continued

4. To apply a pattern, choose Pattern in the Gradient/Pattern palette. Click the down arrow button to display the list of available patterns. Select a predefined pattern or choose Other to select an image to use as a pattern **(9.36)**.

Photoshop does not display gradient or pattern layer effects created in ImageReady, although the information is preserved (and Photoshop displays an icon in the Layers palette to indicate that the effect was created in ImageReady). You cannot edit or remove the effect in Photoshop.

Choose Use Defined Pattern if you have previously defined a pattern using Edit→Define Pattern.

Choose Linked to Layer to maintain the position of the pattern relative to the layer.

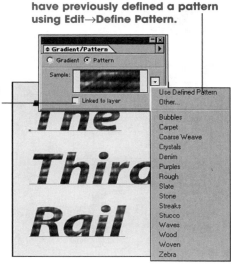

9.36

 I P

Create your gradients in Photoshop if you need to use features that are not available in ImageReady, such as spot or CMYK colors, transparency, or shaped gradients.

ImageReady displays layer effects differently in the Layers palette. You can remove individual layer effects by dragging them to the trash or edit them by double-clicking. You also can control the visibility of individual effects by hiding them.

9.37

 I P

To reverse the order of the gradient, choose Show Options from the Gradient/Pattern palette menu. Then choose Reverse in the Gradient/Pattern palette.

You also can display extra options for a palette by double-clicking the palette tab.

Applying a Preset Layer-Effect Style to a Layer

9.38

9.39

9.40

ImageReady comes with several predefined layer-effect styles, or groups of layer effects that can be applied to layers. You also can define you own layer styles.

Styles are useful for quickly changing the appearance of a background, text, or buttons in an image. By selecting elements or layers and choosing predefined styles, you can go from (**9.38**) to (**9.39**) with just a click of a button. Styles also work especially well with ImageReady's other features, such as rollovers and animation.

To apply a layer-effect style to a layer, select a layer in the Layers palette and double-click a style in the Styles palette (**9.40**). You also can drag a style onto a layer.

To add a layer-effect style to the Styles palette, select a layer with layer effects applied to it and choose New Style from the Styles palette menu. Enter a name for the style and choose OK.

 I P

Edit layer effects by double-clicking the effects icon in the Layers palette. Accessing the context-sensitive menu from this icon also enables you to clear the effects or to turn them off temporarily.

Copying Layer Effects to Other Layers

If you have applied layer effects to a layer, you can copy and paste those effects onto other layers. This makes creating special effects or repeating elements, such as buttons for Web pages, much faster.

1. Create the desired effect in your image. In this example (9.41), the text is on a separate layer and has been embossed.

2. Choose Layer→Effects→Copy Effects, or choose Copy Effects from the context-sensitive menu associated with the effects icon next to the layer in the Layers palette.

3. Select the layer that you want to apply the effects to and choose Paste Effects from the Layer menu or from the shortcut menu. The effects are duplicated on the new layer with all the settings that you have already made (9.42).

Effects also can be copied and pasted between documents.

9.41

9.42

 I P

When editing layer effects, hold down the (Option)[Alt] key and click the Reset button to reset the layer effects without canceling the dialog box.

Breaking Layer Effects into Their Component Layers

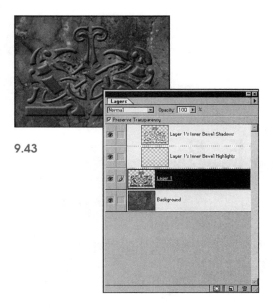

9.43

9.44

Layer effects are achieved by creating intermediate layers using the opacity and transparency information on a layer with the effect settings. These intermediate layers can be viewed and edited directly. By breaking layer effects, you can increase the intensity of effects beyond the maximums permitted in the dialog box (stacking multiple shadows, for example). You also can apply filters or transformations to individual effect components.

1. Choose Create Layers from the shortcut menu or from the Layer menu. After you have broken a layer effect into its component layers, it cannot be put back together again.

2. The layer effect's component layers are grouped with the original layer (9.43).

3. You can edit these layers as you would any other to change the intensity of the effect, alter the components, or see what the effect looks like with select components removed (9.44). In this instance, the shadows have been deleted from the inner bevel.

 **O T E**

Copy either the layer or the effect so that if you need to return the layer to its original state you can easily do that.

CHAPTER 10

In this chapter you learn how to...

Place Text in an Image

Edit Text

Adjust Leading

Adjust Kerning and Tracking

Adjust the Baseline Shift

Apply Special Effects to a Text Layer

Create Wood Text

Create Metal Text

Create Carved Text

Photoshop treats text as a special graphic element and places it on its own layer. A type layer enables you to edit text after it is placed. A type layer can contain only text and the text must be a solid color. To modify the text using filters or to paint on the type layer, you must first render the layer.

ImageReady enables you to fill text with gradients and patterns using a layer effect. To achieve the same effect in Photoshop, use clipping groups.

PUTTING TYPE IN AN IMAGE

While type layers in Photoshop give you considerable control over the text and the ability to continually edit it after it is created, for large quantities of text you might want to consider a page-layout or illustration program.

Photoshop 5.5 adds the ability to control the type of anti-aliasing used for text and also advanced kerning and tracking options. This is especially important for small text in low-resolution images. Photoshop 5.5 also enables you to simulate bold and italicized text for fonts that do not contain these styles by using the Faux Bold and Faux Italic options. You can also easily underline selected text.

ImageReady, like Photoshop, places text on individual type layers. Editing, however, is slightly different. Instead of double-clicking the type layer or text in the image to edit the type in the Type Tool dialog box, you edit the type onscreen and change its properties (font, kerning, and so on) in the Type palette.

Placing Text

Using the Type tool, you can place text anywhere in an image. If you place text in an image mode that supports layers, you can preview and move the text before placing it **(10.1)**. After you choose OK in the Type Tool dialog box **(10.2)**, Photoshop creates an editable type layer. If you place text in an image mode that does not support multiple layers (Indexed Color, for example,) the text is placed without a preview and becomes part of the background canvas. In Indexed Color images, text is also aliased by default. To control aliasing in text, convert the image to RGB. See "Using RGB Instead of Indexed Color for Text and Resampling" on page 67 in Chapter 4, "Image Modes," for more information.

The Type tool has four tools, described in Table 10.1.

When you place vertical text, you can choose to place the letters horizontally (the default) **(10.3)** or vertically **(10.4)** by selecting Rotate in the Type Tool dialog box.

10.1

10.2

10.3   10.4

Table 10.1   Type Tools

Tool	Function
Type	For placing horizontal text in an image.
Type Mask	For placing a selection in the form of type in an image. The Type Mask tool is helpful when creating layer masks.
Vertical Type	For placing vertical text in an image.
Vertical Type Mask	For placing a selection in the form of vertical type in an image.

10.5   **The Photoshop 5.0 TypeTool dialog box has fewer controls for anti-aliasing and does not have a fractional width option or simulated text effects (underline, faux bold, or faux italic).**

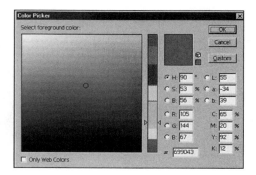

10.6

1. From the toolbar, select the Type tool.

2. Position the cursor in the image and click. The Type Tool dialog box is displayed **(10.5)**.

3. Choose a font, style, and size for the text. When selecting a size, you can choose points or pixels for the units. (If you are working on an image for the Web at 72 ppi, points and pixels produce the same results.)

4. In Photoshop 5.5 and Image-Ready, to underline horizontal text or simulate bold or italicized fonts, select Underline, Faux Bold, or Faux Italic.

5. Choose a color for the text by clicking the color swatch. The Color Picker is displayed **(10.6)**. You can choose a color from the image by clicking with the Eyedropper tool. The foreground color is used by default. The color you select affects all the text you are placing.

6. Choose an alignment for the text: left, right, or center aligned. The point of alignment is based on the point you selected. You can also adjust the leading, kerning and tracking, and baseline shift for selected type. For more information, see the relevant topics later in this chapter.

continues

Placing Text continued

7. In Photoshop 5.5 and ImageReady, choose an anti-aliasing option (Table 10.2).

8. If you are placing vertical text, select Rotate to rotate the letters so that the baseline is vertical. By default, the baselines for all the letters are horizontal.

9. Type the text in the display window of the Type Tool dialog box. If you are working in an image mode that supports multiple layers, a preview displays in the image (10.7).

10. Choose OK when finished.

If you place text in an image mode that does not support multiple layers, the text is selected and floats above the canvas when you exit the Type Tool dialog box. You can reposition it using the Move tool. As soon as you deselect, the type becomes part of the background.

10.7

If you move the cursor into the image, it turns into the Move tool so you can reposition the text.

Table 10.2   Anti-aliasing Options

Option	Description
None	No anti-aliasing is applied.
Crisp	Anti-aliasing is applied to make the text appear sharper.
Strong	Anti-aliasing is applied to make the text appear heavier.
Smooth	Anti-aliasing is applied to make the text appear smoother.

 I P

You can choose only one solid color for each type layer. If you want to use multiple colors or patterns, use a clipping group. See "Filling Text with an Image," on page 152 in Chapter 9, "Layer Effects and Techniques."

Editing Text

10.8

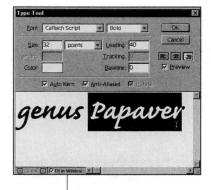

10.9

Fit in Window will zoom your text appropriately to fill the Preview window.

The ability to edit text after it is placed is an invaluable feature of Photoshop. Editable type layers enable you to alter text and its formatting. If the type layer has been rendered or is on a layer other than a type layer, it is editable only as pixels, not as type.

1. Double-click the T next to the layer name (10.8) or on the layer name itself.

2. In the display window of the Type Tool dialog box, select the text that you want to change (10.9).

3. You can change any of the text options that were set when the text was originally placed, including font, size, and color.

4. Choose OK when finished editing the text.

 I P

If you want to use selected fonts only with Adobe Photoshop and other newer versions of Adobe applications (ImageReady, ImageStyler 1.0, and Illustrator 7.0 and later), install them in the Adobe Fonts folder instead of through the operating system.

In Windows, the fonts are located in Program Files\Common Files\Adobe\Fonts on the same hard drive as the operating system. On the Macintosh, it is in System Folder\Application Support\Adobe\Fonts.

Adjusting Leading

Leading is the space between lines of text and is measured from base-line to baseline. A higher leading value increases the distance between the lines **(10.10)** while a very small value creates overlapping lines **(10.11)**.

If you leave the value for the lead-ing blank, Photoshop uses a stan-dard 120% of the text height **(10.12)**.

1. In the Type Tool dialog box, select the line in which you want to adjust spacing. When you select a line of text, the leading between it and the line above it is changed **(10.13)**.

2. Enter a new value for the lead-ing or clear the value to use the default.

3. You can continue to adjust the leading for other lines of text. Choose OK when finished.

10.10

10.11

10.12

10.13

 I P

When using vertical type with horizontal letters, adjust the tracking to change the ver-tical space between the letters.

Adjusting Kerning and Tracking

The Auto Kern in this font is a bit too loose between the O and S in the top word.

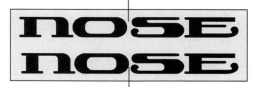

10.14   **The kerning was adjusted manually between the letters of the bottom word.**

10.15

Kerning is the spacing between two letters. Tracking is the spacing of more than two letters and can be used to control the appearance of a word, line, or block of text. Tracking can be changed only when more than one letter is selected in the Type Tool dialog box.

By default, Photoshop uses the kerning built into each font by that font's designer. To manually adjust the kerning, clear the Auto Kern check box in the Type Tool dialog box. You can clear the Auto Kern for selected pairs of letters or for all the text.

Adjust the kerning for headlines and display type or when the Auto Kern yields unacceptable results (**10.14**).

Adjust the tracking when you want to change the overall length of a word or of a line to make it fit into a space or to align it with lines above or below it (**10.15**).

By default, both the kerning and tracking values are set to 0 in the Type Tool dialog box. Positive values add space between the letters or words. Negative values remove space. This space is measured in units that are 1/1000 of an em space. An em space is as wide as the text height. If you use 18 point type, an em space is 18 points.

continues

Adjusting Kerning and Tracking continued

1. In the Type Tool dialog box, place the cursor between two letters to adjust the kerning or select a group of letters to adjust the track.

2. Enter new kerning or tracking values.

3. In Photoshop 5.5 and ImageReady, for small and low-resolution text, clear Fractional Widths if the text is unreadable (10.16 and 10.17).

4. You can continue to alter kerning and tracking for other text. Choose OK when finished.

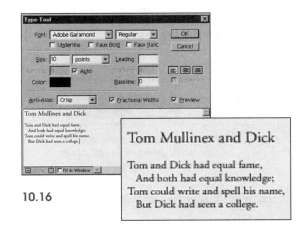

10.16

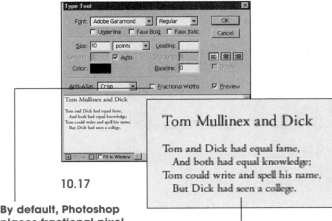

10.17

T I **P**

Kerning for small text in Photoshop version 5.0 is often unacceptable. Download the 5.02 patch if you have not already done so. You can check which version you are using by choosing Help→About Photoshop. The version displays under the banner.

T I **P**

You can use the keyboard to alter kerning or tracking in the Type Tool dialog box. (Option-Arrow keys)[Alt+Arrow keys] changes the value by 20. (Option-Command-Arrow keys)[Alt+Control+Arrow keys] changes the value by 100.

By default, Photoshop places fractional pixel spaces between letters (possible because of anti-aliasing). For small text, some letters may run together. Turning off Fraction Widths forces Photoshop to place text in whole pixel increments.

For small, low resolution text, turning on fractional widths creates better kerning (for example, between the w and r in "write") and prevents tall vertical letters from running together (for example, the double l's in "spell" and "college").

Adjusting the Baseline Shift

10.18

Individual letters or words an be raised or lowered from the baseline of the text **(10.18)**. Entering a positive value for the baseline shift raises the text. Entering a negative value lowers the text under the baseline.

1. In the Type Tool dialog box, highlight the text in which you want to change the baseline shift.

2. Change the baseline shift by changing the Baseline value.

Applying Special Effects to a Text Layer

10.19   **When merging type layers, at least one of the layers must be rendered.**

To apply filters or fills other than solid colors to a type layer, it must first be converted into pixels, or rendered. When you render a type layer, the text is no longer editable. **(10.19)**

1. Select the type layer that you want to render.

2. Choose Layer→Type→Render Layer.

 I P

Render a duplicate of a type layer and hide the original. If you need to make changes to the text, you can delete the rendered version and edit the original type layer.

Similarly, if you apply transformations to a type layer, retain a duplicate of the original layer. You do not need to render a type layer to apply transformations to it.

Creating Wood Text

Photoshop comes with several actions that can be used to create wood textures. These textures can be easily combined with layer effects and clipping groups to fill text. By modifying the actions or their results, you can customize the results to create an even greater variety of wood patterns.

For more information about using actions, see Chapter 19, "Automating Photoshop." For more information about using clipping groups, see "Filling Text with an Image," on page 152 in Chapter 9, "Layer Effects and Techniques."

1. In the Actions palette, choose Load Actions from the menu. From the Actions folder in the Goodies folder, choose the Textures action set **(10.20)**.

2. Create the text that you want to fill with a wood pattern **(10.21)**.

3. Choose the Type layer in the Layers palette **(10.22)**.

4. In the Actions palette, choose the type of wood pattern that you want to create. Once selected, choose the Play Current Selection button.

10.20

The split wood texture was used to fill the background of this image and layer effects were added to enhance the text.

10.21

10.22

 I P

You can fill text with other patterns and textures. Experiment with other textures available in the Textures action set.

C.1

The gray areas show the colors that are out-of-gamut. (See "Previewing Out-of-Gamut Colors" on page 56 in Chapter 4, "Image Modes.")

C.2

Duotone curves affect the application of the second color in the image. (See "Converting to Duotone" on page 73 in Chapter 4, "Image Modes.")

C.3

C.4

C.5

Use Photoshop's History Brush to precisely control the areas, opacity, and blending properties of filters. (See "Painting with Previous Versions of the File with the History Brush" on page 36 in Chapter 2, "Using the History Palette," and "Painting with Previous Versions of an Image" on page 124 in chapter 7, "Painting."

C.6

Use a layer's Blend If options to control how it combines with other layers. (See "Controlling a Layer's Blend If Options for Compositing" on page 146 in Chapter 8, "Using Layers.")

C.7

Use the Sponge tool to increase or decrease the saturation in an area. This figure shows the image before the Desaturation tool was used.

C.8

In this image, the center of the yellow flower is much less saturated. (See "Changing the Saturation in an Area" on page 218 in Chapter 13, "Color Correction.")

C.9

When removing an overall color cast in a CMYK image, move the gamma slider to the left. (See "Removing a Color Cast with Levels" on page 221 in Chapter 13, "Color Correction.")

C.10

Move the middle of the curve down to remove an overall color cast. (See "Removing a Color Cast with Curves" on page 222 in Chapter 13, "Color Correction.")

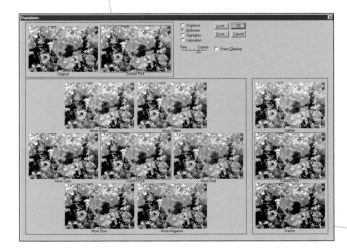

C.11

The Variations dialog box displays several different views of the image. (See "Removing a Color Cast with Variations" on page 219 in Chapter 13, "Color Correction.")

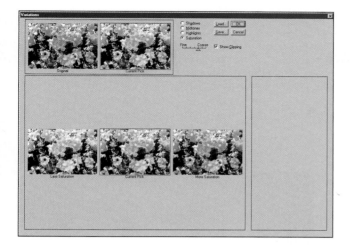

C.12

The Variations dialog box enables you to control the saturation of your images and offers images for comparison. (See "Removing a Color Cast with Variations" on page 219 in Chapter 13, "Color Correction.")

C.13

The before and after images of an image with Hue/Saturation adjustment. (See "Changing Color with Hue/Saturation" on page 223 in Chapter 13, "Color Correction.")

C.14

Selective Color enables you to increase and decrease the amount of a process ink in relation to the other process inks. You can modify the amount of a process color in any primary color selectively without affecting any other primary colors. (See "Changing Color with Selective Color" on page 226 in Chapter 13, "Color Correction.")

C.15

In this image, the blue flowers and ribbons have been partially changed to pink using the Replace Color command. (See "Changing Color with Replace Color" on page 227 in Chapter 13, "Color Correction.")

C.16

Paint or fill areas of an adjustment layer to composite multiple adjustment layers. (See "Creating an Adjustment Layer" on page 228 in Chapter 13, "Color Correction.")

C.17

Combine multiple filters to create increasingly sophisticated effects. (See "Creating a Comic-Book Effect" on page 256 in Chapter 15, "Using Filters.")

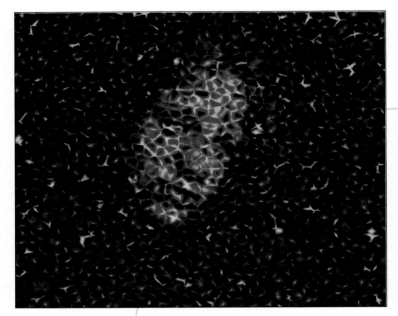

C.18

C.19

You can combine filters with textures and layer blending modes to create increasingly sophisticated compositions. In particular, these images use several layers to create the background textures and multiple copies of the layers with the faces in Overlay mode.

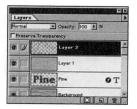

10.23

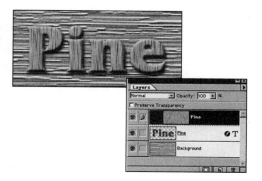

10.24

10.25

5. Many of the wood textures create multiple layers for the wood and for the grain. To make the wood texture easier to work with, merge the layers together. In the case of a wood and grain layer, select the uppermost layer (Grain) and choose Merge Down **(10.23)**.

6. Select the layer that contains the texture and choose Layer→ Group. The text is filled with the wood texture **(10.24)**.

 I P

*Combine the texture with multiple layers and effects to create additional depth. In this image **(10.25)**, an additional text layer, slightly larger than the first, with a smaller emboss depth was used to create the additional ridge.*

 I P

In addition to using a clipping group (see "Filling Text with an Image," on page 152 in Chapter 9, "Layer Effects and Techniques") you can also create a selection or mask from the type layer, create a new layer, and paste or fill into it. Hold down (Command)[Ctrl] and click the layer thumbnail to create the selection.

Creating Metal Text

There are many methods that you can use to create text that appears metallic. The techniques are similar to applying a wood texture to text: create the type, create a layer that contains the texture, and then group the layers together.

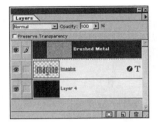

10.26

1. Use the Type tool to add text to the image.

2. Select the new type layer in the Layers palette and create a new layer. The new layer appears above the type layer in the Layers palette so that it can be used as part of a clipping group. Choose Layer→Group with Previous **(10.26)**.

10.27

3. To create brushed metal, fill the new layer with the color of the metal. For aluminum and other white metals, use white. For yellow metals (gold and brass), fill the layer with a yellow/brown color (for example, 170,140,90). Then use Filter→Noise→Add Noise **(10.27)**, and add monochromatic noise to the layer. To complete the effect, use Filter→Blur→Motion Blur **(10.28)** to create the brush effect **(10.29)**.

10.28

10.29

10.30

10.31

To create an irregular oil/chrome effect, use the Rippled Oil action in the Textures action set (10.30) or modify the action to create your own pattern. Choose Layer→Group with Previous to create a clipping group.

To create a bevel or emboss, use an appropriate layer effect.

Combine all these techniques together to enhance the effect (10.31). You can combine the layers together using different blending modes (overlay, for example).

 I P

You may also want to experiment with other color fills to combine with the rippled oil and brush effects. For example, the chrome or copper gradients can enhance the metallic illusion.

Using the Lighting Effects filter can also enhance the metallic appearance because you can control the material that the lights react to. For more information on the Lighting Effects filter, see "Changing the Lighting in an Image," page 262, Chapter 15, "Using Filters."

Creating Carved Text

There are several techniques that you can use to create text so that it appears carved. Although the bevel and emboss filters can begin to create the effect, they do not create the sharp corner that is expected in carved text. You can create the sharp corner by using multiple iterations of the bevel filter.

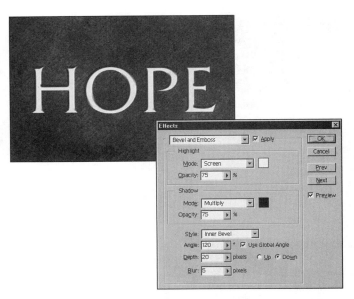

1. Begin by creating the text and applying the bevel and emboss effect. Choose Inner Bevel and use a blur and depth that create a clearly defined angle. Make note of the amount of the blur **(10.32)**.

10.32

2. Select the area defined by the text by holding down (Command)[Ctrl] and clicking the type layer thumbnail in the Layers palette.

3. Choose Select→Modify→ Contract. Enter a value that is less than the value used in the bevel layer effect **(10.33)**. Using a smaller value ensures that there are no seams between the bevels. In this example, the blur was set to 5 and the contraction to 3.

10.33

4. Create a new layer.

5. With the selection still active, fill the contracted text area with the same color as the text.

10.34

10.35

10.36

10.37

6. Copy the layer effect from the original type layer and paste it to the new layer. The angle of the bevel is increased in the text **(10.34)**.

7. Repeat steps 2 through 6 until the desired sharpness of the carving is reached **(10.35)**.

 I P

You can combine the carving technique with clipping groups to use the same texture as the background and with the Lighting Effects filter to create a more dramatic appearance **(10.36)**.

 I P

You can also combine the technique with other layer effects, such as a drop shadow to make the text appear raised instead of carved.

Drop shadows are especially useful for other objects in the image so that the carved text appears unambiguously carved into the background **(10.37)**.

CHAPTER 11

In this chapter you learn to...

Save Selections as Channels

Load Channels as Selections

Manage Saved Selections

Select in Quick Mask Mode

Split and Merge Channels

Photoshop uses channels to determine image composition. For example, an image in RGB mode contains three channels: one each for red, green and blue. Photoshop combines the values of each pixel on a channel using an additive process to determine the composite image. In a CMYK image, the channels show the process color separations.

USING CHANNELS AND MASKS

The ability to influence and edit individual channels gives you unprecedented control over your image. In CMYK, the benefits are clear. If you want to reduce the amount of black ink in an image, you need to lighten only the black channel. In RGB mode, you have similar control over the colors and details in an image. For example, the blue channel often collects the noise when you scan. Using the Smart Blur or Median filter with the Filter Fade command on the blue channel can help eliminate noise throughout the entire image. Similar techniques can be used with images in Lab mode.

In Photoshop an alpha channel is a stored mask or selection. Because channels are saved with the image, you can always recapture the selection information. Photoshop also manages spot color information with channels. For more information about using spot color channels, see "Creating Spot Color Channels" on page 272 in Chapter 16, "Paper Publishing." In file formats that support transparency (such as TGA and PNG), use channels to define the transparency.

ImageReady does not display channel information, and you can not edit it directly. If you want to use channels to make changes to your image, make the changes in Photoshop before switching to ImageReady.

Saving Selections as Channels

A selection is a mask containing 256 levels of gray. Where the mask is white, pixels are completely selected. Where the mask is black, pixels are completely unselected. The levels of gray between black and white indicate selections ranging from unselected to completely selected. When you feather a selection, for example, a smooth transition from selected to unselected, or white to black, is created.

When you save a selection, it is saved as an alpha channel, a grayscale representation of the mask, and stored in the Channels palette with the color channels that define the image and any spot color channels. If you want to save your file in a format that does not support channels, or supports only a limited number of channels (see Table 11.1), you can also save your channels into a separate document. Documents saved in this way contain only the channels that you save. You can open the documents with the original image (or any other image of the same size) and load these externally saved selections.

1. Create a selection (11.1).

2. Choose Select→Save Selection. The Save Selection dialog box is displayed (11.2).

Table 11.1   File Types and Channels Supported

File Extension	Number of Channels Supported
PSD (Photoshop native)	24
DCS 2.0	24 (1 alpha)
PICT (RGB)	1
PIXAR	1
PNG (Grayscale and RGB)	1
TGA	1
TIFF (Grayscale, RGB, CMYK)	24

11.1

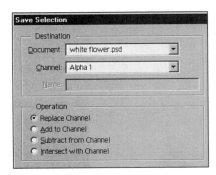

11.2

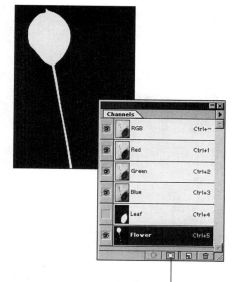

You can also use the
Save Selection as
Channel icon or Save
Selection from the
palette flyout menu.

11.3

3. In the Save Selection dialog
   box, under Document, choose
   where you want to save the
   alpha channel. You can save the
   channel into any document
   with the same pixel dimensions. The default is the current
   image. You can also create a
   new image with the selection
   by selecting New.

4. Under Channel, select an existing saved selection to overwrite
   or New to create a new channel
   (11.3). If you select an existing
   channel, you can choose how
   you want the new selection to
   combine with the existing
   channel by selecting an option
   under Operation. The existing
   channel is overwritten.

5. Under Name, enter the name of
   the selection. If you do not
   enter a name, it is named
   Alpha N, where N is the next
   available number.

6. Choose OK.

 I P

*Save selections incrementally just as you
would save changes to a file in case you need
to recover previous versions of a selection.
You can save selections temporarily and then
delete the channel that is created.*

*You can combine the completed channel with
other selections and channels using any of
the Boolean operations to create increasingly
complicated masks.*

Loading Channels as Selections

You can load any channel as a selection. White areas translate to complete selection. Black areas are not selected. Color channels often provide valuable starting points for complex selections. For example, red channels often contain much of an image's contrast. By duplicating the red channel, modifying it with levels, and using it as a selection, you can often get an excellent start on a complex selection. As another example, holding down (Command)[Ctrl] and clicking the composite channel loads a selection based on the image's luminance. This works particularly well if the image's foreground contrasts with the background.

1. Choose Selection→Load Selection. The Load Selection dialog box is displayed (11.4).

2. In the Load Selection dialog box, choose the document from which to load the selection. You can choose any open document that contains alpha channels and has the same pixel dimensions. The default is the current document.

3. Under Channel, choose the saved selection to load.

4. If you have an existing selection made, choose how you want the saved selection to combine with the current selection by selecting one of the Operation options.

5. Choose OK.

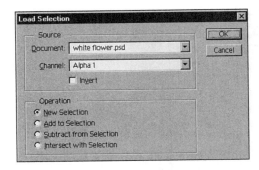

11.4

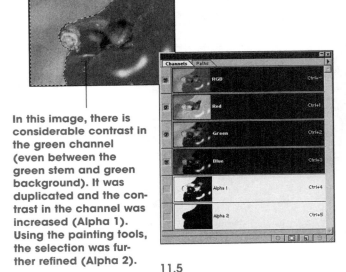

In this image, there is considerable contrast in the green channel (even between the green stem and green background). It was duplicated and the contrast in the channel was increased (Alpha 1). Using the painting tools, the selection was further refined (Alpha 2).

11.5

Table 11.2 Keyboard Shortcuts for Selections

Shortcut	Result
(Command)(Ctrl)-click channel thumbnail	Creates selection from the channel
(Command-Option)(Ctrl+Alt)-click channel thumbnail	Subtracts channel selection from current selection
(Command-Shift)(Ctrl+Shift)-click channel thumbnail	Adds channel section to current selection
(Command-Option-Shift) (Ctrl+Alt+Shift)-click channel thumbnail	Intersects channel selection with current selection

Managing Saved Selections

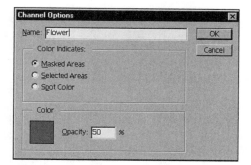

11.6

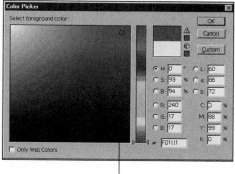

11.7

If your image contains a significant amount of red, change the color for the channel display so that it is easier to see the channel, because the default mask is also red.

Selections that you save are stored as channels in the Channels palette. Alpha channels are saved selections and masks and, like all channels, contain 256 levels of gray. Alpha channels do not print.

1. In the Channels palette, double-click a channel thumbnail to change its properties. The Channel Options dialog box is displayed (11.6). You cannot change the properties for a color channel or the composite channel.

2. Under Name, enter a name for the channel.

3. Under Color Indicates, you can change the way the channel is displayed with other channels. By default, the color indicates the mask or deselected areas. Unless you have a good reason for changing it, leave the setting.

4. Under Color, click the color swatch to choose a color to show when displaying the alpha channel with other channels. Choose an opacity (11.7). By default, the channel is displayed with 50% red to simulate a rubylith mask.

If you are managing multiple saved selections and want to display them at the same time, you can choose different colors to differentiate between them.

continues

Managing Saved Selections continued

5. To display the channel with the color composite, click the eye icon next to the composite and the eye icon next to the alpha channel in the Channels palette **(11.8)**. You can display any combination of channels by clicking the eye icon. If you display the composite channel, all the color channels are also displayed **(11.9)**.

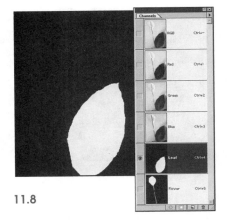

11.8

You can also preview how color channels combine (in a CMYK image, for example) by hiding the channels you do not want to display.

Each channel is numbered, starting at 1. You can switch between the channels by combining the (Command)[Ctrl] key with the number of the channel. Note that if you change from RGB to CMYK mode, the first alpha channel changes from number 4 to number 5. To display the composite channel, press (Command-~)[Ctrl+~].

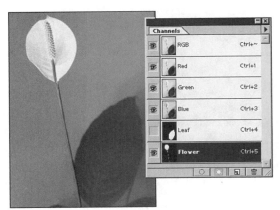

11.9

Alpha channels saved with image files can be used to indicate transparency in page-layout applications and in film and image composition applications. Select the area that you want to remain opaque and save the selection. When you save the image, be sure to select a format that supports alpha channels (such as TIFF or TGA).

Selecting with Painting Tools Using Quick Mask Mode

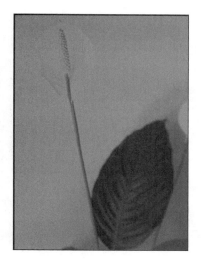

11.10

To move between Quick Mask mode and Standard mode, press Q. You can change the color and opacity used for Quick Mask mode by double-clicking the Quick Mask mode button to open the Quick Mask Options dialog box.

11.11

After you save a selection, you can edit the alpha channel with painting tools from the toolbox and image adjustment tools and then reload the edited channel as a selection. Photoshop enables you to streamline this process using Quick Mask mode.

When you turn on Quick Mask mode, a channel is temporarily created from the current selection and displayed over the image. If nothing is selected, a channel is still created, but the image does not change. When in Quick Mask mode, you can paint with levels of gray in the image with any painting tools. Where you paint with white, you select pixels. Where you paint with black, you deselect.

1. From the toolbox, choose the Edit in Quick Mask mode button ▣. The foreground and background colors in the toolbox are converted to grayscale. If you had a selection, it is displayed in Quick Mask mode. In this instance the leaf was already selected (11.10).

2. Choose a foreground color for painting. Use white to select, black to deselect. Use levels of gray to partially select pixels.

3. Paint in the image with any of the painting tools (11.11). In this example, the Airbrush was used to select the lily's bloom.

continues

Selecting with Painting Tools Using Quick Mask Mode continued

The Airbrush works well for softer selections. The Paintbrush with a large brush size selected is particularly useful for quickly selecting large areas. You can also use filters and image adjustment commands. For example, use Image→Adjust→Invert to invert the selection.

4. When finished editing the mask, choose the Edit in Standard mode button in the toolbox . The selection you created in Quick Mask mode is active in the image (11.12).

11.12

 I P

Create a gradient that fades from black to white to create an even distribution of selection throughout an image. You can use this selection to apply filters or image adjustments gradually over an image. This same selection can be used when compositing layers using a layer mask.

Use the selection tools to create selections while in **Quick Mask** mode. You can stroke and fill the selections to add or subtract from the mask.

11.13

T I P

You can soften a selection by saving it as an alpha channel, selecting the channel, and then using Filter→Blur→Gaussian Blur. A Gaussian blur is also extremely useful for spreading or choking an alpha channel to create a more realistic mask when placing foreground objects against a new background.

Splitting and Merging Channels

11.14

11.15

11.16

You can separate all the channels in an image into separate files. You can also combine separate grayscale files together into a composite image. This can be used to save the individual plates in a CMYK or spot color separation. Merging channels is useful when you are combining separate files from a DCS 2.0 file when the files have lost their links or if you scanned color-filtered images on a scanner.

To split the channels of an image into separate files, choose Split Channels in the Channels palette. A file is created for every channel (11.14).

1. To merge files together into a composite image, all the files that you want to merge must be open and the same size. Choose Merge Channels in the Channels palette (11.15).

2. In the Merge Channels dialog box, select the image mode to use to combine the images. If you have opened three images, CMYK is not available because it requires four channels. Choose the number of channels and the new multi-channel image is built (11.16).

 **N O T E**

If you choose a number of channels that differ from the default (four for RGB, for example), the mode is automatically set to Multichannel.

CHAPTER 12

In this chapter you learn how to...

Check Parts of the Image with the Eyedropper and Samplers

Determine the Tonal Range of an Image with the Histogram

Adjust the Tonal Range with Levels

Adjust the Tonal Range with Curves

Remove Dust and Scratches

Copy Areas with the Rubber Stamp Tool

Blur Areas

Sharpen Areas and Entire Images

Lighten Areas

Darken Areas

Before making significant changes to an image, it is helpful to establish a strategy that can be used on all images. Before beginning to correct an image, you should characterize your monitor and choose appropriate color profile settings. See Chapter 18 "Achieving Consistent Color." When scanning an image, it is best to scan the image at a resolution appropriate to your final output, whether it is Web or print.

IMAGE ADJUSTMENTS AND CORRECTIONS

1. Determine the overall tonal range of the image. Predict what you think the Histogram should look like before opening the Histogram. Look at the flaws in the image. Is it overexposed? Underexposed? Does it lack dynamic range?

2. Adjust the tonal range in Levels or Curves. Set the white and black points. Set the gamma for the image.

3. Remove color casts in the image using Levels or Curves. For more information about color correction, see Chapter 13, "Color Corrections."

4. Remove flaws in the image such as dust or scratches. Adjust the brightness, contrast, and colors of specific areas.

5. Use Unsharp Mask to sharpen the image.

6. If the image will be printed, convert to CMYK and make final color corrections.

Checking Parts of the Image with the Eyedropper and Samplers

The Eyedropper tool enables you to check specific points in the image. The Sample tool places multiple targets in an image that you can monitor as you make adjustments. The eyedropper displays color and position information. You can choose the color model that the eyedropper reports. The sampler only reports values in the current color model.

To control the display of information in the Info palette, choose Palette Options from the flyout menu.

12.1

Both tools display their results in the Info palette (12.1). In an RGB image, you can set the eyedropper to display both RGB and CMYK information simultaneously. Out of gamut colors are displayed with an exclamation point next to their CMYK values (12.2).

12.2

1. To use the eyedropper ![icon], move the cursor in the image. If you click in the image, the foreground color is set to the color under the cursor. To set the background color, hold down (Option)[Alt] and click in the image.

2. To use the sampler ![icon], click up to four points in the image (12.3). Move sampler points by clicking and dragging a sampler target. Delete a sampler target by holding down (Option)[Alt] and clicking on the target.

The Info palette can display the values of up to four samplers.

Sampler points enable you to monitor changes in the image as adjustments are made.

12.3

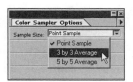

12.4

When using the eyedropper or sampler, watch the Info palette. You can monitor color values when making changes to the image using the image adjustment commands. When working in an RGB image, you also can watch approximate CMYK values or keep track of the total ink density in an area.

You can use the eyedropper to find the lightest and darkest points in the image so that they can be mapped to white and black in Levels or Curves.

(T) I P

*Both the eyedropper and color sampler can be set to point sample, 3×3 average, or 5×5 average (**12.4**). Using one of the average settings provides a better indication of the color in an area when using samplers.*

Using the shortcut menu, you can also Copy Color as HTML. This copies the value of the color under the eyedropper to the clipboard so that it can be pasted directly into an HTML editing program in hexadecimal. For example, COLOR="#AF9A97" was copied using the Copy Color as HTML command.

Determining the Tonal Range of an Image with the Histogram

The Histogram helps determine how you should approach the image correction. Every image has a different histogram. The Histogram displays the number of each pixel at each of the 256 luminosities through an image. The histogram shows the range of luminosities from black to white, left to right. You cannot make any changes to the image using Photoshop's Histogram.

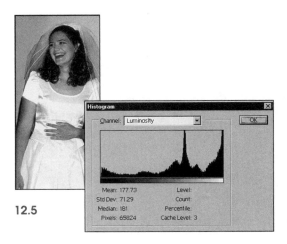

12.5

Figure (12.5) shows a histogram for a high-key image in which the tonal range is predominantly in the highlights.

Figure (12.6) shows a histogram for a low-key image in which the tonal range is predominantly in the shadows.

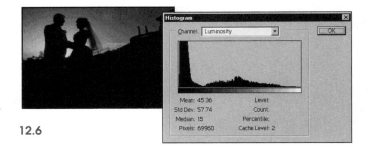

Figure (12.7) shows an image in which the tonal range is too narrow. Note that some detail may be completely lost.

12.6

 T I P

In Photoshop 5.5, you can map the darkest and lightest pixels in the image to black and white using Image→Adjust→Auto Contrast.

When adjusting the contrast, Photoshop ignores the first 0.5% range of both the white and black pixels in the image. This clipping of color values ensures that white and black values are representative areas of the image's content, rather than extreme pixel values.

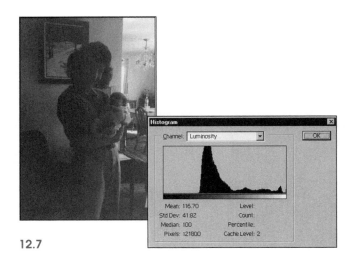

12.7

Adjusting the Tonal Range with Levels

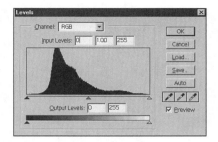

12.8

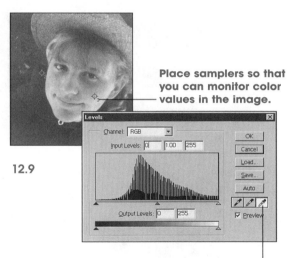

Place samplers so that
you can monitor color
values in the image.

12.9

Double-click the white-point
and black-point eyedroppers
to set the largest white and
black points.

The Levels command is the primary
tool to correct brightness and contrast in an image. Levels is also used
to remove color casts.

The Levels and Curves commands
are very similar. They accomplish
many of the same tasks. Those who
prefer using Levels usually cite the
ability to see the Histogram and edit
it directly. Those who prefer Curves
find that interface more comfortable
and intuitive.

1. Choose Image→Adjust→
   Levels. The Levels dialog box
   is displayed (12.8).

2. Use the white-point eyedropper to select the lightest point
   of the image (12.9). You may
   need to poll with the eyedropper and watch the Info palette
   to determine the lightest point.
   In this image, a sampler (number 1) was placed at the lightest point, the white of the
   subject's eye. You also can
   adjust the white-point slider
   under the histogram preview
   manually and drag it to the
   left.

   Ideally, the target black value
   should be 95, 85, 83, 95 in
   CMYK; 2,2,2 in RGB; or about
   0,0,4% in HSB.

continues

Adjusting the Tonal Range with Levels continued

The target white value should be 5,3,3,0 in CMYK; 244,244,244 in RGB; or about 0,0,96% in HSB.

3. Use the black-point eyedropper to select the darkest point of the image **(12.10)**. You may need to poll with the eyedropper and watch the Info palette to determine the darkest point. In this image, a sampler (number 2) was placed at the darkest point, off the subject's right ear. You also can adjust the black-point slider under the histogram preview manually and drag it to the right.

4. Use the Gamma slider under the histogram preview to adjust the overall brightness and contrast in the image **(12.11)**.

5. Choose OK when finished. You can reset the image without choosing Cancel by holding down (Option)[Alt], which turns the Cancel button into Reset.

I P

If you make image adjustments to images in Grayscale mode, convert to 16 bits/channel (Image→Mode→16 Bits/Channel) before applying Levels or Curves. By increasing the bit depth, the image adjustments that you make will be more accurate. When finished, convert back to 8 bits/channel.

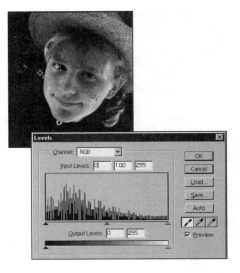

12.10

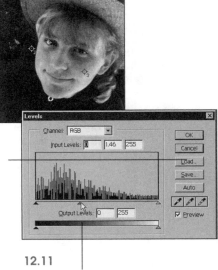

You can save Levels settings for use with similar images. This is useful for batch processing with actions.

12.11

The Output Levels slider enables you to change the maximum highlight and shadow values. You can change the brightest highlight in the image to a light gray instead of white (for broadcast television, for example).

Adjusting the Tonal Range with Curves

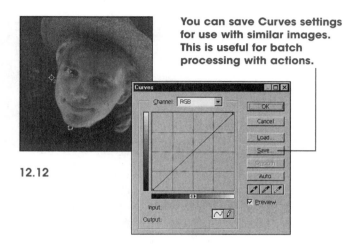

12.12

You can save Curves settings for use with similar images. This is useful for batch processing with actions.

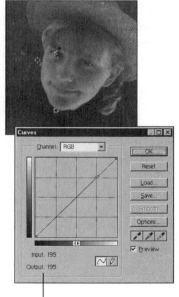

Determine input and output values by (Option)(Alt)-clicking the image with the Eyedropper.

12.13

Like the Levels command, Curves enables you to change the brightness and contrast in an image, to set the highlight and shadow points, and to remove color casts.

The Curves interface shows a baseline relationship between the original values in the image on the horizontal axis (ranging from shadows on the left and highlights on the right), and the modified image on the vertical axis (shadows on the bottom, highlights on the top).

1. Choose Image→Adjust→ Curves. The Curves dialog box is displayed (12.12).

2. You can determine specific input and output levels for points in the image by holding down (Option)[Alt] and clicking with the eyedropper in the image (12.13).

continues

 N O T E

Double-click the white-point and black-point eyedroppers to set the target white and black points.

Adjusting the Tonal Range with Curves continued

3. Use the white-point eyedropper to select the lightest point of the image **(12.14)**. You may need to poll with the eyedropper and watch the Info palette to determine the lightest point. In this image, a sampler (number 1) was placed at the lightest point, in the white of the subject's eye. You also can select the end point of the curve in the upper corner and drag it to the left to decrease the input value. By decreasing the input value and leaving the output value at 255, all colors lighter than the input value are mapped to white.

Ideally, the target black value should be 95,85,83,95 in CMYK; 2,2,2 in RGB; or about 0,0,4% in HSB.

The target white value should be 5,3,3,0 in CMYK; 244,244,244 in RGB; or about 0,0,96% in HSB.

4. Use the black-point eyedropper to select the darkest point of the image **(12.15)**. You may need to poll with the eyedropper and watch the Info palette to determine the darkest point. In this image, a sampler (number 2) was placed at the darkest point, just to the left of the subject's right ear. You also can select the starting point of the curve in the lower corner and

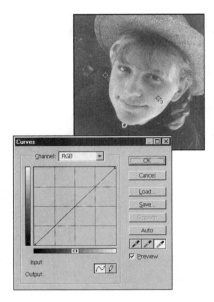

12.14

12.15

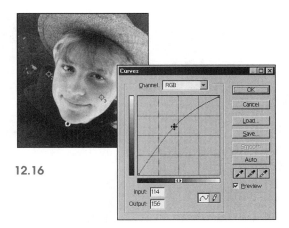

12.16

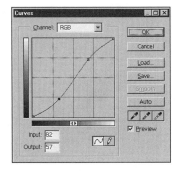

12.17

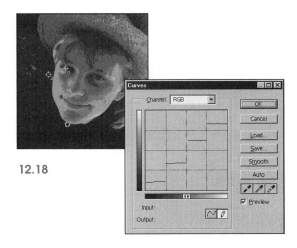

12.18

drag it to the right to increase the input value. By increasing the input value and leaving the output value at 0, all colors darker than the input value are mapped to black.

5. Adjust the overall brightness and contrast by modifying the curve itself. Click the curve to add a point and drag to change the contrast in the image **(12.16)**. Dragging the entire curve up and to the left lightens the image. Dragging the curve down and to the right darkens the image. If you create an S-shape **(12.17)**, highlights and shadows are intensified while improving contrast.

6. Choose OK when finished. You can reset the image without choosing Cancel by holding down (Option)[Alt], which turns the Cancel button into Reset.

 I   P

*You are not restricted to smooth curves in the Curves dialog box. For example, you can posterize an image by setting discrete luminosity levels throughout the image **(12.18)**. Multiple inputs can share the same output level (you can have horizontal lines in the Curves dialog box).*

Removing Dust and Scratches

The Dust & Scratches filter enables you to eliminate small blemishes on a photograph, either occurring in the original photograph **(12.19)** or introduced during the scanning process. The filter eliminates imperfections by making areas of color match by removing pixels in which the color does not match. Dust & Scratches can also be used to remove halftone patterns (caused by scanning images from magazines and other process prints).

12.19

1. Choose Filter→Noise→Dust & Scratches. The Dust & Scratches dialog box is displayed **(12.20)**.

2. Enter a value for the Radius. Measured in pixels, the Radius indicates the area in which pixels of dissimilar colors are sought out. Choose the smallest Radius that still produces acceptable results.

3. Enter a value for the Threshold. The Threshold is the range of acceptable colors within the area set by the Radius. Choose the highest Threshold value that still produces acceptable results.

12.20

4. Choose OK when finished **(12.21)**.

In this particular example, the Dust & Scratches removed some of the medium and smaller blemishes. The larger image correction requires the Rubber Stamp and Blur tools. See the following two sections for more information on these tools.

12.21   **Areas that were repaired with Dust & Scratches**

12.22

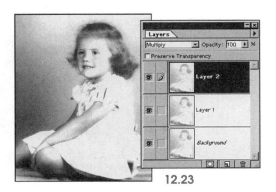

12.23

(T) I P

*When working with older photographs **(12.22)**, you can often build density through the image by combining channels and layers. Look at the Red, Green, and Blue channels and select the channel that contains the greatest contrast. Select the entire channel (Select→All), copy it (Edit→Copy), and after selecting the composite channel and Background layer, choose Edit→Paste. Pasting creates a new layer. Set the new layer's blending mode to Multiply to increase the shadow density, Screen to increase the highlights, or Overlay to do both at the same time **(12.23)**.*

Copying Adjacent Areas with the Rubber Stamp Tool

The Rubber Stamp is the primary retouching tool. Because continuous tone images rarely contain areas of smooth, flat color, it is often necessary to clone the pixels that create the appearance of a texture. The Rubber Stamp tool enables you to copy areas of an image (from a textured wall, for example) over other areas of an image **(12.24)**. You can use the Rubber Stamp tool to remove people, stray electrical wires, or other unwanted objects from photographs by copying background areas into their location. You can also duplicate image elements, such as shadows.

1. Double-click the Rubber Stamp tool ⬚. In the Rubber Stamp options palette **(12.25)**, choose a blending mode and opacity. Lower opacities are useful for making multiple strokes over the same area to help eliminate signs of obvious retouching.

2. Choose Use All Layers to sample data from visible layers. Clear this option to sample pixel data from only the current layer.

3. Select Aligned to apply the sampled area once. Each brush stroke uses a source area relative to the original source area (that is, the displacement between the destination and source always remains constant). Clear Aligned to reset

12.24

12.25

12.26

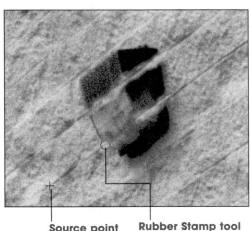

12.27

Source point   **Rubber Stamp tool**

12.28

the destination area for each brush stroke. This is useful when making multiple copies of an area of the image.

4. Choose a brush from the Brushes palette.

5. Choose a source for the Rubber Stamp tool by placing the cursor over the part of any open image **(12.26)** you want to sample, holding down (Option)[Alt] and clicking.

   As you paint, the source point is shown with crosshairs **(12.27)**.

6. Drag to paint with the tool **(12.28)**.

(T) I P

If you are sampling or using a pattern from one image and applying to another, both images must be in the same color mode.

(T) I P

The Pattern Stamp tool is located with the Rubber Stamp and paints with a pattern saved in the pattern buffer. To define a pattern, select a rectangular area and choose Edit→Define Pattern.

Blurring Areas

The Blur tool gives you significant control over the details seen in a particular area. Blurring is useful to de-emphasize areas of an image or to clean up obvious color breaks created by the Rubber Stamp tool.

1. Double-click the Blur tool in the toolbox.

2. Select a blending mode for the blur and the Pressure **(12.29)** to determine how quickly an area blurs when you hold the cursor over it.

3. In the Brushes palette, select a brush size.

4. Click and drag in the image to blur an area **(12.30)**.

In this particular image, the Blur tool was used to blend the crease in the image and to eliminate some of the obvious rubber-stamped areas.

(T) I P

You also can select areas and use any of the blur filters. If you use the Gaussian Blur, you can control the intensity of the blur. At the same time, by selecting a specific area and performing only one task, you can easily undo and try different settings.

If you want to add film grain back into an image or area, you can use Filter→Noise→ Add Noise **(12.31)** *or Filter→Artistic→ Film Grain* **(12.32)**. *This is also useful if areas of the image look too smooth after using the Rubber Stamp or Smudge tools.*

A higher pressure setting blurs the image more quicly while lower settings apply more subtle distortions.

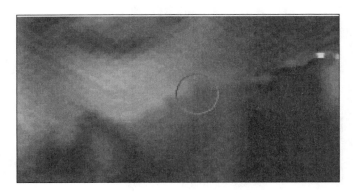

12.29

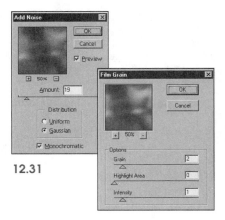

12.30

12.31

12.32

Sharpening Areas

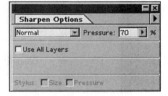

12.33

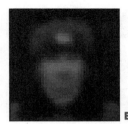

Before

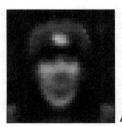

After

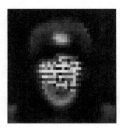

Use the sharper tool sparingly to avoid introducing unwanted artifacts.

12.34

The Sharpen tool increases the apparent sharpness of an area by increasing the contrast between colors. You can use sharpening to help bring slightly blurry areas into focus. Note that you cannot actually add detail by sharpening, you can only give the appearance of added clarity. Use the Sharpen tool with caution because it is easy to create unwanted artifacts in the area you are sharpening.

1. Double-click the Sharpen tool in the toolbox. The Sharpen Options palette is displayed **(12.33)**.

2. Select a blending mode for the sharpen and the Pressure to determine how quickly an area sharpens when you hold the cursor over it.

3. In the Brushes palette, select a brush size.

4. Click and drag in the image to sharpen an area **(12.34)**.

(T) I P

You also can select areas and use any of the sharpen filters. In particular, you can use Unsharp Mask to precisely sharpen an entire image or a selection.

Sharpening an Image

The Unsharp Mask filter should be run as part of your image workflow. You can run the filter after scanning, after retouching, or after converting to CMYK. If you are converting to CMYK, consider running Unsharp Mask in CMYK mode only, or in Lab mode on the Lightness channel. Running Unsharp Mask in Lab mode on the Lightness channel sharpens the image without changing any of the color values in the a and b channels. Whenever you perform an operation that produces interpolation such as resampling or using free transform, run Unsharp Mask to help counteract the effects of interpolation.

12.35

1. Choose Filter→Sharpen→ Unsharp Mask. The Unsharp Mask dialog box is displayed (12.35).

2. Enter an Amount. The Amount determines the overall quantity of sharpening that occurs.

12.36

3. Enter a Radius. The Radius determines how far from any one pixel Photoshop should increase the contrast to sharpen an area. Generally, this translates into the thickness of the edges. Smaller values create crisper edges.

4. Enter a Threshold. The Threshold determines the number of levels allowed before sharpening occurs.

80,2.2,0

500,1.3,0

400,4.0,0

12.37   **The Unsharp Mask applied to the same file with various settings.**

When set to 0, all pixels can be sharpened. When set to 100, only pixels that vary by more than 100 levels are changed, that is edges must have higher levels of contrast for sharpening to occur.

5. Use the zoom tools and the preview in the dialog box to compare different parts of the image with different settings.

6. When finished, choose OK (12.37).

 T I P

To work specifically with highlights or shadows, apply curves to the luminance of the image. Hold down (Command)[Ctrl] and click the composite channel in the Channels palette. This creates a selection based on the luminance. In the Layers palette, create a levels adjustment layer. The luminance-based selection is used as a mask. In the Levels dialog box, you can increase or decrease the highlights throughout the image. If you invert the selection before creating the adjustment layer, you can increase shadow density and bring up shadow detail. For more information, see "Pulling Detail Out of Shadows" on page 230 in Chapter 13, "Color Correction."

Lightening Areas

You can lighten areas to bring objects out of shadows and to increase highlights using the Dodge tool . You can only pull objects from the shadows if detail exists in shadow areas (that is, if the area is not completely black).

To brighten the highlights of the image, choose Highlights. To pull objects out of shadows (by increasing the contrast between the midtones and the shadows), choose Midtones.

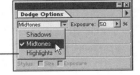

12.38

1. Double-click the Dodge tool in the toolbox. The Dodge Options palette is displayed **(12.38)**.

2. Choose which types of values you want to affect: Highlights, Midtones, or Shadows.

3. Choose an Exposure setting. The higher the setting, the faster the image lightens.

4. In the Brushes palette, select a brush size.

5. Click and drag in the image to lighten an area **(12.39)**.

12.39   **Before lightening**   **After lightening**

(N) O T E

Despite Photoshop's power, it cannot reproduce detail that does not exist in an image. If your image does not contain any detail in the shadow areas, nothing in the process of scanning or making changes in Photoshop will correct this. The same is true for images that are blurry or out of focus—details cannot be added, only deleted.

Darkening Areas

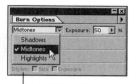

12.40

To dull highlights, choose
Highlights. To pull objects into
shadows, choose Midtones. To
intensify shadow areas,
choose Shadow.

12.41

12.42

You can darken areas to increase the
intensity of shadows using the Burn
tool . You can also use the Burn
tool to add shadows behind objects
by darkening specific areas.

1. Double-click the burn tool in
   the toolbox. The Burn Options
   palette is displayed **(12.40)**.

2. Choose which types of values
   you want to effect: Highlights,
   Midtones, or Shadows. Choose
   Shadows to intensify shadow
   areas. Choose an Exposure setting. The higher the setting, the
   faster the image darkens.

3. In the Brushes palette, select a
   brush size.

4. Click and drag in the image to
   darken an area. **(12.41)** shows
   an original image, and **(12.42)**
   shows a more dramatic shadow created with the Burn too.

(T) I P

*Instead of using the Burn or Dodge tools,
you can select an area and use Levels or
Curves. This gives you higher levels of control should you need to undo and also makes
the process repeatable for other areas or
images. Use Color Range to specifically
select highlights, midtones, or shadows.*

©HAPTER 13

In this chapter you learn how to...

Change the Saturation in an Area

Remove a Color Cast with Variations

Remove a Color Cast with Levels and Curves

Change Color with Hue/Saturation

Change Color with Selective Color

Change Color with Replace Color

Create an Adjustment Layer

Pull Detail Out of Shadows

Correct High-Key and Low-Key Images

In Chapter 12, "Image Adjustments and Corrections," the proposed strategy for adjusting and correcting images includes two steps that involve correcting color:

- Remove color casts in the image using Levels or Curves.

- Adjust the brightness, contrast, and colors of specific areas using the Burn, Dodge, and Sponge tools, Hue/Saturation, or Levels and Curves.

COLOR CORRECTION

You can change color globally and locally. Start by eliminating widespread color casts, then correct smaller areas. After converting to CMYK mode, it is often necessary to make additional color corrections. For example, you can use Selective Color, Levels, or Curves to further correct an image after you have created a color proof.

Ideally, in a properly calibrated workflow, scanners, monitors, and printers would handle color seamlessly as it is passed from device to device (see Chapter 18, "Achieving Consistent Color"). However, there are many differences in how individuals perceive colors.

The best rule for color correction is to learn Photoshop's tools well enough so that you can make an image's color match what you consider its ideal color. However, you may also want to seek the opinions of other image professionals. Certainly, if you are creating print images, your printer may have definite ideas about what works best for a specific image, job, or piece of equipment. If you are preparing images for the Web, have others preview your images in as many browsers, monitors, and operating systems as possible.

Changing the Saturation in an Area

The Sponge tool increases and decreases saturation or color intensity in areas of an image. You can use the Sponge tool when dealing with out-of-gamut colors before converting to CMYK mode. You can also use the Sponge tool after converting to CMYK to intensify some colors.

Like out-of-gamut colors, when converting from RGB to CMYK, you can use the Sponge tool to desaturate colors that cause problems when output to video.

1. Double-click the Sponge tool in the toolbox. It is grouped with the Burn and Dodge tools. The Sponge Options palette is displayed **(13.1)**.

2. Select a mode for the Sponge tool. You can either saturate or desaturate.

3. In the Brushes palette, select a brush size.

4. Click and drag in the image to change the saturation in an area **(13.2)** (see Figures **C.7** and **C.8** in the color insert).

(T) I P

Select an area and use any of the color adjustment commands to provide precise and repeatable numeric changes. You can also combine the Sponge tool and color adjustment commands with Color Range selections. For example, you can select all the reds in an image.

Set a Pressure to determine how quickly an area saturates or desaturates when you hold the cursor over it.

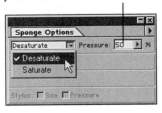

13.1

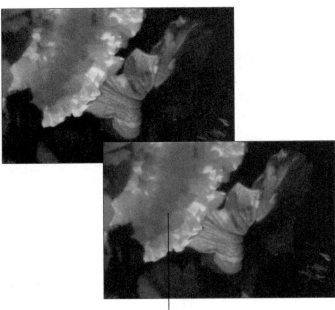

13.2   **It's difficult to tell in this black-and-white version, but this flower has been desaturated with the sponge tool.**

Removing a Color Cast with Variations

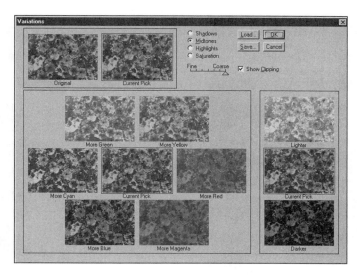

13.3

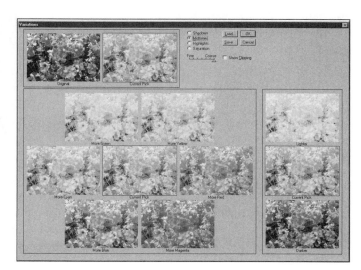

13.4

In general, you should use Levels or Curves to remove a color cast because they permit greater control, you can see the preview of the change in the image window, and you can zoom to inspect areas of the image. Variations is useful, however, to help you determine how an image should be altered overall, especially if the ways that colors combine in Photoshop is new to you.

1. Choose Image→Adjust→ Variations. The Variations dialog box is displayed (13.3) (see also Figure C.11 in the color insert). The Variations dialog box displays several different views of the image. The upper-left corner shows the Original and next to it, the image altered by Variations.

2. Choose Shadows, Midtones, or Highlights to determine where colors should be added to the image and where the image should be lightened or darkened. To add a color to the image, click in the appropriate preview. For example, to reduce the amount of blue in an image, click the More Yellow preview. All the previews in the image except for the original will be updated (13.4).

continues

Removing a Color Cast with Variations continued

3. The amount of color added is determined by the Fine/Coarse slider. For each notch coarser, the amount of change is doubled. For each notch finer, the amount of change is halved.

4. You can make the image darker or lighter using the Lighter and Darker previews.

5. Choose Saturation to adjust the saturation in the image. The Variations dialog box changes to show the more and less saturated previews **(13.5)** (see also Figure **C.13** in the color insert). Click the More or Less saturated previews to change the saturation.

6. Choose Show Clipping to display a gamut warning for the pixels in the image that fall outside of the CMYK gamut.

7. Choose OK.

You can return the original state of the image when Variations was started by clicking the Original image or holding down (Option)(Alt) and choosing the Reset button (when it replaces the Cancel button).

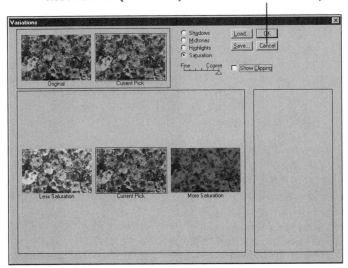

13.5

When working in the Variations dialog box, you can only return to previous versions by applying the opposite effect (instead of adding Yellow, add Blue, for example).

Removing a Color Cast with Levels

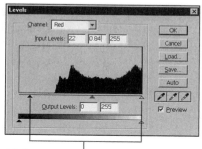

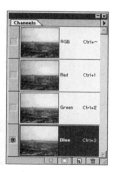

13.6   **Use the highlight and shadow sliders if the selected white point or black point is not completely neutral (that is, the red, green, and blue values are not the same).**

13.7

When changing individual channels, channels that contain the dominant colors can often be changed only in small increments before significantly altering the image. You may find that adjusting the channel or channels for the nondominant colors produces the desired effect.

Levels can be used to alter the tonal range in an image or, by changing the levels for an individual channel, you can alter the color composition of an image. Each channel in the Levels command controls a primary color in the image and its complement. For example, to change the amount of red in an image, you add or subtract cyan. To remove a greenish cast, add magenta. In general, you change the gamma slider in the Levels dialog box to change the overall cast.

1. Choose Image→Adjust→ Levels. The Levels dialog box is displayed (13.6).

2. Choose the channel based on the color cast. For example, if the image is reddish overall, or if there is too much red in the highlights or shadows, choose the Red channel.

3. Move the gamma slider to the right to remove an overall color cast (see Figure C.10 in the color insert). Adjust the highlight and shadow sliders as necessary.

4. Choose OK.

 I   P

Place color samplers on points for which you know the desired colors and monitor them as you change the color in the image (13.7).

Removing a Color Cast with Curves

Like Levels, Curves can be used to alter the tonal range in an image or, by selecting an individual channel, alter the color composition of an image. When you select an individual channel, pulling the curve up intensifies the color throughout the image, whereas pulling the curve down removes the color. You can also select an area of an image to change the color composition in a area or among a range of colors.

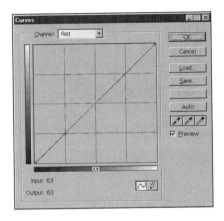

13.8

1. Choose Image→Adjust→ Curves. The Curves dialog box is displayed **(13.8)**.

2. Choose the channel based on the color cast. For example, if the image is reddish overall, or if there is too much red in the highlights or shadows, choose the Red channel.

3. Move the middle of the curve down to remove an overall color cast (see Figure **C.10** in the color insert). Adjust the ends of the curve to change the highlights and shadows as necessary **(13.9)**.

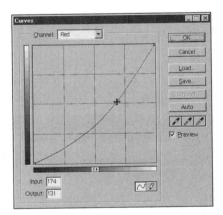

13.9

4. Choose OK.

T I P

You can use the zoom keyboard shortcuts while in the Levels or Curves dialog boxes to inspect specific areas. To pan, use the space-bar. (Command-Space)[Ctrl+Space] will zoom in, while (Command-Option-Space)[Ctrl+Alt+Space] zooms out.

Changing Color with Hue/Saturation

13.10

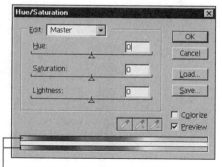

The top color strip shows the current spectrum. The bottom color strip reflects changes to the Hue, displaying the rotation through the color wheel.

13.11

The Hue/Saturation command provides one of the easiest ways to change color in an image. You can apply Hue/Saturation on an entire image to shift the color or increase the saturation for every pixel. To change the color of a car, flower, jacket, or any object or area of an image, select the pixels you want to change and use Hue/Saturation. See also "Changing Color with Replace Color" on page 227 later in this chapter.

When you change the Hue, you are rotating the colors through the color wheel. Red is at 0 degrees, Yellow at 60, Green at 120, and so on until the circle completes with Red at 360 degrees. At the bottom of the Hue/ Saturation dialog box the color wheel projected onto a strip is displayed.

1. Choose a layer or select an area of the image (13.10) (see also Figure C.13 in the color insert).

2. Choose Image→Adjust→ Hue/Saturation. The Hue/Saturation dialog box is displayed (13.11).

3. Under Edit, choose Master to change the entire image. Choose a specific color to alter only those colors in the image. For example, you can alter all the blues in an image, either add a little green, or radically change them all to yellow.

continues

Changing Color with Hue/Saturation continued

If you chose a specific color, sliders are displayed between the color strips so that you can set the range of colors (13.12). For example, if you choose Reds, the dark gray band is centered at 0 degrees and stretches for 15 degrees along the color wheel in either direction. This is the range of colors that is changed when you alter the Hue. The light gray bars extend for another 30 degrees, indicating the falloff of the hue change.

Note that if you move a range into a completely different color area (moving the red range to yellow, for example), Photoshop will change the color selected in the Edit list (from Reds to Yellows 2, in this example).

4. Drag the Hue slider to alter the color in the image.

The eyedropper centers the color range. Use the plus eyedropper to expand the color range and the minus eyedropper to contract the color range.

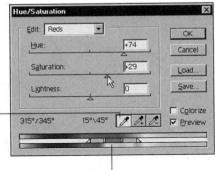

13.12 **When you change the Hue, only the colors indicated by the slider are altered.**

Drag the light gray bars to widen or narrow the range of colors without changing the length of the falloff.

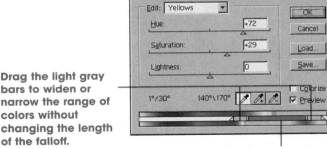

13.13 **Drag the dark gray bar to change which range of colors is affected.**

TIP

The Hue/Saturation command can be used to convert areas of an image to grayscale. Select the areas that you want to change to grayscale, choose Image→Adjust→ Hue/Saturation and move the Saturation slider all the way to the left. You can also use Image→Adjust→Desaturate.

The angles for the range and falloff along the color wheel are displayed above the color strips.

Drag the triangular ends to change the falloff in either direction.

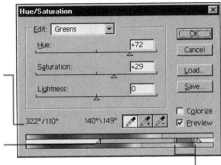

13.14 **Drag the small rectangles that enclose the dark gray bar to widen or narrow the range of colors while leaving the falloff endpoint fixed.**

13.15

5. Drag the Saturation slider to alter the Saturation in the image. Drag the slider all the way to the left to leach out all the color in the image.

6. Drag the Lightness slider to alter the lightness of the colors in the image.

7. Choose OK. The colors in the image are altered (13.15) (see also Figure C.13 in the color insert).

 T I P

When you increase the gamma of an image using Levels, you can use Hue/Saturation to replace some of the saturation that might be lost.

 T I P

You can also use Hue/Saturation to tint grayscale areas of an RGB image like a monotone. Select the area that you want to add color to and choose Image→Adjust→ Hue/ Saturation. Choose Colorize and use the Hue and Saturation sliders to select a color. Use the Lightness slider to lighten or darken the image. Black pixels in the image are replaced by the color you create.

Changing Color with Selective Color

The Selective Color command is especially useful when making color corrections to images in CMYK mode. Like selecting an individual color for adjustment in the Hue/Saturation command, Selective Colors alters all colors within a range. You can use Selective Color to increase the amount of magenta used in all the reds in an image, or to increase the intensity of the magentas.

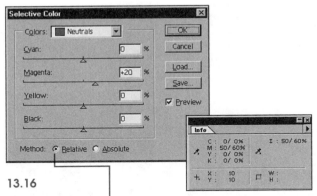

13.16

For a pixel that contains 50% magenta, increasing magenta by 20% increases the proportion of magenta to 60% (increases by 20% of 50%). For a pixel that contains 60%, the proportion is increased to 72%.

1. Choose Image→Adjust→ Selective Color. The Selective Color dialog box is displayed.

2. Under Colors, choose the color range in the image that you want to adjust.

3. Choose Relative to increase or decrease the amount of color based on the current amount of color (13.16).

   Choose Absolute to add the amount specified to the pixel's value (13.17).

4. Drag the sliders to change the way in which colors are mixed in the image (see Figure C.14 in the color insert).

5. Choose OK.

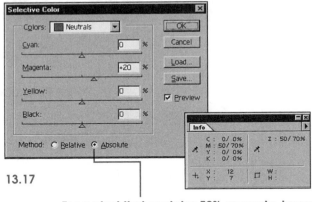

13.17

For a pixel that contains 50% magenta, increasing magenta by 20% increases the proportion of magenta to 70%. For a pixel that contains 60%, the proportion is increased to 80%.

Changing Color with Replace Color

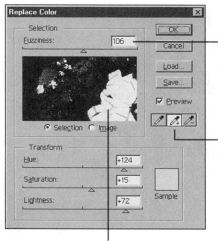

Like the Magic Wand tolerance setting, Fuzziness values control the range of colors selected.

To add colors to be used for the basis of the selection, use the add eyedropper. To subtract color, use the subtract eyedropper.

13.18   **Areas shown in white are selected. Areas shown in black are not selected. Areas shown in gray are partially selected.**

13.19

13.20

The Replace Color command combines a Color Range selection with the capability to change hue, saturation, and lightness for the selection, like the Hue/Saturation command, to alter a range of colors in an image. Use Replace Color to alter the color of objects or to replace specific hues throughout an image.

1. Choose Image→Adjust→ Replace Color. The Replace Color dialog box is displayed (13.18).

2. Select a color to use as the basis for selection by clicking either in the preview or in the image with the eyedropper (13.19). If the window in the Color Range dialog box is set to Preview, a preview of the selection is displayed.

3. To control the range of colors chosen beyond those selected with the eyedropper, adjust the Fuzziness. values for Fuzziness range from 0 to 200. If you set the Fuzziness to 0, only the colors you select with the eyedropper are selected. Larger values select larger ranges of colors.

4. Drag the Hue, Saturation, and Lightness sliders to alter the selected colors (13.20) (see Figure C.15 in the color insert)

5. Choose OK.

Creating an Adjustment Layer

Most of the image adjustment and color correction commands can be used with adjustment layers. Adjustment layers apply the image effect to all layers under it. You can turn adjustment layers off, delete them, and change their settings after they are created to give you maximum flexibility over your changes.

13.21

You can paint on adjustment layers to create a mask. Using a mask, you can precisely control the area of the effect, or vary the effect by using a gradient mask. You don't need to add a layer mask to an adjustment layer, just paint on it. Using masks, you can combine multiple adjustment layers **(13.21)** (see also Figure C.16 in the color insert).

You also can change the blending mode and opacity of an adjustment layer to combine the adjustment with the underlying layers with unlimited variety.

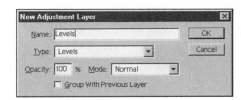

13.22

Adjustment layers do not take the same space as normal layers, because component channel information is not stored for them.

1. In the Layers palette, choose New Adjustment Layer from the Layers palette menu. The New Adjustment Layer dialog box is displayed **(13.22)**.

2. Enter a name for the adjustment layer. The default name is based on the type of adjustment layer you create.

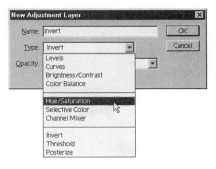

13.23

13.24

13.25

3. Under Type, choose the type of adjustment layer from the list **(13.23)**.

4. Choose an Opacity and Mode for the layer. You can change these after the layer is created in the Layers palette just as you can with ordinary layers.

5. You can group an adjustment layer with another layer. Only the grouped layer is affected by the adjustment layer.

6. Choose OK. The dialog box that is displayed is based on the type of adjustment layer that you selected.

7. Enter the information required by the type of adjustment layer you selected. Choose OK **(13.24)**.

The adjustment layer appears in the Layers palette. You can manage an adjustment layer just like any other layer.

 I P

You can also group an adjustment layer together with another layer by holding down the (Option)[Alt] key and clicking the line between the two layers. The adjustment layer must be above the layer with which it is grouped **(13.25)**.

Pulling Detail Out of Shadows

Adjustment layers can be combined with masks to limit their areas of effect. If you have an active selection when you create the adjustment layer, it is automatically used as a mask. You can edit the mask further by clicking the mask in the Layers palette and painting on it as you would a layer mask. For more information, see "Creating and Editing a Layer Mask by Painting" on page 156 in Chapter 9, "Layer Effects and Techniques."

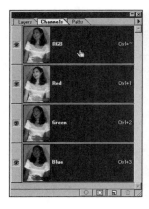

13.26

1. Create a selection from the luminance in the image by holding down (Command) [Ctrl] and clicking the composite channel in the Channels palette (13.26).

2. Currently the highlights in the image are selected. To select the shadows in the image, choose Select→Inverse.

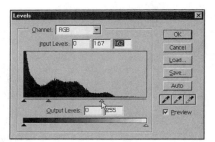

13.27

3. In Layers palette menu, choose New Adjustment Layer. Choose Levels (Curves also works).

4. In the Levels dialog box, move the gamma slider to the left to pull detail out of the shadows. You can also make adjustments with the other sliders (13.27).

5. When finished in the Levels dialog box, choose OK. An adjustment layer is added using the selection as a mask (13.28).

This is one example of using a mask with an adjustment layer. Specifically, Curves or Levels are applied to the luminance in the image. You can also create gradients to composite adjustments along with layers.

13.28

Correcting High-Key and Low-Key Images

13.29

13.30

13.31

Adjustment layers enable you to quickly correct underexposed **(13.29)** or overexposed images by changing their blending modes. You can achieve a similar effect by adjusting the blending mode of a duplicated layer, although adjustment layers are more efficient because they do not have the same channel overhead as normal layers.

1. In the Layers palette, choose New Adjustment Layer from the Layers palette menu. The New Adjustment Layer dialog box is displayed.

2. Under Type, choose Levels. If the image is overexposed (too light), choose Multiply for the mode. If the image is underexposed (too dark), choose Screen for the mode.

3. Choose OK.

4. In the Levels dialog box, choose OK. You do not need to make any alterations. The image should be partially corrected **(13.30)**.

5. To refine the correction, change the opacity of the adjustment layer. If further correction is needed, duplicate the adjustment layer. You can apply masks to the duplicated adjustment layers to precisely control their effect **(13.31)**.

CHAPTER 14

In this chapter you learn how to...

Create, Select, and Edit Paths

Save a Work Path

Save an Image with a Clipping Path for Use in a Page-Layout Program

Save a Path for Use in an Illustration Package

Convert a Path into a Selection

Convert a Selection into a Path

Fill a Path

Stroke a Path

Blur an Object Along a Path

Bézier paths are common to almost all illustration applications, such as Illustrator, FreeHand, and CorelDRAW. These applications all use Bézier paths as the fundamental method for defining vector objects. Vector objects are defined mathematically and can be made arbitrarily large. A circle in Illustrator, for example, can be made 10 times larger, and that object remains a circle. In Photoshop, on the other hand, you work primarily with *pixels.* A circle in Photoshop cannot be scaled up, because it consists of small squares (pixels). When scaled, the squares become larger, and aliasing is apparent.

WORKING WITH PATHS

Although Photoshop is primarily a raster-based editing program, you can create Bézier paths in Photoshop. Paths serve four purposes:

- To create clipping paths for use in illustration and page-layout applications

- To provide interoperability with Adobe Illustrator

- To create selections

- To create highly controllable stroke and fill effects

Photoshop 5's addition of the Freeform Pen tool and the Magnetic Pen tool takes some of the difficulty out of creating complex paths. Many of the tools operate largely the same in Photoshop and Illustrator, and the products are able to seamlessly exchange path information.

The Paths palette organizes the paths in a Photoshop document and enables you to add, delete, rename, copy, and change the visibility of paths.

Creating, Selecting, and Editing Paths

A path in Photoshop is a collection of open or closed subpaths. A subpath contains path segments defined by control points and direction lines. Creating path segments in Photoshop is similar to creating paths in illustration applications such as Adobe Illustrator. You click to choose control points and drag direction lines to determine the smoothness or curve of the path segment between direction points **(14.1)**.

Keep the segments as long as possible—it is easier to edit paths that contain fewer segments, and they tend to be more accurate. Paths are easy to edit, though, so don't worry too much about precision when creating a path.

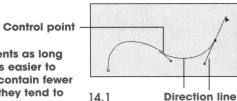

14.1

To create a new path, click and drag with the Pen tool . If you already have created a path segment, clicking and dragging with the Pen tool appends segments to the existing subpath. To start a new subpath, click the Pen tool in the toolbox before clicking and dragging in the image area.

14.2 Creates new path

If you already have created a path, choose the Creates New Path button in the Paths palette **(14.2)** to create a new path, and click and drag with the Pen tool. When you create a new path in the Paths palette, you create a container for Bézier path information. You create the Bézier path itself with the Pen tool.

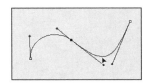

14.3

Edit path segments by clicking and dragging them or by clicking on direction points and modifying the direction lines with the Direct Selection tool **(14.3)**. To create a path with straight line segments, click without dragging direction

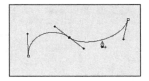

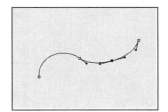

14.4

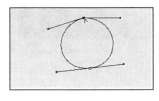

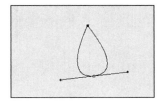

14.5

To convert a smooth point to a corner point, click on a control point with the Convert Point tool . Click and drag on a corner point with the Convert Point tool to create a smooth point.

lines. To delete a segment, select it with the Direct Selection tool and press Delete. To delete a subpath, select it by dragging a marquee around the subpath and press Delete. To delete an entire path from the Paths palette, drag the path to the Trash icon or, after clicking on a point on the path, press Delete twice.

Add and delete direction points by using the Add Anchor Point and Delete Anchor Point tools (14.4).

To move a subpath, select it by dragging a marquee with the Direct Selection tool. Then click on the subpath and drag to move it.

After the subpath is closed, the Pen tool cursor switches to the Add Anchor Point or Delete Anchor Point tool when you move the cursor over the subpath. When the cursor is on a line segment, you can add an anchor point. When the cursor is over an anchor point, you can delete it. Press and hold (Option) [Alt] for the Convert Anchor Point tool.

(T) I P

By default, each control point blends two path segments smoothly. To create a corner or cusp, you need to create direction lines that are not parallel. Press (Option)[Alt] while dragging the direction line. Press Shift while dragging to constrain the direction line.

Saving a Work Path

When you create a path by using the Pen tool, Photoshop creates a work path. The last work path created is saved with the image but is easily replaced by the Path Creation tools in the Paths palette. To make the path a permanent part of the image, you must save it and give it a name in the Paths palette.

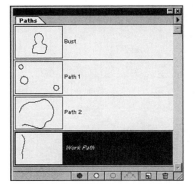

1. Choose Window→Show Paths to display the Paths palette (**14.6**).

14.6

2. Double-click the work path.

3. In the Save Path dialog box, enter a name for the path.

Saving an Image with a Clipping Path for Use in a Page-Layout Program

When you save a Photoshop Encapsulated PostScript (EPS) file for use in a page-layout or illustration package, all the pixels are opaque by default. A clipping path isolates the areas that you want to be opaque. The page-layout program uses transparency for areas outside the clipping path so that only the object inside the clipping path is displayed. Some page-layout programs also let you use the clipping path to define text runarounds.

Instead of using the Magnetic Lasso tool, use the Magnetic Pen tool. The Magnetic Pen tool is configured like the Magnetic Lasso tool, but the result is a path that you can edit using the Path tools. When the path is complete, choose Load Path as a selection to convert it.

14.7

1. Create a closed subpath around the object you want to be opaque (**14.7**).

2. Double-click the work path to save it. In the Save Path dialog box, enter a name for the path.

14.8   Smaller values create clipping paths with shorter segments. Larger values create clipping paths with longer segments.

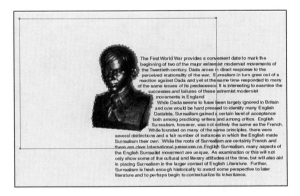

14.9

3. Choose Clipping Path from the Paths palette.

4. In the Clipping Path dialog box **(14.8)**, select the path.

5. Enter a value for flatness. Flatness values range from 0.2 to 100. Unless you are receiving printing errors, leave the Flatness value blank to use the printer's default value.

6. Choose OK.

7. Save the image as an EPS or DCS file if you are printing on a PostScript printer. Save the image as a TIFF if you are printing on a non-PostScript printer.

When you print the image from a page-layout program, only the pixels bounded by the clipping path print. Note that EPS files with TIFF previews print correctly but do not display correctly in some page-layout programs. Most illustration programs, however, display and print the image and clipping path correctly **(14.9)**.

Saving a Path for Use in an Illustration Package

Although Photoshop does not let you place text along a path, you can save a path you create in Photoshop for use in Illustrator to create text effects and then place the Illustrator file into Photoshop. You can export any or all paths as Adobe Illustrator (AI) files. You also can export a path that shows the document bounds for placement purposes in Illustrator.

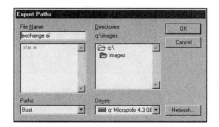

14.10

1. Create a path.

2. Double-click the work path to save it. In the Save Path dialog box, enter a name for the path.

3. Choose File→Export→Paths to Illustrator. The Export Paths dialog box appears (14.10).

4. In the Paths drop-down list, select the path you want to export. Select Document Bounds to export a path that indicates the size of the image. Select All Paths to export all the paths in the Photoshop document.

14.11

5. Enter a filename and choose OK.

To use the path in Illustrator, open the Adobe Illustrator file or choose File→Place. Place text on the path or make other modifications using the path and save the file. Then choose File→Place in Photoshop to import the new Adobe Illustrator file (14.11).

You also can copy and paste path information from Illustrator into Photoshop. When you paste path information from Illustrator, Photoshop asks whether the information should be placed or used as a path.

You also can drag and drop paths between Illustrator and Photoshop. If you drag and drop a path from Illustrator into Photoshop, it is rasterized.

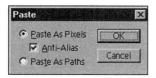

14.12

Converting a Path into a Selection

14.13

**Click here to show
the selection but
not the path**

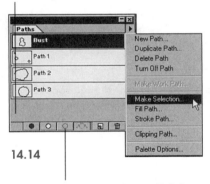

14.14

You also can convert a path into a selection by using the
Loads Path as a Selection button in the Paths palette (or
just press (Command)(Ctrl) and click on the path). This
action uses the current values in the Make Selection dialog
box to create the selection. To select feathering, anti-
aliasing, and operation options, press (Option)(Alt) and
click the Loads Path as a Selection button.

You can use paths to create selections. Objects with hard edges that
lack contrast with the background
or that do not have a single range of
color often can be selected easily
using paths.

1. Use the Pen tool to create a
   path. To select an object in an
   image, trace the object using
   one of the Pen tools. Use the
   Path tools to edit the path.

   If you already have a path,
   select it in the Paths palette.

2. Choose Make Selection in the
   Paths palette menu. The Make
   Selection dialog box appears
   (14.13).

3. In the Feather Radius field,
   enter an amount to fade the
   selection. Enter 0 to create a
   solid selection with anti-
   aliasing. Clear the Anti-Aliased
   check box to create an aliased
   selection.

4. If you had a previous selection,
   go to the Operation section
   and specify how the new selection should combine with the
   previous one.

5. Choose OK.

A selection is created that matches
the current path. To display the
selection without showing the path,
click in the gray area under the
thumbnails in the Paths palette
(14.14).

Converting a Selection into a Path

You can convert path information into a selection and selection information into a path. You can use selection techniques to create regular geometric objects such as rectangles and circles and then convert these to paths. You also can use advanced selection tools, such as the Magic Wand or Color Range command. After you define a selection, you can convert it to a path.

1. Create a selection.

2. Choose Make Work Path from the Paths palette menu. The Make Work Path dialog box appears **(14.15)**.

3. Enter a Tolerance value. The tolerance determines how closely the path follows the selection shape. Tolerance values range from 0.5 to 10 **(14.16)** and **(14.17)**.

4. Choose OK.

A work path is created in the Paths palette. If you already had a work path, it is replaced. Save the work path by double-clicking its thumbnail and renaming it before you create your new path.

 I P

You also can convert a selection into a path by clicking the Make Work Path button at the bottom of the Paths palette. To set the tolerance information, press (Option)[Alt] while clicking the button.

14.15

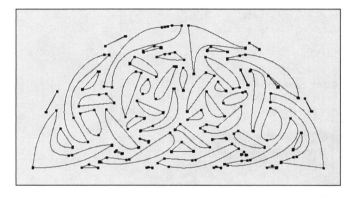

14.16   **If you choose a high value for the tolerance, fewer anchor points are created, resulting in a smoother but not necessarily as accurate path.**

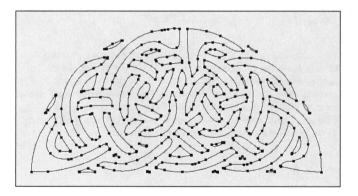

14.17   **Lower tolerance values create a more accurate but data-heavy path.**

Filling a Path

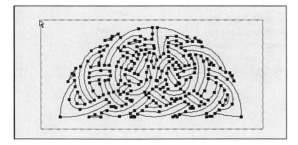

14.18

14.19

To display the Fill Paths or Fill Subpaths dialog box, press (Option) (Alt) while clicking the Fill Paths or Fill Subpaths button in the Paths palette.

14.20

Like selections, paths can be filled with continuous colors, history, or patterns. You can use paths to create repeatable and predictable fills, particularly within actions. Filling paths also enables you to control the feathering and anti-aliasing as you fill.

1. Select a path in the Paths palette **(14.18)**, or select a subpath using the Direct Selection tool.

2. Choose Fill Paths or Fill Subpaths from the Paths palette menu. The Fill Paths or Fill Subpaths dialog box appears **(14.19)**.

3. From the Use drop-down list, choose a fill option.

4. In the Blending section, choose an opacity and Blending mode for the fill. If a layer has transparent areas, the Preserve Transparency check box will be available. If you do not want to preserve a layer's transparency, clear the Preserve Transparency check box.

5. In the Rendering section, choose a Feather Radius value and specify whether you want to anti-alias the filled area.

6. Choose OK.

The area bounded by the path is filled **(14.20)**. If the path is open, the endpoints are joined along the shortest path, and this closed path is filled.

Stroking a Path

Like stroking a selection, you can stroke a path. By stroking open paths, you can control the location of brushstrokes in an image.

1. Determine which tool you want to use to stroke the path or subpath. Double-click the tool in the toolbox, and set the tool options in the Options palette. Choose a brush to use with the tool.

2. Select a path in the Paths palette (14.21), or select a sub-path using the Direct Selection tool.

3. Choose Stroke Paths or Stroke Subpaths from the Paths palette menu. The Stroke Paths or Stroke Subpaths dialog box appears (14.22).

4. From the Tool drop-down list, choose a tool to use to stroke the path.

5. Choose OK. The path is stroked using the tool you selected (14.23).

To create a path from text, use the Text Mask tool to create a selection based on the text you enter, and then convert the selection to a path.

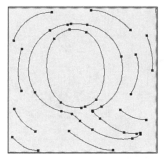

14.21

14.22

14.23

(T) I P

You also can choose the Stroke Paths or Stroke Subpaths button in the Paths palette. To choose a tool from the Stroke Paths or Stroke Subpaths dialog box, press (Option)[Alt] while clicking the tool.

Blurring an Object Along a Path

14.24

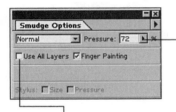

14.25

The Pressure setting specifies the length of the blur along the path.

Clear the Use All Layers check box to smudge only the current layer.

By choosing the Smudge tool when stroking, you can blur an object along an irregular path. This creates an effect similar to a motion blur, but with a controlled path. The object should be on its own layer that also contains transparency. This technique demonstrates some of the variety of effects you can achieve by stroking along a path.

1. Create a path for the blur starting at the center of the object and moving away from it **(14.24)**.

2. Double-click the Smudge tool on the toolbar. The Smudge tool is with the Blur and Sharpen tools. In the Smudge Options palette **(14.25)**, turn on Finger Painting. Choose a pressure.

3. Select the layer of the object you are blurring in the Layers palette. Choose Duplicate Layer from the Layers palette. This is the layer for the blur, so you can call it Blur.

4. Choose New Layer from the Layers palette. You will use this layer to create a custom brush for the blur. Call the layer Temp, and delete it when you are finished.

continues

Blurring an Object Along a Path continued

5. Select the object on the original layer by pressing (Command)[Ctrl] while clicking the layer thumbnail in the Layers palette.

6. Select the Temp layer in the Layers palette. Choose Edit→Fill. In the Fill dialog box, choose Black from the list of colors, which fills the object with black **(14.26)**.

7. In the Brushes palette, choose Define Brush. Then select the brush you just defined. Choose Select→Deselect.

8. Select the Blur layer in the Layers palette.

9. In the Paths palette, select the path you defined in step 1. Choose Stroke Paths from the Paths palette. From the Tool drop-down list, select **Smudge** **(14.27)**. Then choose OK.

The object is smudged in Finger Painting mode using the brush you created from the object **(14.28)**. (In this example, an additional layer effect also was applied to the original object.)

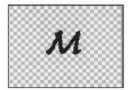

14.26

14.27

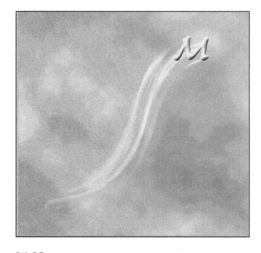

14.28

©HAPTER 15

In this chapter you learn how to…

Use Other Plug-ins

Fade a Filter's Effect

Apply a Blur

Create Depth-of-Field Effects

Use Artistic Effects

Create a Comic-Book Effect

Apply Texture to an Image

Apply a Displacement Map to an Image

Change the Lighting in an Image

Add Noise

Photoshop's filters provide a wide range of special effects, ranging from artistic and stylistic transformations to utilitarian blur and sharpen commands. Photoshop's filters are organized by general categories on the Filter menu.

Other filters typically are added according to the filter's manufacturer. The Watermark filters are added to the menu under Digimarc, for example.

USING FILTERS

This chapter does not cover each of the more than 100 filters installed with Photoshop. Instead, it presents an overview of general filter behavior and covers the most important filters, such as Gaussian Blur and Unsharp Mask. This chapter also demonstrates how you can combine filters to produce certain effects.

The best way to learn the filters is through experimentation. You must have an idea of a filter's effects before you can choose how filters behave in combination. You also should understand how layers behave and blend.

The ability to predict the behavior of filters and blending modes enables you to create increasingly sophisticated and precise effects using the Filter Fade command. For example, you can set the Unsharp Mask filter to Luminosity mode to sharpen without allowing any of the colors in the image to shift.

Once you determine how to create a desired effect using combinations of filters, you can save the entire procedure as an action for use with other images. This is particularly useful when creating an effect that requires a series of filters. For more information about actions, see Chapter 19, "Automating Photoshop."

Using Other Plug-ins

All of Photoshop's filters are plug-ins—files stored in Photoshop's Plug-ins folder by default. Photoshop uses plug-ins for other features of the application, such as support for various file formats (GIF and PhotoCD, for instance).

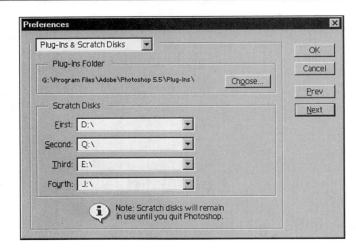

15.1

You can purchase sets of plug-ins from other manufacturers, download free plug-ins from the Web, and even create your own. Photoshop comes with the Filter Factory plug-in, which enables you to define your own filter effects. If you are familiar with programming, you might be interested in Photoshop's Software Development Kit (SDK), which is freely available from its Web site.

To add plug-ins for use with Photoshop, follow the installation instructions or copy the plug-ins directly into Photoshop's Plug-ins folder. To simplify organization, you can create a folder for your new plug-ins.

To change where Photoshop looks for plug-ins, choose File→Preferences→Plug-Ins & Scratch Disks **(15.1)**. Click Choose to set a search path for Photoshop to look for plug-ins. By default, it looks in all subdirectories. Be careful not to set the search path too high (that is, don't have it search an entire hard drive), because it searches for all plug-ins on startup. ImageReady has similar controls for searching for plug-ins on startup. By default, it searches its Plug-ins folder, and you also can specify an additional search folder.

Fading a Filter's Effect

15.2

15.3

15.4

Immediately after applying a filter, you can fade the effect of the filter. This enables you to fine-tune effects and usually is much quicker than undoing and reapplying the filter with different settings. With the Fade command, you also can change a filter's Blending mode so that a motion blur also multiplies or so that you can add clouds in Exclusion mode.

1. Apply a filter. In this example, Filter→Pixelate→Color Halftone is used (**15.2**).

2. Choose Filter→Fade Filter. The Fade dialog box appears (**15.3**).

3. Enter an opacity.

4. Select a Blending mode for the filter effect and choose OK.

   The filter effect is replaced by the faded version, and its blending mode is changed (**15.4**).

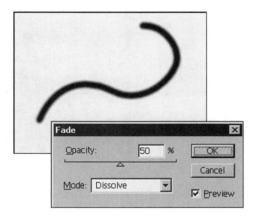

15.5

T I P

*You also can use the Filter→Fade command to fade the last brushstroke from one of the painting tools (**15.5** and **15.6**).*

T I P

To experiment with a filter's effect, apply the filter to a duplicate of the selected layer. Before starting extensive experimentation, save a snapshot in the History palette.

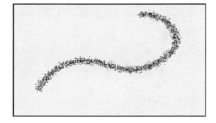

15.6

Applying a Blur

You can use blurs to create shadows, glows, diffusion effects, and depth of field, and to smooth areas retouched using the Rubber Stamp tool. One of the most commonly used Photoshop filters, the Gaussian (pronounced *gowseeun*) Blur, enables you to set a specific blur amount. Many prefer the Gaussian Blur over the Blur and Blur More filters because the blur can be precisely controlled and repeated. In addition, the filter displays a preview of the effect.

1. Select the area or layer that you want to blur **(15.7)**.

2. Choose Filter→Blur→Gaussian Blur. The Gaussian Blur dialog box appears **(15.8)**.

3. Enter a blur amount, measured in pixels. Images at different resolutions may require different blur radii to produce the same blur effect.

Be sure that Preserve Transparency is turned off if you want the pixels to blur into transparent areas.

15.7

If generating a full preview in the image area is taking too long, clear the Preview check box. The preview still appears in the Gaussian Blur dialog box.

15.8

 I P

*Photoshop also has a Radial Blur filter that produces blurs emanating radially from a center point **(15.9)**. You also can use the Radial Blur filter to produce a zoom blur so that it looks like areas of the image are accelerating forward or backward **(15.10)**.*

15.9

15.10

15.11

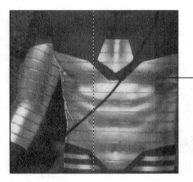

Photoshop's Smart Blur filter attempts to maintain contrasting edges while blurring areas of similar color and tone. Smart Blur is useful for removing patterns introduced when scanning printed images (from magazines, for example).

15.12

To create a diffusion effect, duplicate the layer that you want to diffuse, place it above the original layer, apply a Gaussian blur, and adjust the opacity of the new layer.

15.13

4. Click and drag in the Preview window to pan to the image. Use the plus (+) and minus (–) buttons to zoom in and out on the preview image. The Preview window displays only the current layer.

5. Choose OK. The blur is applied to the selection or layer (15.11).

 I P

You can record a variety of Gaussian blurs as actions so that you can repeat the blur with identical settings.

 I P

Some filters do not work in image modes other than RGB (for example, the Lens Flare and Lighting Effects filters). If your original image is in RGB, run the filter in the original image before converting image modes. If the image is in a different image mode, use Image→Mode→RGB to convert the image, run the filter, and convert back to the original mode. Note that you should convert back and forth between image modes only when absolutely necessary because of color loss during the conversion.

Creating Depth-of-Field Effects

Depth of field is the area between the nearest and farthest points from the camera that are acceptably sharp in the focused image. Everything beyond the farthest point or in front of the nearest point appears blurry or out of focus. By making a selection and applying a blur, you can alter the apparent depth of field in a photograph. Change the depth of field to emphasize the sharper objects and deemphasize the blurry objects. This also can be an effective technique when compositing images together.

15.14

1. Select the areas of the image that should appear out of focus (15.14).

2. Copy and paste to place the foreground or background objects on their own layer (15.15). In Photoshop 5.5, the Extract command works well to isolate foreground objects on their own layer.

15.15

This layer was defringed, and Preserve Transparency was enabled so that areas in the background would not be blurred into the foreground.

   You also may want to consider using Layer→Matting→ Defringe to eliminate any extra pixels selected along the edges that would create odd-colored areas when blurred.

 I P

You also can use other blurs—such as a Motion Blur, Radial Blur, or Zoom Blur— to alter the depth of field.

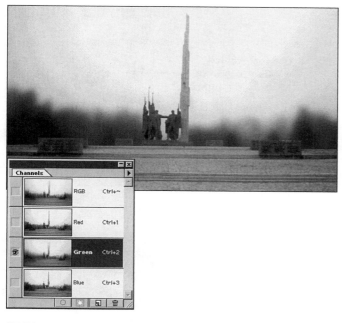

15.16

15.17

3. Select the layer that contains the area of the image that you want to blur in the Layers palette and choose Filter→Blur→Gaussian Blur.

4. In the Gaussian Blur dialog box, select a radius appropriate to blur the image and choose OK. The area that you selected is blurred. In this example, the foreground objects gain greater emphasis as the background recedes (15.16).

You can blur foreground areas as well as background areas to set a specific start and stop point for in-focus regions (15.17).

 T I **P**

To preview a filter's effect on a large image, run the filter on a small selected area or on an individual channel.

Run an artistic effect on a small area to determine the appropriate settings, for example. For filters that affect the entire image, such as Radial Blur, applying the filter to an individual channel helps you set the center point and amount of the blur in Radial or Zoom mode.

Using Artistic Effects

Most of the Artistic, Stylize, Brush Strokes, and Distort filters share a common interface. You can use these filters alone or in groups. Experiment on your own to discover what the filters do and to find your favorite combinations. For an example of using the Watercolor filter in combination with others, see the next section "Creating a Comic-Book Effect."

Use the Preview window to pan and zoom in the image.

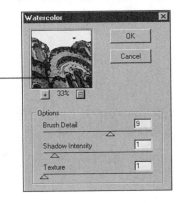

15.18

1. Choose Filter, and then select the filter you want to apply. Artistic→Watercolor was chosen for this example, so the Watercolor dialog box appears (15.18).

2. Each filter has settings that determine its effect. The Watercolor filter uses Brush Detail, Shadow Intensity, and Texture. Brush Detail determines the randomness of the brushstrokes and how noisy the edges are. Shadow Intensity determines the point at which black is used to replace colors from the image. Texture determines the width of the brushstrokes, providing more or less texture in the final image.

Other filters use different settings to control how they affect an image (15.19 and 15.20).

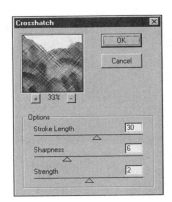

15.19

15.20

15.21

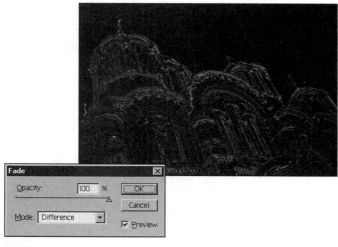

15.22

15.23

3. Choose OK. For large images or complex effects, the status bar tracks the progress of the filter. You can press Esc to cancel the effect before it is applied.

The filter is applied to the image (15.21). You can use Fade→Filter to alter the effect of the filter, either by adjusting its opacity or its blending mode (15.22).

 I P

Many filters cannot be applied to an empty layer (15.23). To quickly fill a layer, choose Edit→Fill and choose an appropriate color for the layer.

(T) I P

If you apply filters that take a while to run, you can set Photoshop to alert you with a beep when the filter is complete. Choose File→Preferences→General and choose Beep When Done.

Creating a Comic-Book Effect

This section presents an example of combining filter and image-adjustment effects. This procedure creates the linework for a simulated comic-book page and then alters the colors in the image in a comic-like style.

15.24

Before you run any process that significantly alters the image, create a copy of the file, duplicate the layer, or—for the most efficient use of space—create a snapshot in the History palette. By creating a snapshot, you can return to the point before the process was performed and try it a different way.

1. The comic-book effect requires two layers that contain the same image (15.24). If there is only one layer in the image, drag the background layer to the New Layer icon in the Layers palette.

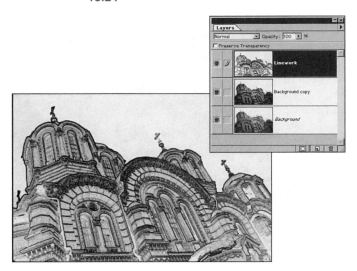

15.25

2. Select the uppermost layer. This layer will contain the linework for the image. To create the linework, choose Filter→Stylize→Find Edges (15.25). The linework temporarily obscures the rest of the layers in the Layers palette.

15.26

15.27

15.28

3. Find Edges creates colored edges based on the color of the pixels in the original image. The edges need to be black to simulate the linework in a comic book. To convert a single layer to grayscale, choose Image→Adjust→Desaturate. Use Image→Adjust→Levels to increase the contrast of the layer. To convert the layer to completely black and white, choose Image→Adjust→ Threshold (**15.26**).

4. You want the white areas of the linework layer to show through to the layer with the image while preserving the black linework. In the Layers palette, change the mode for the layer to Multiply. In this example, part of the bottom layer was filled with white so that the linework would be clearly visible (**15.27**).

5. To change the structure of the underlying image so that it is more comic-like, choose Image→Adjust→Posterize. In the Posterize dialog box, set the number of levels to use in the image. You also can experiment with Artistic filters for the underlying image layer. This example uses the Watercolor filter (**15.28**).

Applying Texture to an Image

Photoshop has several filters that use a texture map to change the apparent texture of an image or a selected area. Using the Texturizer filter, you can create your own textures and apply them to an image. You apply textures by reducing or increasing the tile depth to replicate the highlights and shadows based on a texture map and a light direction.

15.29

Before using the Texturizer filter, you should create a texture map (15.29). The texture map should be an image saved in the Photoshop native format. Only the grayscale information in the texture map is used to determine which parts of the image come forward or recede. In particular, the edges between areas of black and white are important.

1. Choose Filter→Texture→ Texturizer. The Texturizer dialog box appears.

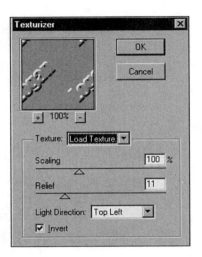

15.30

2. Choose a predefined texture. Or, to use one of your own textures, choose Load Texture. Browse to find a texture and choose Open.

3. Adjust the scaling and relief. The Scaling setting determines how large to make the texture map. The Relief setting determines the strength of the texture.

4. The areas of emboss and deboss are determined by the areas of black and white in the texture map. Enable the Invert check box to flip the embossed and debossed areas (15.30).

15.31

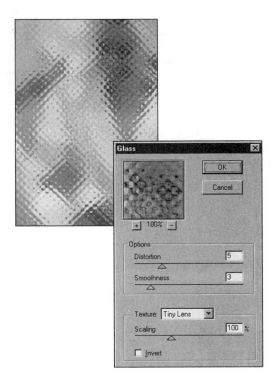

15.32

5. Choose a light direction for the relief.

6. Choose OK. The texture fills the image (**15.31**).

 I P

The Glass filter is similar to the Texturizer filter, although it also distorts image data to produce a shiny, glass effect (**15.32**).

 I P

You can use multiple textures and displacement maps to create a variety of effects. Many techniques that create the appearance that an image is on a particular surface (a puzzle, tiles, stone, and so on) are combinations of effects.

Applying a Displacement Map to an Image

A displacement map offsets pixels in an image based on the colors in the map. Specifically, the displacement map scales the image the maximum negative amount where the map is black and the maximum positive amount where the map is white. A 50 percent gray value has no effect.

The displacement map should be a file in Photoshop native format in any mode other than Bitmap (15.33). The file should be flattened or contain composite layer information.

1. Choose Filter→Distort→ Displace. The Displace dialog box appears (15.34).

2. Specify the Horizontal Scale and Vertical Scale settings, or the amount that the pixels are displaced by the map.

3. Determine how a displacement map that is not the same size as the image being altered should be handled: scaled or tiled.

4. When edge pixels are offset, Photoshop needs to know how to fill in the information from the edges. Select Repeat Edge Pixels or Wrap Around to acquire pixel information from the other side of the image.

15.33

15.34

15.35

15.36

5. Choose OK.

6. Choose a file to use as the displacement map and choose Open. The image is displaced.

The Displace filter offsets the pixels based on the displacement map that you select (15.35). The Displace filter works particularly well when combined with other effects, such as the Texturizer filter (15.36).

 T I P

High contrast displacement maps create the most significant shifts. Use Image→Adjust→Levels to increase the contrast in the displacement map file by moving the white and black sliders closer to one another.

 T I P

You can use the same maps for both the Displace and Texturizer filters by saving a flattened grayscale image in Photoshop's native format.

Changing the Lighting in an Image

You can use the Lighting Effects filter to create an endless variety of changes to an image. You can use Lighting Effects to change the lighting in an image, to add special lighting and color effects, and to add texture to areas of an image. The Lighting Effects filter is available only for images in RGB mode.

1. Choose Filter→Render→ Lighting Effects. The Lighting Effects dialog box appears (15.37).

2. In the Style section, choose a predefined lighting style. After you create a group of lights and settings, you can save your own lighting style.

3. Click and drag the Add Light icon into the Preview window to add a new light. You can change the light type by selecting it and choosing Spotlight, Omni, or Directional from the Light Type drop-down list. See Table 15.1

4. Set the Intensity value for each light. For spotlights, set the focus.

Each light is represented by its white center point. To move any light, click on its center point and drag it to a new position.

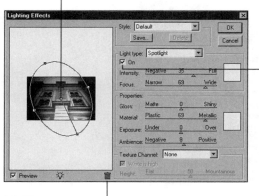

To turn a light on or off, select the light and use the On check box.

15.37

To delete a light, drag it to the Trash icon.

Table 15.1   Spotlight Types

Type	Features	How to Edit
Spotlight	Direction, area of effect, and position	To change the direction or area of effect, click and drag the control handles on the elliptical perimeter.
Omni light	Area of effect and position	Change the area of effect by dragging any of the handles on the outside circle.
Direction light	Direction and position	The length of the direction line controls the height and effect of the light.

Intensity ranges from −100 to 100. At −100, the light darkens the image. At 100, the light applies the maximum lighting effect. Set the color for each light by clicking in the color swatch.

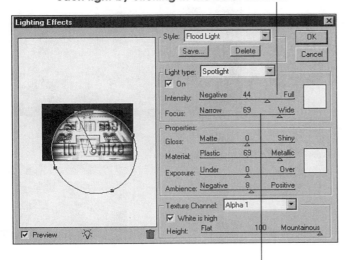

15.38

At −100, the spotlight has a very narrow effect. At 100, the spotlight fills its bounding ellipse evenly.

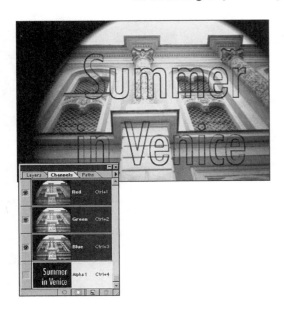

15.39

5. Set the properties, or the way the light should interact with the surface of the image. The properties apply to every light in the scene.

Change the Gloss value to determine the shininess of the surface. High Gloss values increase the size of the specular highlight. Change the Material property to control the intensity of the specular highlight.

Change the Exposure property to set the overall additive or subtractive effect of the lights on the image, whether overexposed or underexposed. Change the Ambience property to set a default light throughout the image. You also can control the color of the ambient light by clicking on the color swatch in the Properties section.

6. To apply a texture through the Lighting Effects filter, you must have an alpha channel in the image that contains that texture information. Select a channel from the Texture Channel drop-down list. The texture, based on the areas of black and white in the channel, is applied where the light interacts with the surface of the image (15.38).

7. Choose OK. The lighting effects are applied to the image (15.39).

Adding Noise

The Noise filters add and remove noise in an image. The Add Noise filter changes the color of pixels randomly throughout an image by a specified amount (15.40). You can use a Noise filter when you have blurred an image or made an area too smooth with the Rubber Stamp or Smudge tool. You also can add the Noise filter and use it as a basis before running other filters. For example, try combining Noise filters with the Artistic filters to create textures.

15.40

1. Choose Filter→Noise→Add Noise. The Add Noise dialog box appears (15.41).

2. Choose an amount of noise to add by entering a value or dragging the slider. Values range from 1 to 999. At 1, very little noise is added. At 999, the image is almost completely obliterated.

15.41

 I P

You can add noise in individual channels to help remove obvious banding in gradients. You also may need to combine this method with the Gaussian Blur filter.

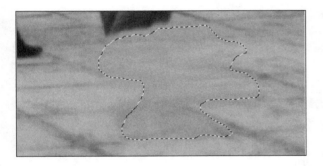

15.42

3. Choose Uniform or Gaussian for the noise type. Uniform determines the color values for changed pixels by selecting randomly from a range of colors determined by the Amount setting. Gaussian uses the same range, but the color values are selected along a bell-curve distribution. Uniform noise typically is smoother, whereas the Gaussian noise tends to be speckled.

4. Enable the Monochromatic check box to add noise while preserving the underlying color.

5. Choose OK. Noise is added throughout the image or area **(15.42)**.

 I P

Another filter in the Noise submenu, Median, is designed to remove noise in an image by blending the brightness of pixels. Use Median to remove moiré patters by applying it to individual channels (especially Green and Blue). You also can use Median to smooth over artifacts and noise introduced by motion.

CHAPTER 16

In this chapter you learn how to...

Choose a CMYK Model and Conversion Method

Create Spot Color Channels

Apply Trapping

Choose an Appropriate File Format

Set Halftone Screens

Create Transfer Functions

Add Crop Marks, Registration Marks, and Calibration Bars

The world of onscreen images is concerned solely with three colors: red, green, and blue. If you work with paper, you often must consider these colors in the first step of the workflow, although your final output is in four or possibly more colors. Knowing how the image will be printed often requires a relationship with your printer or prepress service bureau, or a bit of trial and error if you are creating the output.

PAPER PUBLISHING

Whether you are creating images that will be printed by a service, or you create the film or proofs, Photoshop provides a broad range of tools to simplify the process. Photoshop 5, in particular, added several features, such as support for spot color channels and the capability to save DCS 2.0 files, that secured its position as the standard for prepress professionals.

When preparing images for print, you can choose from the outset whether you want to start in RGB and convert to CMYK, or whether you want to start the process in CMYK. Both methods have advantages and disadvantages. Images in RGB are smaller and therefore faster to work with. Furthermore, all the filters are available when working in RGB. Images in CMYK are 25% larger than those in RGB (because there are four channels), but there is less concern about out-of-gamut colors when working entirely in CMYK.

If you scan an image in RGB, you should try to keep it in RGB as long as you can and save an RGB version of the file before converting to CMYK. If you scan in CMYK, don't convert back and forth between RGB.

Choosing a CMYK Model and Conversion Method

Before converting to CMYK mode from RGB, you should specify a CMYK Setup. The CMYK Setup is used to process the image as it is converted from RGB, through Lab. After an image is in CMYK mode, changing the CMYK Setup affects the appearance of the image onscreen but does not actually change the image itself. You must correctly configure the CMYK Setup before converting from RGB. Changing the CMYK setup is similar to setting a preference. After it is set, it remains in effect for all conversions between RGB and CMYK until it is changed. For more information about converting between RGB and CMYK mode, see "Converting from RGB to CMYK" on page 54 in Chapter 4, "Image Modes."

Like setting the resolution, you need to know information about your output method before using the CMYK Setup.

1. Choose File→Save a Copy and save an RGB master version of the file in case you need to make changes to the original.

2. Choose File→Color Settings→CMYK Setup. Then choose a method for defining the CMYK color space: Built-in, ICC, or Tables. (See Table 16.1 for more information.)

3. Select Built-In (16.1) to manually adjust the separation settings. Choose a color set from the Ink Colors drop-down list.

Table 5.1 How to Find the Conversion Method You Need to Use

CMYK Model	Use	Go to
Built-in	Use to manually adjust separation settings.	Step 3, page 268
ICC	Use to control the CMYK setup based on the ICC color profile of your printer	Step 8, page 270
Tables	Use to load separation tables defined in Photoshop 4.0 or other applications.	Step 12, page 271

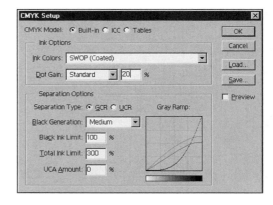

16.1

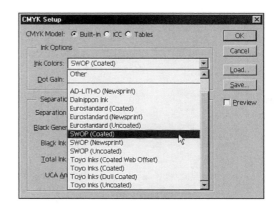

16.2

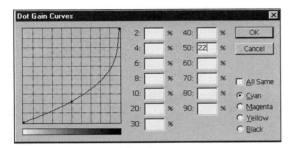

16.3

Table 16.2 Typical Dot Gain Settings

Newsprint	25 to 35%
Sheet-fed, coated stock	10 to 15%
Sheet-fed, uncoated stock	18 to 22%
Web, coated stock	15 to 22%

Table 16.3 Separation Methods

| GCR (Gray Component Replacement) | Neutral colors in the image are removed from the cyan, magenta, and yellow plates and replaced with corresponding grays on the black plate. If you choose GCR, you also can choose UCA (Undercolor Addition) to replace some of the color depleted by GCR. Choose a Black Generation option to determine the level of replacement, or choose Custom to define your own replacement curve. GCR commonly is used when printing on coated stock. |
| UCR (Undercolor Removal) | Cyan, magenta, and yellow inks are removed from the shadow and midtones and replaced by black, often significantly reducing the total amount of ink used to print the image. Colors may appear more vibrant at the cost of the overall tonal range of the image. UCR commonly is used when printing on uncoated stock. |

4. Dot gain is compensation for the way ink spreads on different papers through the midtones of an image. From the Dot Gain drop-down list (16.2), choose Standard; then specify a standard dot gain based on the paper, ink, and press you will use to print (Table 16.2).

Choose Curves from the Dot Gain list to precisely control the dot gain for each process color (16.3), but talk to your printer or service bureau before getting too deep into this.

5. Choose a separation method to control how black is managed in the printed image (Table 16.3).

6. Specify a percentage for the Black Ink Limit setting, or the total amount of black ink used at the darkest points of the image.

continues

Choosing a CMYK Model and Conversion Method continued

7. Specify a Total Ink Limit percentage, or the total amount of ink printed at any one point in the image (Table 16.4).

Your choices for the Separation options are represented by the Gray Ramp.

8. Choose the ICC model to control the CMYK setup based on the ICC color profile of your printer **(16.4)**.

Choose the ICC profile for your output device, define your own using third-party profiling software, or load a profile provided with your printer.

9. From the Engine drop-down list **(16.5)**, choose a Color Management Module (CMM) to use to interpret ICC profile information.

Table 16.4 Total Ink Limit Percentage Settings

Coated stock	300 to 340%
Uncoated stock	270 to 300%
Newsprint	220 to 280%

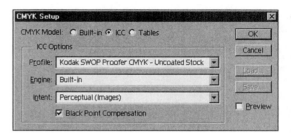

16.4

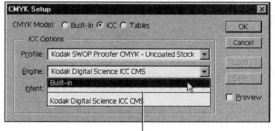

16.5   **By default, you can choose between Photoshop's built-in engine and the Kodak Digital Science ICC CMS. If you have other CMMs installed on your system, you can select one of those instead.**

T I P

Enable the Preview check box to display a preview of how the changes made in the CMYK setup affect the image. The preview affects images only in CMYK mode and changes only how the image is displayed onscreen. To apply the changes, you must convert from RGB to CMYK.

To preview the changes, create a smaller copy of the image before converting the original to CMYK.

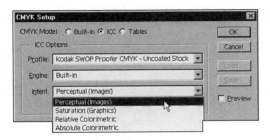

16.6

Table 16.5 Out-of-Gamut Color Handling

Perceptual (Images)	Maintains the relationships among the colors in the image. Most of the colors in the image will change as out-of-gamut colors are mapped to the CMYK gamut. Colors that are not out of gamut also will change as Photoshop attempts to maintain the relationship between these colors and the out-of-gamut colors. This is the best choice in most cases.
Saturation (Graphics)	Maintains the relative saturation values of the colors. Colors that are out of gamut are converted to colors inside the CMYK gamut while maintaining their saturation values.
Relative Colorimetric	Typically converts out-of-gamut colors to colors inside the CMYK gamut while maintaining lightness values. This setting does not change the values of colors inside the CMYK gamut.
Absolute Colorimetric	Disables white-point matching during the conversion process and therefore might not produce acceptable results.

10. Use the Intent drop-down list (16.6) to tell Photoshop how you want it to handle out-of-gamut colors (colors that cannot be accurately reproduced in CMYK) (Table 16.5).

11. Enable the Black Point Compensation check box to map the darkest neutral color in the unconverted image to the darkest neutral color in the target color space. If you do not enable Black Point Compensation, Photoshop maps the darkest color in the unconverted image to black.

12. Choose the Tables Model (16.7) to load tables you defined in Photoshop 4.0 or other applications that produce compatible separation tables.

13. Choose OK.

16.7   **To save CMYK settings as an ICC profile, choose Tables after entering CMYK setup information. Then choose Save.**

(T) I P

To save the CMYK settings you specify in the Built-In option as an ICC profile, select the Separation Table option and choose Save. (You may need to choose Save and then immediately choose Cancel under Built-In so that the built-in settings are used with the Tables selection.)

Creating Spot Color Channels

You can indicate areas to be printed with a spot color. An example of using spot colors is adding a fifth plate that contains a special ink such as gold or fluorescent pink. You also can add plates that carry a spot color to add punch to a particular color (called bump plates). Another example is creating a two-color print job so that only two colors are used.

Many spot colors that you use cannot be reproduced accurately on a monitor because they fall outside of the RGB gamut. The image displayed onscreen is only a preview of the final print. Keep this in mind when choosing a preview color to represent the spot color.

1. Choose New Spot Channel from the Channels palette menu.

2. In the New Spot Channel dialog box **(16.8)**, click on the color swatch to display the color picker **(16.9)**. Usually, you choose a custom color for a spot color channel, so if the Custom Colors dialog box does not appear, choose Custom in the color picker. The color you choose is only a preview of the actual color. When printed, it is the name of the color that is important.

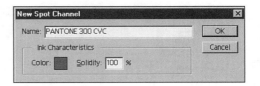

16.8

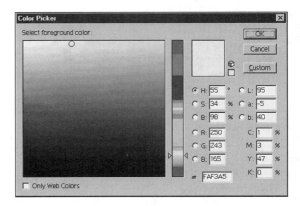

16.9

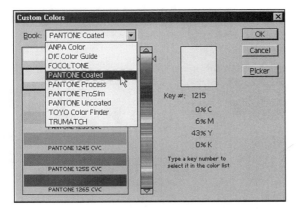

16.10

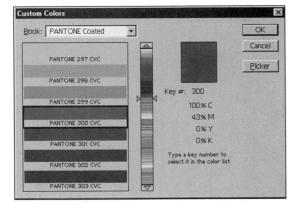

16.11

3. In the Custom Colors dialog box, select a set of colors to use from the Book drop-down list **(16.10)**. Pantone or Pantone Matching System (PMS) colors often are used **(16.11)**. If you want to print a color that is not listed, choose the color closest to the one you want to print. Choose OK.

4. You can change the name of the color you selected in the Custom Colors dialog box. Enter a different name if you need compatibility with other applications that support spot colors or to specify a color not available in the Custom Colors dialog box.

5. Enter a value for Solidity. Solidity determines how the spot color is displayed onscreen. It does not change the way the spot color is printed. The tonal range of the spot color is determined by what you "paint" on the layer (see Step 7).

6. Choose OK.

continues

 I P

Spot color channels always overprint in the order in which they appear in the Channels palette. To move a spot color channel above a color channel, convert the image to Multichannel mode.

Creating Spot Color Channels continued

7. Paint on the spot color channel using any of the painting tools. You also can use any of the filters or tools that are supported in Grayscale mode. Where you paint with black, you add 100% of the spot color. Where you paint with white, you remove the spot color **(16.12)**.

You also can copy information from other channels, layers, or images and paste it into a spot color channel. The result always is grayscale in the individual channel. If your image is missing any or all of the CMYK channels, Photoshop converts the image to Multichannel mode.

Images can have, at most, 24 channels total. This includes color, alpha, and spot color channels.

16.12

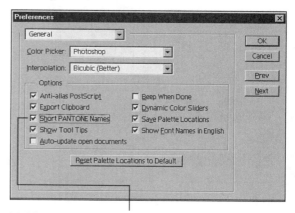

16.13

T I P

When you print, you can specify a different color for the spot color plate (silver instead of gold, for example).

In fact, this is how print jobs that contained spot colors were prepared before Photoshop added support for spot color channels. You could create an image that contained only black and magenta, for example, create the separations, and then specify that the printer use a Pantone color instead of magenta ink.

If you are exporting the image to an application that requires short Pantone names, choose File→Preferences→ General and choose Short Pantone Names.

Applying Trapping

16.14

16.15   **Trapping is typically the very last step before printing. To apply trapping, the image must be in CMYK or Multichannel mode. Photoshop applies spread trapping and does not apply choke trapping.**

You can apply trapping in Photoshop, but like most of the print configurations in this chapter, consult your printer before doing so. Your printer may have specialized trapping software. Letting your printer do it not only guarantees better trapping results but saves you the time and trouble of tedious trapping work.

Photoshop obeys the following rules when applying trapping:

- All colors spread under black.
- Lighter colors spread under darker colors.
- Yellow spreads under cyan, magenta, and black.
- Pure cyan and pure magenta spread under each other equally.

1. Choose Image→Trap.

2. In the Trap dialog box (16.14), enter the width of the overlap. You can set the size of the overlap in pixels, points, or millimeters. Consult your printer to determine the amount of expected misregistration.

3. Choose OK.

The overlap is applied to the appropriate elements in the Photoshop image (16.15). In this image, an extreme trap was used for illustration purposes.

Choosing an Appropriate File Format

When you save an image for print, you have several file format options. Consult your service bureau to find out what formats it supports and prefers. Some printers accept the Photoshop native file format but prefer that layers are flattened to minimize file size. For more information about saving files, see Chapter 1, "Opening, Placing, and Saving Images." For more information about exporting a file for use with a page-layout program and clipping paths, see Chapter 14, "Working with Paths."

Table 16.6 File Format Options

Format	Pros	Cons
DCS 2.0	Can contain spot color channels, one alpha channel, clipping paths	Not always supported
EPS	Widely supported, can contain clipping paths	No support for spot colors or alpha channels
TIFF	Widely supported, can often be edited in page layout programs, page layout programs often show the actual image instead of a preview, can contain one alpha channel	Raster only format; sometimes larger and slower to process

Setting Halftone Screens

In conventional halftoning, images consist of a regular array of tiny dots that vary in size. In process printing, each ink color has its own screen. Photoshop enables you to customize the angles of the screens for each ink and to adjust the shape of the dot used on the screen. As with the rest of Photoshop's print setup, you should consult your printer before changing the default settings.

1. Choose File→Page Setup (16.16).

2. Choose Screens. The Halftone Screens dialog box appears (16.17).

3. Clear the Use Printer's Default Screens check box to specify the screen frequency, screen angle, and dot shape.

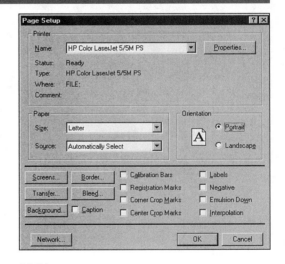

16.16

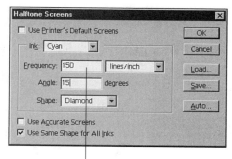

16.17 Enter the line screen that will be used to print the job. Be sure that the image's resolution is sufficient (1.5 to 2 times the screen frequency).

Table 16.7 Screen Angles

Cyan	15 degrees
Magenta	75 degrees
Yellow	0 degrees
Black	45 degrees (This screen angle should be used for the most prevalent color in the image, because it is the angle least noticeable to the eye.)

Elliptical dots provide smoother gradations in the midtones.

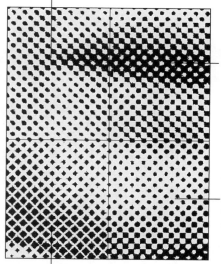

Square dots are used for sheet-fed, web off-set, and letterpress printing.

Round dots minimize midtone and high-light gain and are used for high-speed web offset printing.

Diamond dots maintain detail in the midtones and three-quartertones.

16.18

4. In the Frequency box, enter a value for the screen frequency or line screen. The screen frequency is the number of printed dots per inch on each separated plate.

5. Choose a color from the Ink drop-down list.

6. In the Angle box, enter a screen angle for the color you selected. Setting the screen angles is important to eliminate moiré patterns. Table 16.7 shows typical screen angles.

For additional colors or screens, consult your printer for the proper angles.

7. In the Shape drop-down list, choose a shape for the halftone dot (16.18). Table 16.8 shows typical uses for each dot shape follow.

You also can select Custom and specify your own spot shape by entering the Post-Script code in the dialog box.

8. Enable the Use Accurate Screens check box if you are outputting to a printer that supports PostScript Level 2 or higher, or has an Emerald controller.

9. Choose OK.

You can save the halftone screen information with EPS and DCS 2.0 files.

Creating Transfer Functions

You can create transfer functions to compensate for a miscalibrated imagesetter. Specifically, transfer functions compensate for dot gain between an image and its film. For example, the Transfer function makes 50% dots in the image print as 50% dots on film.

1. Choose File→Page Setup.

2. Choose Transfer. The Transfer Functions dialog box appears (16.19).

3. Enter values in the Transfer Functions dialog box. Typically, you enter a desired value for the 50% dot. You can set the same dot for all inks used by enabling the All Same check box, or you can set the dot individually for each ink.

To determine the values you should enter in this dialog box, use the measurements from a transmissive densitomiter (used to measure the density of printed halftones).

The transfer functions are applied when the image is rasterized by a PostScript imagesetter.

You can save the transfer function information with EPS and DCS 2.0 files.

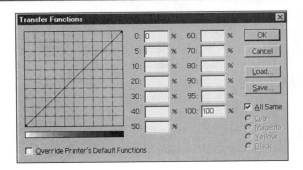

16.19

Adding Crop Marks, Registration Marks, and Calibration Bars

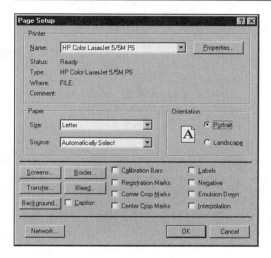

16.20

You can use the Page Setup option to include a variety of printing information, including crop marks and calibration bars.

1. Choose File→Page Setup.

2. In the Page Setup dialog box (16.20), choose a printer, paper size, and paper orientation.

3. Choose the features you want to print (16.21).

4. Click Background to select a color for the blank area around the image (by default, the paper color, or on film, clear).

5. Click Border to print a black border around the image. Half the border width overlaps with the edges of the image.

6. Click Bleed to reposition the corner crop marks inside the image. Bleed is necessary so that an image fills a page to the edges, even if the trimming is a little off.

7. Enable the Caption check box to print the caption set in the File Info command.

8. Click Screens or Transfer to set those options. See the previous sections in this chapter for more information about creating halftone screens or transfer functions.

9. Choose OK.

Star target   **Label**   **Registration marks**

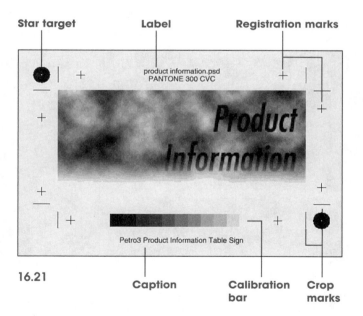

16.21   **Caption**   **Calibration bar**   **Crop marks**

© H A P T E R **17**

In this chapter you learn how to…

Save GIFs, JPEGs, and PNGs for the Web

Save Images with Transparency

Use the Web Palette

Create Seamless Backgrounds

Lay Out a Web Page in Photoshop and ImageReady

Slice Images

Create Imagemaps

Create Button Rollovers

Create Animations

Paralleling the proliferation of the Web, Photoshop has evolved and been widely accepted by Web designers for its capability to create graphics specifically suited for online viewing. Photoshop 5.5 is a significant advance in the development of Photoshop, particularly for those interested in creating graphics targeted for use on the Web. The Save for Web command enables you to choose the most appropriate optimization level by visually

ELECTRONIC PUBLISHING

comparing different versions of the image. New options have been added when converting to Indexed Color mode, including new dithering and compression capabilities. The Type tool also has been improved to support small type at low resolutions.

The most significant change to Photoshop's capability to create Web graphics is the inclusion of ImageReady 2.0. Similar to Photoshop in look and feel, ImageReady's focus is entirely on images destined to appear onscreen. Slices let you break up large graphics into small, quick-loading files. You also can use slices to define hotspots and even JavaScript rollover effects. ImageReady automatically generates the HTML, scripts, and optimized images necessary to work in standard browsers. ImageReady also provides support for GIF animation and is integrated tightly with the Layers palette.

Even without Photoshop 5.5 and ImageReady 2.0, Photoshop 5.02 can be used effectively as a tool for those designing Web graphics. The most basic functions of exporting GIFs, JPEGs, and PNGs have been included in Photoshop for years. These functions will evolve alongside the Web and the needs of Web designers.

IR 5.5 Saving GIFs for the Web

The GIF (Graphics Interchange Format) is one of the most commonly used file formats on the World Wide Web. GIF files compress considerable amounts depending on their contents, can contain transparent areas, and can be used to create animations. Although GIFs can contain at most 256 colors, this is often enough for many graphics applications, which makes this file format well-suited to flat-color images and banner ads.

Using the Save for Web command in Photoshop 5.5 or the Optimize palette in ImageReady 2.0, you can choose a variety of optimization and compression settings and compare the results side-by-side with the original to determine whether too much image data has been discarded. The significant factors that affect the size of the final file are number of colors, dithering method, and Lossy compression setting.

1. In Photoshop 5.5, choose File→Save for Web. Choose 2-Up or 4-Up in the Save for Web dialog box to display multiple versions of the file (17.1). In ImageReady, you can display multiple versions in the document window.

2. Select one of the panes of the 2-Up or 4-Up display to set a different optimization level. You should leave one of the panes set to the original image for comparison purposes.

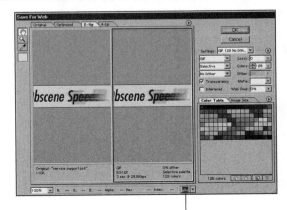

17.1

You can view the image in different browsers by selecting the Preview in Browser button. The image is opened in the selected browser along with other image information. This enables you to see exactly how a specific browser displays an image, including dithering and color shifts.

17.2

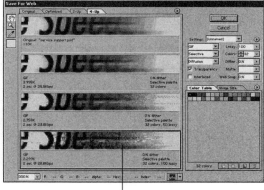

17.3

To minimize file size in a GIF image, create large areas of the same color. For example, for an image that appears over a textured background, create large areas of transparency to fully utilize the compression used in the GIF. In fact, the GIF compresses based on horizontal patterns. Vertical color changes (such as gradients) compress more than horizontal color changes.

3. Select a preset GIF optimization type either from the Settings list (17.2) in the Save for Web dialog box or in ImageReady's Optimization palette. You can also enter your own settings.

4. Choose a Color Table, set a Dither method, choose the number of Colors, set the Matte color (the color to blend transparent pixels against), and set the value for Web Snap (the tolerance used to change colors to their nearest color in the Web palette). For more information about dithering options, see "Converting to Indexed Color" on page 61 in Chapter 4, "Image Modes." Choose larger Dither values to minimize banding.

5. Check Interlaced to turn on interlacing for the file.

6. Choose a value for Lossy. Lossy controls the amount of lossy compression. Use the highest Lossy setting that still produces acceptable results (17.3). You cannot use the Lossy option with the Interlaced option, or with Noise or Pattern Dither algorithms.

   Whenever you change any settings, watch the preview in the selected pane of the 2-Up or

continues

Saving GIFs for the Web continued

4-Up display. Make sure that the image quality is still acceptable. The goal is to maintain image quality while reducing the file size displayed at the bottom of the pane to the lowest possible value. Any increase in compression or reduction in the number of colors reduces image quality as well as image size (17.4).

7. Choose Image Size in the Save for Web dialog box to resize the image when you save the file (17.5). Enter a new width and height or percentage. Under Quality, choose Bicubic for most images. Choose Nearest Neighbor if the image is a flat color or line drawing.

   After you have specified a resizing option, choose Apply to preview the resampling.

8. When finished, choose OK in the Save for Web dialog box or File→Save Optimized As in ImageReady.

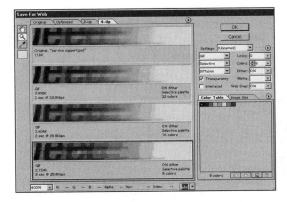

17.4

17.5

 I P

Always crop images as tightly as possible. If you need extra space around the image, you can use a transparent 1×1-pixel GIF as a spacer.

Saving JPEGs for the Web

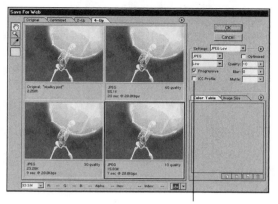

17.6   **Choose ICC Profile in the Save for Web dialog box to embed ICC Color Profile information in the file.**

17.7

JPEGs support 24-bit color and are an excellent choice when displaying continuous-tone images or photographs on the Web. JPEG (Joint Photographic Experts Group) is a file format as well as a compression scheme that reduces the size of images by discarding image data. You can set the amount of compression used when saving a JPEG. Larger compression settings produce smaller files, but can create artifacts in the image.

1. In Photoshop 5.5, choose File→Save for Web. In the Save for Web dialog box, choose 2-Up or 4-Up to display multiple versions of the file **(17.6)**. In ImageReady, you can display multiple versions in the document window.

2. Select one of the panes of the 2-Up or 4-Up display to set a different optimization level. You should leave one of the panes set to the original image for comparison purposes.

3. Choose one of the preset JPEG optimization types from the Settings list **(17.7)** in the Save for Web dialog box or in ImageReady's Optimization palette. You can also enter your own settings.

continues

Saving JPEGs for the Web continued

4. Choose a compression quality or enter the value directly. You can also set a blur value to reduce artifacts caused by compression and choose a matte color.

   Whenever you change any settings, watch the preview in the appropriate pane of the 2-Up or 4-Up display. Make sure the image quality is still acceptable. The goal is to maintain image quality while reducing the file size displayed at the bottom of the pane to the lowest possible value. Any increase in compression reduces image quality as well as image size.

5. Choose Image Size in the Save for Web dialog box to resize the image when you save the file **(17.8)**. Enter a new width and height or percentage.

   After you have specified a resizing option, choose Apply to preview the resampling.

6. When finished, choose OK in the Save for Web dialog box or File→Save Optimized As in ImageReady.

17.8

Choose Bicubic for most images. Choose Nearest Neighbor if the image is a flat color or line drawing.

 I P

Use the Eyedropper tool to select the Matte color from the image or preview. Under Matte, select Eyedropper Color.

Saving PNGs for the Web

PNGs are a royalty-free alternative to the GIF. The PNG (Portable Network Graphics) format supports both RGB and Indexed Color images. The PNG format supports alpha channel transparency and uses lossless compression so that no image data is discarded. Some older browsers do not support the PNG format.

17.9

You can load and save optimization settings by using the Optimize menu. You can also load and save color tables using the Color Table menu.

17.10

1. In Photoshop 5.5, choose File→Save for Web. Choose 2-Up or 4-Up in the Save for Web dialog box to display multiple versions of the file (17.9). In ImageReady, you can display multiple versions in the document window.

2. Select one of the panes of the 2-Up or 4-Up display to set a different optimization level. You should leave one of the panes set to the original image for comparison purposes.

3. Select a preset PNG optimization type either from the Settings list (17.10) in the Save for Web dialog box or in ImageReady's Optimization palette. You can also enter your own settings.

4. If you choose PNG-8, choose a Color Table, set a Dither method, choose the number of Colors, set the Matte color (the color to blend transparent

continues

Saving PNGs for the Web continued

pixels against), and set the value for Web Snap (the tolerance used to change colors to their nearest color in the Web palette). For more information about dithering options, see "Converting to Indexed Color" on page 61 in Chapter 4, "Image Modes." Choose higher Dither values to minimize banding.

If you choose PNG-24, choose a Matte color.

5. If you choose PNG-8, you can edit the color table. For more information about editing the color table, see "Modifying a Color Table in ImageReady" on page 70 in Chapter 4, "Image Modes."

6. Check Interlaced to turn on interlacing for the file.

Whenever you change any settings, watch the preview in the selected pane of the 2-Up or 4-Up display. Make sure the image quality is still acceptable. The goal is to maintain image quality while reducing the file size displayed at the bottom of the pane to the lowest possible value. Any increase in compression or reduction in the number of colors reduces image quality as well as image size (17.11).

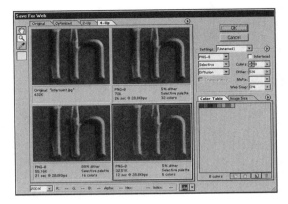

17.11

17.12

7. Choose Image Size in the Save for Web dialog box to resize the image when you save the file (17.12). Enter a new width and height or percentage. Under Quality, choose Bicubic for most images. Choose Nearest Neighbor if the image is a flat color or line drawing.

After you have specified a resizing option, choose Apply to preview the resampling.

8. When finished, choose OK in the Save for Web dialog box or File→Save Optimized As in ImageReady.

 I P

You can use the DitherBox filter to precisely control dithering and, therefore, image quality. For more information about the DitherBox filter, see "Using DitherBox to Control Dithering" on page 68 in Chapter 4.

Saving Images with Transparency

You can save GIF and PNG files with transparent areas. To save a file with transparency, the image must contain transparent areas (17.13).

If your image is in Indexed Color mode and you use the GIF89a Export filter, you also can create areas of transparency by selecting the colors you want to be transparent.

1. Choose File→Save for Web.

2. Choose GIF, PNG-8, or PNG-24, depending on your needs. GIF is most common, but the PNG has better control over transparent areas.

3. Make sure the Transparency check box is enabled.

4. Choose the rest of the optimization options (see the appropriate file format earlier in this chapter).

5. Choose OK.

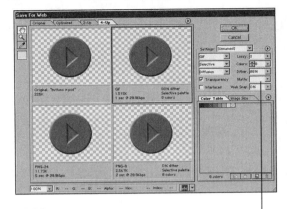

17.13

GIFs support only one level of transparency, so some aliasing may be apparent. Choose an appropriate Matte color to help reduce this.

 I P

You also can use a single alpha channel to define transparency in a PNG. Use File→Save a Copy to save the PNG with the alpha channel. The alpha channel is used to define transparency by browsers that display PNGs.

 I P

Photoshop also provides a wizard to step you through the export of transparent images for both online and print. Choose Help→Export Transparent Image.

Using the Web Palette

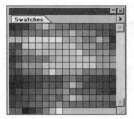

17.14

To load the Web-safe swatches so that you can select only Web-safe colors when creating and editing an image, choose Replace Swatches in the Swatches palette. Navigate and choose Web Hues Swatches and choose Load. The Web Hues swatches are in the Color Swatches folder in the Goodies folder.

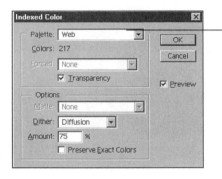

17.15

To use the Web palette when you convert to Indexed Color mode or export the file, select Web from the list of color tables in the Indexed Color dialog box or the Save for Web dialog box (17.16).

When creating flat color images, you can reduce or eliminate dithering by using the Web palette and Web-safe swatches. The Web palette contains the 216 colors common to both the Windows and the Mac 256-color palettes. When an image is displayed in a browser on an operating system set to 256 colors, any colors that fall outside of the system palettes are dithered. Using the Web palette forces all the colors in an image to stay within the fixed limits of the two system palettes so that dithering does not occur.

Note that if you want to strictly use Web-safe colors, you should disable or not use Photoshop's features that create color blends (for example, layer effects and anti-aliasing).

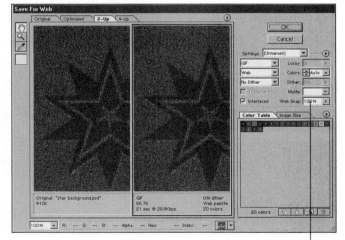

17.16   **When using a color table other than Web, such as Selective or Adaptive, you can force the resulting image to use only colors from the Web palette by setting the Web Snap option to 100%.**

Ⓝ O T E

Watch Web-safe colors carefully when using and converting between ICC color profiles. If your display is set to use only 256 colors, Web-safe colors may appear dithered based on the RGB profile you have selected.

In addition, colors may appear to shift when you open Photoshop 5.02 and Photoshop 5.5 images in ImageReady 2.0. Choose Monitor RGB in the RGB Setup dialog box in Photoshop to achieve consistent color between Photoshop and ImageReady.

Creating Seamless Backgrounds

Backgrounds for Web pages often are tiled. You can eliminate the seams between the tiles by using the Offset filter and the Rubber Stamp tool.

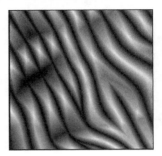

17.17

1. Select an area of an image that you want to tile. You can constrain the aspect ratio of the rectangular marquee to select an area of a particular size. This is the area that will be made tilable. You can use the same technique on an entire image.

2. Choose Image→Crop (17.17). If you want to preserve the original image, be sure to use Save As to give the new image a new name.

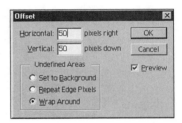

17.18

3. Choose Filter→Other→Offset. In the Offset dialog box (17.18), choose a horizontal and vertical offset about half the total image size. Be sure to select Wrap Around in the Undefined Areas section.

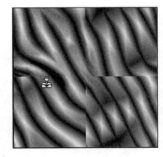

17.19

4. Use the Rubber Stamp tool to blend the obvious seams created by the Offset filter (17.19). You also can use the Smudge and Blur tools to help blend the edges. Try varying the opacity of the Rubber Stamp tool and adding noise if the rubber stamp creates areas of obvious repetition.

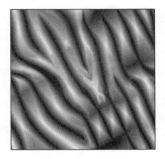

17.20

17.21

17.22

5. When finished (17.20), because the pixels on the top match the pixels on the bottom, and the pixels on the sides match one another, the image creates seamless patterns when tiled. Choose Filter→Other→Offset and use the opposite values from those used previously to undo the offset.

6. To test the pattern, choose Select→All. Then choose Edit→Define Pattern. Create a new image that is larger than the tile, choose Edit→Fill, and select Pattern. The tile fills the larger image seamlessly (17.21).

 I P

If the image is 256×256 pixels or a multiple of that size, the Clouds filter will automatically tile the image **(17.22)**. *Choose Filter→Render→Clouds.*

 I P

To display the pixel dimensions of an image in Photoshop, press (Option)[Alt] while clicking on the file size numbers in the status bar. Photoshop displays the dimensions, number of channels, and resolution.

Laying Out a Web Page in Photoshop and ImageReady

You can create an entire Web page from within Photoshop and Image-Ready if it consists solely of images. You can even let ImageReady create HTML files for you. Obviously, for text content, an HTML editor is necessary.

1. Begin by starting a new file. In the New dialog box **(17.23)**, choose an appropriate image mode for the page (either RGB or Grayscale), select a background option, and enter the size of the page.

2. Lay out the graphics and buttons on the page **(17.24)**. Keep the buttons on separate layers, and don't worry about rollover states—those are handled in ImageReady. If you started the image in Photoshop, switch to ImageReady by using the Jump to ImageReady button .

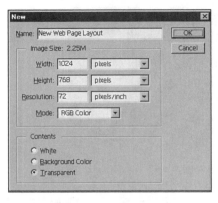

17.23

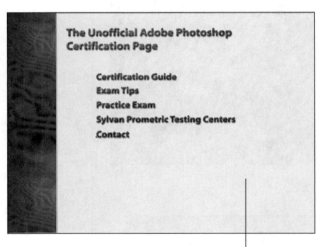

17.24

(T) I P

You can use the browser itself as a guide when laying out your page by taking a screen shot of an open browser window and using it as your background layer in Photoshop. To capture the screen, press Print Screen to copy the screen to the Clipboard in Windows and (Command-Shift-3) to create a screen dump file on your startup hard drive on the Macintosh.

When choosing a size, you should consider appropriate screen sizes (640×480, 800×600, 1024×768, and so on). You also should consider the amount of space lost for the browser controls (although some browsers, such as Microsoft Internet Explorer, can be run in full-screen mode). Choosing 640×480 or smaller ensures that even viewers with smaller screen settings can view the page without scrolling.

In reality, the height of the page can be anything you want; the viewer can scroll vertically.

17.25

You can force Photoshop to save all the files you create with lowercase extensions. Choose File→Preferences→Saving Files. In the File Extensions drop-down list, choose Use Lower Case. Lowercase extensions commonly are used in HTML. Although some operating systems used on Web servers are case preserving and not case sensitive, UNIX servers—which host the vast majority of Web sites—are case sensitive.

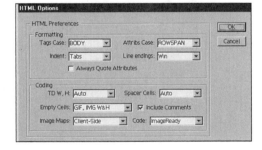

17.26

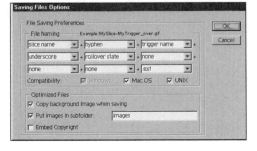

17.27

3. Use ImageReady's Slice tool to separate the page and assign URLs to regions. For more information, see the next section, "Slicing Images and Creating Imagemaps." After you create slices, you can create rollover effects.

4. When finished creating the page, select the optimization settings and choose File→Save Optimized As (17.25).

5. Click HTML Options to configure how the HTML is created (17.26). Click Saving Files Options to determine a file-naming convention, operating system compatibility, and control for handling optimized files (17.27).

6. Choose Save.

An HTML file is created with the appropriate IMAGE and HREF tags. If you create an image rollover, the necessary scripts are included in the file.

(T) I P

Photoshop 5.5 and ImageReady both support the entry of colors based on their hexadecimal codes in the color pickers. Web-safe colors are based on combinations of 00, 33, 66, 99, CC, and FF.

Slicing Images and Creating Imagemaps

You can use ImageReady to separate images into smaller, faster-loading pieces and to create button maps using the Slice tool. When you use the Slice tool, the image is divided into rectangular regions, each of which is saved as a separate file (17.28). When you save from ImageReady in HTML, tables are formatted automatically to put the images together seamlessly on the page.

Slices can cut across any layer in your ImageReady document. ImageReady supports two kinds of slices. You create user slices (displayed with blue header information) with the Slice tool. Auto slices (displayed with gray header information) are created by ImageReady around user slices. New Image-Ready documents contain one large image-sized slice representing a single-cell HTML table. You can turn in auto slices into user slices by choosing Slices→Promote to User Slice to gain greater control of the slice. You can set different optimization levels for each user slice, for example, whereas all auto slices share the same optimization level.

Although Photoshop does not display ImageReady information (such as slices), it does preserve that information.

1. Choose the Slice tool ![slice tool icon] from the ImageReady toolbox.

User slices (displayed with dark blue header information) are those that you create. You can set different optimization levels for each user slice. User slices can also be used in rollovers.

Auto slices (displayed with light gray header information) are created by ImageReady to fill in areas around user slices. You can promote auto slices to user slices by choosing Slices→Promote to User Slice to gain greater control of the slice. Auto slices all share the same optimization level.

17.28 **Slices can cut across any layers in your ImageReady document. New ImageReady documents contain one large image-sized slice representing a single-cell HTML table.**

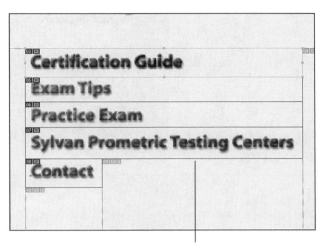

17.29   **The Slice tool automatically snaps to other slice boundaries and corners. The Slice tool also snaps to guidelines created in Photoshop or in ImageReady.**

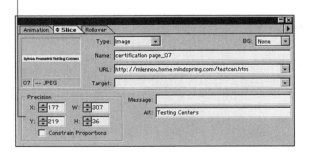

17.30

Like the rectangular marquee, you can set the Slice tool to select areas of a fixed size or constrained aspect ratio.

17.31

2. Click and drag rectangular regions around each area of the image you want to be separate (17.29). The slices are numbered automatically, starting at the top and moving left to right.

3. Use the Slice Select tool to select the region or slice you want to edit.

4. In the Slice palette (17.30), enter a name for the slice if you do not want to use ImageReady's default naming structure. The name of the slice is used as the image's filename when ImageReady generates the HTML and images.

5. Enter a URL to link to the slice. If you enter a URL, you also can enter a target for the referenced page.

continues

(T) I P

You can display more information about the slice you have selected by clicking on the up/down arrow in the Slice tab. This extra section of the Slice palette (17.31) enables you to enter alternative text (the text that shows as the image is loading) and message information (the ToolTip information displayed over images by some browsers).

Slicing Images and Creating Imagemaps continued

By default, slices contain images. Choose No Image in the Slices palette if you want an empty cell in the HTML table (for text or a solid color). You also can set a background color for slices to be used in the HTML table.

6. Repeat the association of slices and URLs for each slice that you want to reference another page.

7. When finished, select the optimization settings you want to use for the images and choose File→Save Optimized As (17.32). Enter the name of the HTML file you want to create, as well as the HTML and image options, and choose Save.

An HTML file with the appropriate HREF and IMAGE tags is generated (17.33). You can cut and paste the HTML directly into other pages you are working on.

You also should save in ImageReady format to preserve the original editable image in case you need to make changes.

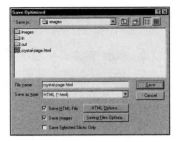

17.32

 I P

You can create guides in ImageReady as you would in Photoshop by dragging from the rulers, or choose View→Create Guides to create a grid. After you set up guides, you can use Slices→Create Slices From Guides.

```html
<HTML>
<HEAD>
<TITLE>Crystal Page Entrance</TITLE>
<META HTTP-EQUIV="Content-Type" CONTENT="text/html;
charset=iso-8859-1">
</HEAD>
<BODY BGCOLOR=#FFFFFF>
<!-- ImageReady Slices (crystal page.psd) -->
<TABLE BORDER=0 CELLPADDING=0 CELLSPACING=0>
<TR>
<TD COLSPAN=3>
<IMG SRC="images/crystal-page_01.gif" WIDTH=800
HEIGHT=108<</TD>
</TR>
<TR>
<TD ROWSPAN=2>
<IMG SRC="images/crystal-page_02.gif" WIDTH=36
HEIGHT=425></TD>
<TD>
<A HREF="http://www.crystal.com/enter.html">
<IMG SRC="images/crystal-page_03.gif" WIDTH=208 HEIGHT=74
BORDER=0></A></TD>
<TD ROWSPAN=2>
<IMG SRC="images/crystal-page_04.gif" WIDTH=556
HEIGHT=425></TD>
</TR>
<TR>
<TD>
<IMG SRC="images/crystal-page_05.gif" WIDTH=208
HEIGHT=351></TD>
</TR>
</TABLE>
<!-- End ImageReady Slices -->
</BODY>
</HTML>
```

17.33

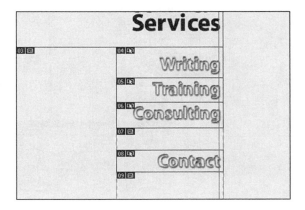

17.34

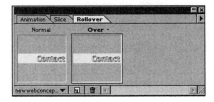

17.35

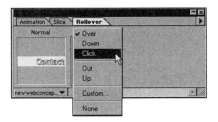

17.36

ImageReady enables you to easily create rollovers that are activated on a Web page when the cursor interacts with a region, defined in ImageReady by a slice. You can use layer visibility and effects to control the states of the rollover (for example, when the mouse moves over an area or when the mouse moves out of an area). ImageReady remembers the changes you make to the image for each state. The Rollover palette provides extensive controls over the various configuration options for the rollover and shows each state. ImageReady generates HTML and JavaScript that works with the major browsers when you save as HTML.

1. Begin by creating slices in the image for all the areas for which you want to assign URLs or create rollover effects (17.34). Assign URLs to slices in the Slice palette.

2. In the Rollover palette, choose the Create New Rollover State button. A new state is created in the palette (17.35).

3. The default state is Over. That is, the image changes when the cursor is moved over the region defined by the slice. To change the state, click on the word Over and select a different state (17.36). You can create as many unique rollover states as you want for each slice. For exam-

continues

Creating Button Rollovers continued

ple, you can create a button that appears to go down when the mouse is moved into the area and glows when the mouse is moved out of the area.

4. With the new state selected in the Rollover palette, alter the image. In this example, the text is on a separate layer and the Color Fill layer effect was added **(17.37)**. Using layers and layer effects (such as glows and emboss/deboss changes) works especially well.

17.37

5. Continue to create rollover states for additional slices. You can copy and paste rollover states between slices and copy and paste layer effects between the new states.

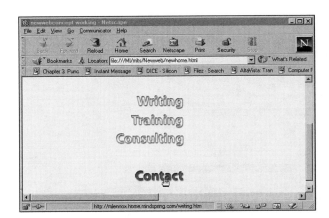

6. When finished, select the optimization settings you want to use for the images and choose File→Save Optimized As. Enter the name of the HTML file you want to create, as well as the HTML and image options, and choose Save.

An HTML file with the appropriate HREF and IMAGE tags is generated **(17.38)**. ImageReady also includes the necessary JavaScript code to make the rollovers work in browsers that support JavaScript.

17.38

Creating Animations

17.39

When you open an existing animated GIF, ImageReady displays the frames in the Animation palette and adds a layer for each frame.

17.40   The Duplicate Current Frame icon

17.41

Choose Tween from the Animation palette menu to create a smooth transition from one frame to the next. Tween adds to the file size, but your results are more fluid.

17.42

ImageReady provides tools to easily create GIF animations. Begin by combining each frame of the animation into one file, with each frame on a separate layer **(17.39)**. You can do this in Photoshop before switching to ImageReady, or you can do it in ImageReady. The frames are analogous to traditional animation cels. The actual frames are controlled in ImageReady's Animation palette, where you set the order and timing for each frame.

1. Start with all the layers in the image visible. In the Animation palette, choose the Duplicate Current Frame icon **(17.40)**.

2. Repeat for each frame of the animation. In this example, there are seven layers, so seven frames were created **(17.41)**.

(T) I P

You can flatten animation frames into layers if you want to use an animation in a rollover. A single composite layer is created for each frame, containing all of the layers in the frame. The original layers in the frame are hidden but preserved and are available if they are needed for another rollover state.

If you save the animation as a GIF, the animation frames are flattened. You should save the original file in Photoshop file format to preserve the layers.

3. Select the first frame in the Animation palette. Set the layer visibility for the frame. Repeat for each frame in the animation **(17.43)**.

4. To preview the animation, click the Play button in the Animation palette.

5. Set the timing of each frame **(17.44)**.

6. Set the loop behavior for the animation by selecting from the list of loop options **(17.45)**.

7. When finished with the animation, choose the optimization settings for the file. Choose a GIF format and try to make the file as small as possible by increasing the lossy compression and decreasing the number of colors.

8. Choose File→Save Optimized As. Enter the name of the GIF file to create and choose Save.

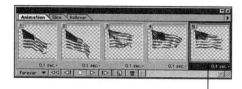

17.43 You can drag frames in the palette to change the order. You also can add and delete frames.

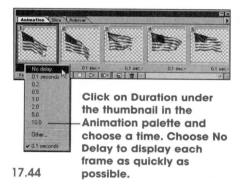

Click on Duration under the thumbnail in the Animation palette and choose a time. Choose No Delay to display each frame as quickly as possible.

17.44

You can set the animation to play forever, once, or a set number of times.

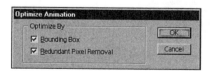

17.45

 I P

Choose Optimize Animation from the Animation palette menu to remove redundant pixels and crop to a bounding box around the animation **(17.46)**. *Using Optimize by Bounding Box crops each frame to preserve only the area that has changed from the preceding frame. (The resulting GIF animation may be incompatible with some GIF editors.)*

17.46

©HAPTER 18

In this chapter you learn how to...

Characterize Your Monitor with Adobe Gamma

Choose an RGB Profile

Choose a Grayscale Profile

Change Your Image's Profile

Achieving consistent color among scanner, monitor, and printer is one of the most significant goals of the entire digital-imaging community. In addition, the capability to define colors so that they appear the same on any monitor displaying any operating system is not only the dream of prepress professionals, but Web designers as well. The International Color Consortium (ICC) was established to create, promote, and encourage the standardization and evolution of an open, vendor-neutral, cross-platform color management system architecture and components. Adobe Systems is one of the eight founding members of the ICC.

ACHIEVING CONSISTENT COLOR

At the heart of the ICC's color management system are profiles. Device profiles provide the information necessary to convert color data between native device color spaces and device-independent color spaces. This information enables the conversion of color data between different devices (for example, a monitor and a printer). The actual conversion is done by a color management module (CMM). The ICC profiles are embedded in image files so that the color information can be read and converted correctly by ICC-aware applications (such as Photoshop). Photoshop's support for ICC color profiles enables smooth color transitions from screen to print. In addition, by embedding color profiles in images, you can ensure that everyone with a properly characterized monitor will see the same colors.

If you are creating images for the Web, you only need to characterize your monitor and choose an appropriate RGB setup. If you are creating images for print, you also need to configure a CMYK setup.

Characterizing Your Monitor with Adobe Gamma

The first step to achieving consistent color is to define an ICC profile for your monitor. This process is called characterization. Because the monitor is not calibrated to the images, the images are calibrated for display on your monitor.

You are not required to use the Adobe Gamma Utility to characterize your monitor. You can use any ICC profile generator that is ICM 2.0 (Windows 98 and 2000) or Color-Sync (Macintosh) compatible. You only need to characterize your monitor once (unless there are changes to the ambient lighting or brightness and contrast of the monitor).

You can start the Color Management Wizard to go through the settings one at a time from within Photoshop by choosing Help→Color Management.

1. Start the Adobe Gamma Utility. On the Macintosh, choose Apple menu→Control Panels→Adobe Gamma. In Windows, choose Start→ Settings→Control Panel and double-click the Adobe Gamma Utility.

2. In the Adobe Gamma Utility, if you have already characterized your monitor, choose Load to load the ICC profile (**18.2**). You can stop after the profile is loaded or modify the characterization using the utility.

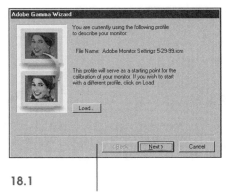

18.1

If you are using Photoshop 5.0, you should run the Adobe Gamma Utility in the Control Panel before running Photoshop for the first time. When you start Photoshop 5.02 or 5.5 for the first time, the Adobe Color Management Wizard prompts you to run through the Adobe Gamma Utility and then asks whether you want to use a preset color management configuration. You can run the Adobe Gamma Utility as a wizard so that it asks you to specify your settings one at a time, or as a unified dialog box where you enter all the information at once. If you have a previous profile describing the monitor, this is used as a starting point. You can follow the steps in the wizard or enter the characterization information manually.

Make the gray squares as dark as possible while keeping the white bar as bright as possible.

Adjust the slider to make the center box blend into the background line as much as possible.

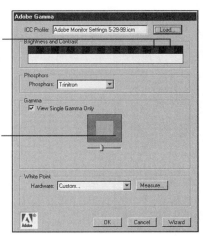

18.2

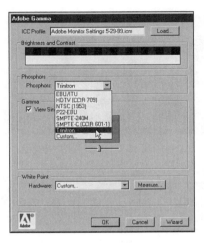

18.3

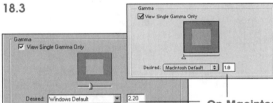

18.4

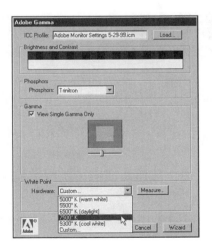

18.5

On Macintosh and Windows systems with monitors controlled by the operating system, you can specify a target gamma. For Windows systems, the default gamma is between 2.2 and 2.5. For Macintosh systems, the default gamma is 1.8.

3. Adjust the Brightness and Contrast controls on your monitor so that the gray squares under Brightness and Contrast are as dark as possible (but not black), while still maintaining a bright white bar.

4. From the Phosphors drop-down list, select a description of the phosphors in your monitor (18.3). Choose Custom to enter the chromaticity coordinates if they were provided with your monitor.

5. In the Gamma section, drag the slider until the center box matches the patterned frame as closely as possible. Back away from the monitor until the pattern appears to be a continuous gray. You also can adjust the red, green, and blue gamma independently by clearing the View Single Gamma Only check box.

6. In the White Point section, select the white point from the Hardware drop-down list (18.5). The white point is the whitest (hottest white) that monitor is capable of displaying. If you don't know the white point for your monitor but were provided with the values, choose Custom.

continues

Characterizing Your Monitor with Adobe Gamma continued

Click Measure to determine the white point manually. Three squares are displayed. Click on the left or right squares until the center square is a neutral gray, and then click on the center square (18.6).

7. When finished, choose OK. The utility asks whether you want to save the profile for the characterized monitor (18.8). Choose Save.

After you characterize your monitor, you can use the RGB and CMYK setup to determine how colors should be displayed in Photoshop.

18.6

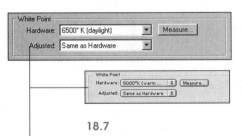

18.7

On Macintosh and Windows systems with monitors controlled by the operating system, you can specify an adjusted white point. Don't change this value unless you know the color temperature used to view an image, and it is different than the white point of the monitor being characterized.

18.8

 T I P

On a Macintosh, set the target gamma to 2.2 in the Adobe Gamma Utility to preview Web images as they will appear on PC monitors.

Choosing an RGB Profile

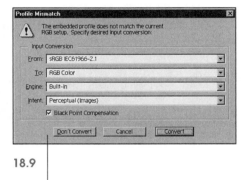

18.9

When you open an image that contains an embedded profile that differs from the current RGB profile, the colors are converted from the image's profile to the working profile. If you open images that do not contain embedded profiles, they can be converted using assumed Photoshop 4.0 settings, or you can choose another assumed profile in Profile Setup.

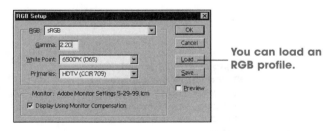

You can load an RGB profile.

18.10

Whether you are preparing images for display on the Web or for print, you should choose an RGB profile to accurately display color information on your monitor. The color space described by the RGB setup is independent of your monitor's color space. This means that when creating RGB data, you are not limited to your monitor's RGB range. In addition, because of the independence between RGB color space and monitor color space, colors can be displayed accurately on any monitor. In many cases, the default choice for an RGB color space is acceptable.

You can change the RGB setup and configure how Photoshop responds to profile mismatches (18.9). (See "Handling an ICC Profile Mismatch" on page 9 in Chapter 1, "Opening, Placing, and Saving Images.")

1. Choose File→Color Management→RGB Setup.

2. In the RGB Setup dialog box, choose an RGB color space from the list (18.10). Choose a color space based on the final use for the image.

   The profile you specify can contain colors that your monitor cannot display, because the two profiles are independent. Photoshop uses the CMM to translate the colors from one profile to another.

continues

Choosing an RGB Profile continued

Table 8.1 RGB Profiles

Profile	Use
sRGB	The default and best option if you are creating images that will be displayed online.
Adobe RGB	Based on the SMPTE-240M profile that originally appeared in Photoshop 5.0. Uses a wider RGB gamut appropriate for general print work, outputting to a film recorder, or creating transparencies.
Apple RGB	Reproduces the color space used by previous versions of Photoshop and other desktop publishing applications. Use this profile if your images will be displayed only on Macintosh computers.
ColorMatch RGB	Use this profile with a PressView monitor.
PAL/SECAM, SMPTE	Use these profiles for images that will be output to video.
Wide Gamut RGB	Use this gamut to choose colors from the largest possible RGB gamut, although many of the colors cannot be viewed on a monitor or printed.
Custom	Use Custom to define a profile by entering the gamma, white point, and primaries information. Use this profile to define ICC profiles for scanners or digital cameras so that you can edit in the same space as the device. You also can use a custom profile if you want to define your own profile.
Monitor RGB	Use the monitor's profile to make Photoshop behave like earlier versions. This profile is useful if you are working with older applications (PageMaker 5.0 or earlier, for example) that do not read embedded profile information, and you want a consistent display between those applications and Photoshop.

3. The gamma, white point, and primaries information is updated to match the RGB profile you select. Change any of the information to create a custom profile.

4. Clear the Display Using Monitor Compensation check box to edit using the RGB profile you selected, but to not display the conversion from the RGB profile to the monitor profile created in the Adobe Gamma Utility. The color display is less accurate but slightly faster.

When converting from RGB to CMYK, both the RGB and CMYK setups are used. For information about configuring the CMYK setup, see "Choosing a CMYK Model and Conversion Method" on page 268 in Chapter 16, "Paper Publishing."

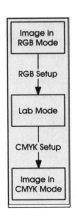

18.11

Choosing a Grayscale Profile

18.12

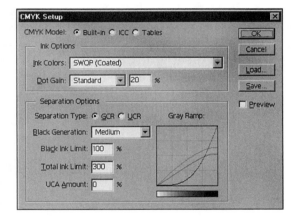

18.13

Grayscale profiles are applicable only to images in Grayscale mode. You configure the Grayscale profile based on the final output of your image. You can set the grayscale behavior as black ink or as equal amounts of red, green, and blue inks.

1. Choose File→Color Settings→Grayscale Setup.

2. In the Grayscale Setup dialog box, select RGB if your grayscale image will appear onscreen (18.12). Select Black Ink if it will be printed.

   If you select Black Ink, Photoshop uses the Dot Gain settings specified in the CMYK Setup dialog box (18.13). (For more information on Dot Gain, see "Choosing a CYMK Model and Conversion Method," on page 268 in Chapter 16, "Paper Publishing."

 I P

You often can work with grayscale images using the RGB profile and convert to the Black Ink profile as a final step. Note that very few applications, even those that are ICC aware, can handle embedded Grayscale profiles. If errors occur, you can choose not to embed Grayscale profiles in the profile setup.

Changing Your Image's Profile

You can translate an image from its current profile to any other defined profile, including the working spaces defined for Grayscale, RGB, CMYK, and Lab modes. This action shifts the colors in the image. It does not alter the profile embedded in the file when it is saved.

Use the following steps after you change the working space and need to convert open images, or if you ignored the ICC profile when opening an image but subsequently need to convert the file to a working space.

1. Choose Image→Mode→Profile to Profile.

2. The Profile to Profile dialog box appears **(18.14)**. In the From drop-down list, choose the profile to assume for the current image.

3. Choose the profile to which you want to convert the image.

4. From the Engine drop-down list, choose a CMM. Choose Built-In to use Photoshop's, or choose any other CMM installed on your system.

5. Choose a rendering intent listed in Table 18.2 from the Intent drop-down list.

6. Enable or disable the Black Point Compensation box.

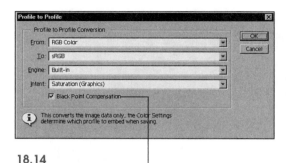

18.14

Enable the Black Point Compensation check box to map the darkest neutral color in the unconverted image to the darkest neutral color in the target color space. If you do not enable Black Point Compensation, Photoshop maps the darkest color in the unconverted image to black.

Table 18.2   Rendering Intents

Intent Option	Description
Perceptual (Images)	Maintains the relationship between colors in the image. Most of the colors in the image change as colors are mapped to the new gamut. Colors in both color gamuts also change as Photoshop attempts to maintain the relationship between colors.
Saturation (Graphics)	Maintains the relative saturation values of the colors. Colors that are not in the new gamut are converted while maintaining their saturation values.
Relative Colorimetric	Typically converts colors while maintaining lightness values. This setting does not change the values of colors inside the new gamut.
Absolute Colorimetric	Disables white-point matching during the conversion process. This might not produce acceptable results.

©HAPTER 19

In this chapter you learn how to...

Load and Save an Action Set

Run an Action

Choose the Commands in an Action to Run

Control User Input While Running Actions

Record an Action

Edit Actions

Insert a Stop in an Action

Insert a Path in an Action

Insert a Menu Item in an Action

Run Actions on Batches of Images

Create and Use Droplets

Photoshop actions enable you to create macros for frequently used commands and procedures. You can combine a series of filters or image adjustments to create a specific, repeatable effect. You can also create an action with a single command to assign a keyboard shortcut to your most frequently used commands or to display a palette.

AUTOMATING PHOTOSHOP

Actions can record any command that affects the entire image or an area of an image. You can also record tools that affect areas of an image, such as the Paintbucket and selection tools. The painting tools (Airbrush, Paintbrush, and so on) and toning tools cannot be recorded directly (although you can stroke paths). Paths and menu commands (such as view commands) can be inserted into an action after it has been recorded.

Actions are collected into action sets. Actions themselves contain individual commands, which can, in turn, have settings that can be configured. Actions can also be nested into other actions.

You can save actions sets to distribute and share them with others. You can also load action sets to use actions created by other people. Photoshop has a variety of actions in the Goodies folder that you can use and modify.

You can also apply an action to a collection of images using Photoshop's Batch option. For example, you could convert an entire folder of images to CMYK mode or convert a series of images to GIFs using the same color table.

ImageReady records actions the same way Photoshop does, but handles them very differently. For more information, see "Creating and Using Droplets," page 323.

Loading and Saving an Action Set

Photoshop enables you to group sets of actions together by type and purpose. When you install Photoshop, several action sets are also installed in the Goodies folder.

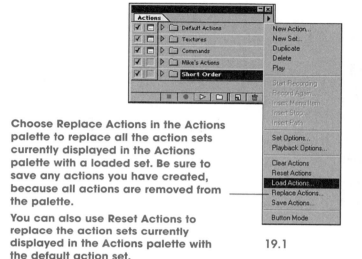

You can also download sets of actions from the Web or load actions that you have previously saved.

1. Choose Load Actions from Actions palette (19.1) menu.

2. Browse and choose the action set that you want to load. Choose Load.

The action set is displayed in the Actions palette.

To save an action set, choose Save Actions from the Actions palette.

Choose Replace Actions in the Actions palette to replace all the action sets currently displayed in the Actions palette with a loaded set. Be sure to save any actions you have created, because all actions are removed from the palette.

You can also use Reset Actions to replace the action sets currently displayed in the Actions palette with the default action set.

19.1

Running an Action

19.2

After you have created an action, you can run it from the Actions palette.

To run an action inside an action set, open the set by clicking the arrow next to the folder (19.2). Select the action and choose the Play button at the bottom of the Actions palette.

Running Selective Commands and Controlling User Input

19.3

19.4

Because some commands in an action are based on previous commands, you should take care before disabling commands. For example, disabling a Conditional Mode Change step may leave an image in Indexed Color mode and subsequent filters will not work.

You should always test the action to make sure it functions the way you want.

You can begin playing an action from any command in the action. Open the action to display the individual commands, select the command where you want to start playing the action, and choose the Play Current Selection button.

You can select specific commands to run in an action. Usually, this is used to turn off commands that you don't want to run. For example, you might have duplicate commands that differ only in their settings for different size images (different Radius settings for the Gaussian Blur filter, for example). By turning on only one of the commands, you eliminate the need to create multiple actions.

You can also choose which commands should prompt for user input. If you want to enter information in a dialog box, you can turn the modal control on. If you want to use the settings that were used when the action was first created, you can turn the modal control off.

To turn off specific commands in an action, clear the check box next to the command in the action (19.3).

To turn off user input for a command, clear the dialog toggle next to the command (19.4).

You can also turn off user interaction for an entire action by clearing the toggle next to the action.

 I P

If you use third-party plug-ins in an action or use a plug-in manager, any plug-in that you used must be available when you run the filter.

Recording an Action

Recording an action is the primary method of creating new actions. Unless you are certain of the steps you are going to take in an action, it is useful write them down or rehearse the steps before actually recording the action.

When you record an action, only tools and commands that affect the entire image or areas of an image can be recorded. See Table 19.1.

1. Choose the New Action button 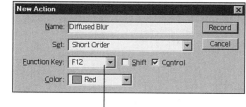 in the Actions palette.

2. In the New Action dialog box (19.5), enter a name for the action. You can also choose an action set, function key, and color for the action button (for use in button mode).

3. To begin recording immediately, choose Record.

4. Make modifications to the image. Photoshop records every change to the image as a whole or changes to areas of the image including selections and fills. Photoshop also records layer changes, such as grouping, layers masks, and layer effects. You may need to select a specific layer before starting the action or insert a stop to prompt the user to select a layer.

5. When finished recording, choose the Stop button in the Actions palette.

19.5

Be careful when recording selections and other tools that affect specific areas. Some commands work differently on images that have different pixel dimensions, just as many filters produce different results depending on the size of the image.

You can also run actions by using their function key equivalents. To change an action's function key, double-click the action and change the properties.

Table 19.1   Recordable Commands

Recordable Commands and Tools	Commands and Tools That Cannot Be Recorded Directly
Selection tools and commands	Painting tools
Fill command and Paintbucket tool	Pen tools
All image adjustment commands	Zoom tools and View commands
Mode change commands	
All filters	
Layer changes	

Because some commands do not work with all image modes (Indexed Color doesn't support any filters, for example), you may want to start the action with the File→Automate→ Conditional Mode Change command.

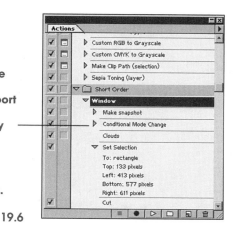

19.6

Editing Actions

Table 19.2   Editing Actions

To do this...	Do this...
Add commands	Choose the location in the action where you need to add the command and choose the Record button in the Actions palette. Choose stop when finished.
Move commands	Click and drag them to new positions in the action.
Delete commands	Select it and choose the trash button.
Duplicate commands	Select it and choose Duplicate from the Actions palette menu.

You can edit actions after they are created by adding, rearranging, and deleting commands. See Table 19.2.

You can also include several similar commands with different parameter settings so that one action can be used for a variety of images. For example, you can add several Gaussian Blur commands to a single action, each with different radii. You can turn these commands on or off based on the resolution of the image. You can use the same technique with foreground or background colors for a variety of consistent buttons.

Inserting a Stop in an Action

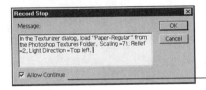

Choose Allow Continue if the user should be able to continue the action from the Message dialog box.

19.7

19.8

Stops can be used to tell the user something valuable about what is happening in an action, tell the user values to enter in an upcoming dialog box, or to stop the action entirely so that the user can do something else before continuing. For example, you can tell the user which file and settings to use in the Displace filter's dialog box.

1. Select the command after which the stop should occur.

2. From the Actions palette menu, choose Insert Stop.

3. In the dialog box (19.7), enter the information that the user should see.

Inserting a Path in an Action

You can insert a path into an action after it has been recorded. Although you can't record painting tools in an action, you can use a path to create fill and stroke effects. You can also use paths in actions to create irregular selections that can be repeated in multiple images. Path sizes are absolute, so their sizes in relationship to images with different pixel dimensions are different.

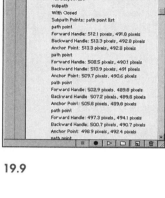

19.9

The path must already exist in the image to be inserted into an action.

1. Choose a path in the Paths palette.

2. Choose a command in an action. The path will be inserted immediately after the selected command.

3. Choose Insert Path from the Actions palette menu.

The path is inserted into the action. The insertion includes all the data required to create the path **(19.9)**.

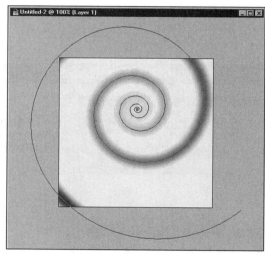

19.10

 I P

*After a path is inserted, you can use painting tools in the action by stroking the path with a specific tool **(19.10)**.*

Note that in this example, the inserted path is larger than the canvas size.

Inserting a Menu Item in an Action

19.11

19.12

Like inserting a Path, you can insert a menu item to perform tasks that don't record when the action is created (for example, View Commands).

1. Choose a command in an action. The menu item will be inserted immediately after the selected command.

2. Choose Insert Menu Item from the Actions palette menu.

3. In the Insert Menu Item dialog box, choose the menu item from the application menu or type the first few letters of the item and choose Find **(19.11)**.

4. Choose OK.

When the action is run, if the menu item uses a dialog box, it will be opened. The user can make whichever settings or selections are necessary and close the dialog box. The action will then continue.

(T) I P

Actions can also be run from button mode. Choose Button Mode from the Actions palette menu. Then click a button to run the action **(19.12)***. You can change an action's button color by double-clicking the action when not in Button mode.*

Running Actions on Groups of Images

One of the most powerful features of actions is their ability to process more than images. You can set a batch process in motion and leave it while Photoshop processes.

You can use batch processing for repetitive tasks, such as changing sizes or levels of information for hundreds of images. You can place a border on every image or add copyright information.

1. Choose File→Automate→ Batch.

2. In the Batch dialog box **(19.13)**, choose the action set and action that you want to apply.

3. Choose the Source of the images to modify **(19.14)**.

4. Choose a Destination. Choose None to keep the files open after running the action. Choose Save and Close to save the files and overwrite the originals. Choose Folder to save the files to a different folder using the same names as the originals.

   Note that Photoshop does not warn you if original files are being overwritten.

5. Choose OK.

If your action begins with an Open command, you should override it for batch processing. The first step of the batch processing is to open the next file in the batch and an Open command in an action points to only one specific file.

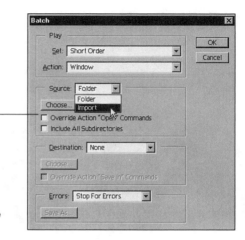

19.13

If the action contains a Save command, choose Override Action "Save In" Command (or else every processed image is saved to the same file, so you'll only see the last image you processed).

19.14

You can either process images as they are scanned using the TWAIN interface, or open images in a specified folder. If you choose Folder, use the Choose button to select the folder that contains the images. The folder can contain any collection of image formats that Photoshop can open.

Creating and Using Droplets

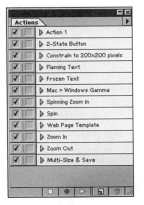

The Action palette in ImageReady resembles the one in Photoshop 4. Actions are not grouped into sets. Batch processing and other action processing is accomplished entirely in the Actions palette. ImageReady actions can be very useful, especially when creating animation effects.

19.15

19.16

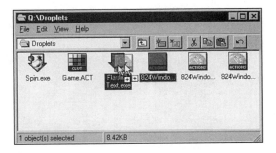

19.17

ImageReady treats actions differently than Photoshop does. In fact, they are incompatible. ImageReady's actions are ASCII text files that can be edited in a text editor. In addition, ImageReady's actions can be saved as small applications called droplets. Droplets can contain all the same commands as ImageReady actions (19.15).

1. To create a droplet from an action, select the action in the Actions palette and choose Create Droplet from the Actions palette menu (19.16).

2. To create a droplet from optimization settings, choose Create Droplet from the Optimize palette menu.

3. To apply a droplet to a series of images, in the operating system, drag a group of files and drop them on the droplet (19.17). The droplet starts ImageReady and batch processes the images.

(N) O T E

After you create an action in ImageReady, it is saved in ImageReady's Actions folder. You can copy action files from this folder and distribute them or load actions created on another computer into this folder. The actions are read each time ImageReady is restarted or the Rescan Actions Folder is selected in the Actions palette.

©HAPTER **20**

In this chapter you learn how to...

Enter Copyright Information, Captions, and Keywords

Embed and Read a Watermark

Create Thumbnails

Create Contact Sheets

Create Picture Packages

Create a Web Photo Gallery

In the age of the Internet, protecting images from copyright infringement has become a significant concern for all artists, digital and traditional. An image is protected legally as soon as you create it. Images that you create cannot be used without your permission, and derivative images cannot be created from them. Your copyright of an image exists whether or not the copyright symbol is on the image or you have embedded a watermark.

PROTECTING AND SORTING YOUR IMAGES

Photoshop provides several tools that enable you to add protection to your images, both in print and on the Web. These tools provide support and documentation for your claim of ownership.

If you are particularly concerned about legal protection for an image, you should register your work with the U.S. Copyright Office. The registration process is relatively inexpensive and straightforward. Obtain the forms, including instructions, from the Copyright Office. After you return the application (typically Form VA for visual arts), copies of the work, and the registration fee of $30, the work is officially protected under U.S. copyright law. For more information about copyright and its procedures, see the U.S. Copyright Office's Web site at http://lcweb.loc.gov/copyright/.

Photoshop also provides several methods to help you keep track of your images by adding keywords, search categories, and other image information. You also can keep track of your images visually by creating contact sheets, web photo galleries, and picture packages using Photoshop's automation tools. Web photo galleries and picture packages are new to Photoshop 5.5. Contact sheets existed in Photoshop 5.0 but are improved in Photoshop 5.5.

Entering Copyright Information, Captions, and Keywords

The File Info command enables you to enter information compatible with standards established by the Newspaper Association of America and the International Press Telecommunications Council. On Macintosh systems, any file format can contain file information. On Windows systems, only JPEG, TIFF, and Photoshop files support the extra file information.

1. Choose File→File Info.

2. The File Info dialog box appears (20.1). From the Section drop-down list, choose Caption. Enter the caption information for the image. You can print the caption you enter with the image by enabling the Caption check box in the Page Setup dialog box.

3. Choose Keywords from the Section drop-down list (20.2). Enter a keyword and click Add. The keyword is added to the list. To delete or replace a keyword, select it from the list and click the appropriate button.

   Keywords can be used when searching by a variety of applications that sort and categorize your images.

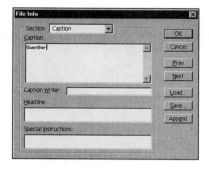

20.1

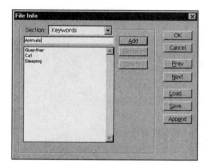

20.2

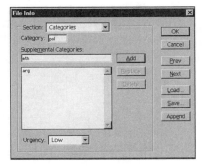

20.3

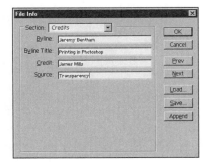

20.4

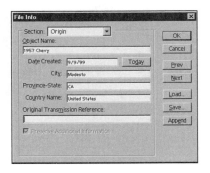

20.5

4. Choose Categories from the Section drop-down list **(20.3)**. Enter a three-character alphabetic category code. To include the image in supplemental categories, type the code and click Add.

   Where available, the local Associated Press Regional Registry maintains a list of categories.

   From the Urgency drop-down list, specify the editorial urgency of the image (not its handling priority).

5. Choose Credits from the Section drop-down list **(20.4)**. Enter the byline, credit, and source information.

6. Choose Origin from the Section drop-down list **(20.5)**. Enter information about the history of the image. Enter a brief description in the Object Name field. In the Date field, enter the date in any format. Choose Today to enter the current date. Enter the appropriate location information in the remaining fields.

continues

Entering Copyright Information, Captions, and Keywords continued

7. Choose Copyright & URL from the Section drop-down list **(20.3)**. In the Copyright Notice, enter the copyright notice. The Copyright Notice field should include the word "Copyright," your name, and the year. Enable the Mark as Copyrighted check box to tag the image. The copyright symbol appears in the file bar with the filename .

You also can enter URL information. This capability is useful when tagging JPEG images that will appear on the Web.

URL information is entered automatically if you embed a digital watermark with the Digimarc filter. (See the next section, "Embedding and Reading a Watermark.")

8. Choose OK.

The information is included with the image when the image is saved.

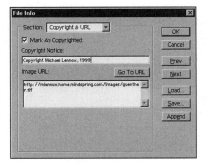

20.6

(N) O T E

Like the copyright symbol added to images and registration with the U.S. Copyright Office, the addition of copyright information or a watermark does not prevent others from violating a copyright.

Embedding and Reading a Watermark

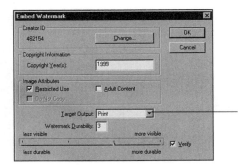

20.7

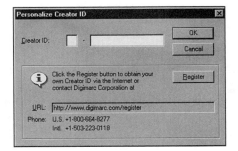

20.8

If you choose Print and the image is too small, or if you choose Screen or Web and the image's resolution is too high, the plug-in warns you and suggests appropriate changes.

Photoshop uses the Digimarc Watermark system to embed a typically invisible digital signature in an image. This signature is not perceptible in the image but can be read from within Photoshop using the Digimarc plug-in. Furthermore, you can set the digital watermark so that it remains even after the image is printed. The image retains its copyright protection if scanned from a print and reused.

1. Choose Filters→Digimarc→ Embed Watermark. The Embed Watermark dialog box appears **(20.7)**.

2. If you have not yet registered for a Digimarc ID, you'll see a Personalize button in the Creator ID section. Click Personalize. Enter your ID if you have one **(20.8)**. If you don't have an ID, click Personalize, and then choose Register to register with Digimarc. Basic registration is free, and you can include which information is displayed when the watermark is read. You also can register with Digimarc by phone (503-968-2908) or fax (503-968-0219).

3. In the Copyright Year(s) field, enter the copyright year.

continues

Embedding and Reading a Watermark continued

4. Enable the Restricted Use or Adult Content check box to tag the image with additional specific information.

5. From the Target Output dropdown list, choose where the image will be used.

6. Change the durability and visibility of the watermark by dragging the slider. A more durable watermark is more visible. Enable the Verify check box to display a verification of the watermark embedding.

7. Click OK. You should notice very little change in the image as minor adjustments are made to pixels throughout the image based on the Digimarc algorithm.

To read a watermark, choose Filter→Digimarc→Read Watermark. The watermark information for the image appears **(20.9)**. Click Web Lookup to see the creator's specific information **(20.10)**.

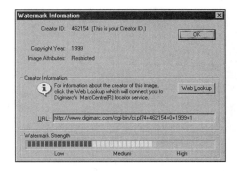

20.9

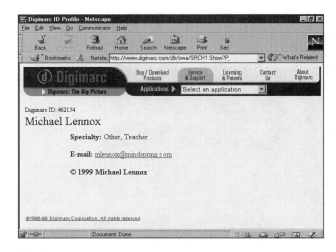

20.10

T I P

If you do not want to wait for Photoshop to detect the watermark for every image you open, go to the Plug-ins folder and remove the Digiopen filter from the Digimarc folder. You still will be able to read embedded watermarks manually and to embed watermarks.

Creating Thumbnails

20.11

20.12

20.13

You can create thumbnails for any image that can be opened in Photoshop. You then can use the thumbnails on a Web page, print them, or use them with a document or image-management system.

1. Choose File→AutomateFit Image.

2. In the Fit Image dialog box (20.11), enter the maximum horizontal and vertical dimensions for the thumbnail. The aspect ratio of the image is preserved as the image size is changed to match the width or height.

3. Choose OK.

If you want to create an action to process a series of images, before starting this procedure, create a new action in the Actions palette and click the Begin Recording button. The action contains only one command: Fit Image (20.12).

To process the action on a series of images, choose File→Automate→ Batch. Select the action in the Batch dialog box (20.13). Because you probably want to maintain your original images, choose Folder in the Source and Destination drop-down lists. (You might need to create a new folder for the destination in your operating system.) For more information on recording actions and batch processing, see Chapter 19, "Automating Photoshop."

Creating Contact Sheets

The Contact Sheet II automation command uses the Fit Image command to create thumbnails and place them in rows and columns on a page specifically designed for printing. To create a series of thumbnails for use as a Web page, see the section "Creating a Web Photo Gallery" later in this chapter.

1. Choose File→Automate→ Contact Sheet II.

2. In the Contact Sheet II dialog box (20.14), click the Choose button to select a folder that contains images from which to make the contact sheet.

3. In the Document section, enter settings for the new contact sheet file.

4. In the Thumbnails section, choose a number of columns and rows, and how the images should be placed. Photoshop calculates the appropriate size of the thumbnails.

5. Enable the Use Filename as Caption check box to place the filename below each thumbnail.

6. Choose OK.

Photoshop processes all the files in the folder you chose, resizing and placing them in a new document (20.15). Photoshop creates additional documents to make more pages as required.

Choose Include all Subdirectories if you want Photoshop to search for images in all the subfolders of the selected folder.

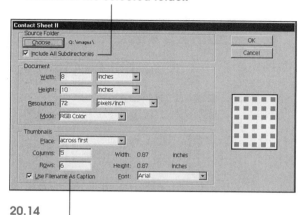

20.14

Filenames can be used as captions although the font size of the filenames cannot be controlled or edited, and this is the only additional information that can be included on the contact sheet.

20.15

Creating Picture Packages

20.16

Photoshop enables you to create picture packages. A picture package is a single page that contains several sizes of the same image (20.16). This page contains the following sizes of images:

- One 5×7
- Two 2.5×3.5
- Four 2×2.5 (wallet-sized)

1. Choose File→Automate→ Picture Package.

2. In the Picture Package dialog box (20.17), click Choose to select an image to process, or if a file is already open, enable the Use Frontmost Document check box.

3. Select a layout from the Layout drop-down list.

4. Choose an image mode and resolution for the resulting page. If you intend to print the page, choose Grayscale or CMYK mode and choose a resolution appropriate for your output device.

5. Choose OK.

20.17

Creating a Web Photo Gallery

A Web photo gallery is an HTML page containing thumbnail images of a group of images. Each thumbnail is linked to a page that contains larger versions of the image and a navigational structure to move to the next and previous image or back to the home page containing the thumbnails.

1. Choose File→Automate→Web Photo Gallery.

2. In the Web Photo Gallery dialog box (20.18), choose a source and destination folder.

3. Enter a site name, photographer, and date.

4. Choose a size for the thumbnails.

   If you want the filename to be placed below the thumbnail, enable the Use Filename as Caption check box.

The source folder can contain images in any format Photoshop can open. The filenames can contain spaces, although depending on where you plan on posting the Web photo gallery, you might want to consider removing the spaces.

20.18

Three folders are created in the destination folder: one for the JPEG images, one for the JPEG thumbnails, and one for the HTML pages that contain the images.

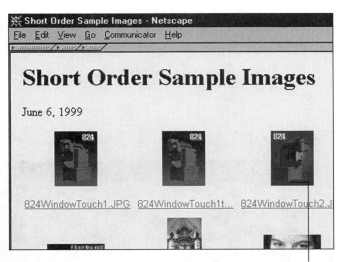

20.19

Clicking an image thumbnail opens a larger view of that image (20.20).

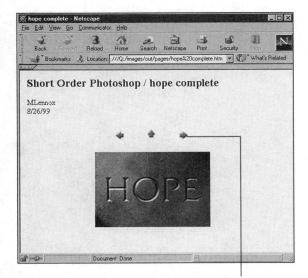

20.20

You can change the arrows used in the photo gallery by creating new arrows in Photoshop or ImageReady and editing the HTML. You also can combine the Web photo gallery with other ImageReady effects, such as rollovers and animation.

5. Choose a size and compression quality for the JPEG images that are linked to the thumbnails.

6. Choose OK.

An HTML page is created, which you can view in a browser (20.19). Photoshop launches your default browser and opens the HTML file that contains the thumbnails, called `Index`.

I P

Only the first page of multipage PDF files is used when creating thumbnails and images for the Web photo gallery. If you want to create a Web photo gallery that contains all the pages of a PDF, choose File→ Automate→ Multi-Page PDF to PSD.

I P

The Web Photo Gallery command converts any GIF images to JPEG. You can replace the JPEG images with the original GIFs in the Images folder and in the appropriate HTML files.

INDEX

A

Action palette, 316
action sets
  executing, 316, 321
  loading, 316
  saving, 316
actions. *See also* macros
  editing, 319
  executing images, 322
  inserting
    menu items, 321
    paths, 320
    stops, 319
  recording, 318
Actions palette, 180
Add Layer Mask command
  (Layer menu), 60
Add Noise command (Filter
  menu), 264
Add Noise dialog box, 264
adding
  borders, selections, 90-91
  carved text, 184-185
  crop marks, 279
  cut-out effects, 158-160
  drop shadows, 158-160
  glows, 161
  layer masks, 154
    painting, 156
  metallic textures, 182-183
  noise, 264-265
  perspective, 103-104
  pixels, 82
  registration marks, 279
  selections, 82
  wood textures, 180-181
Adjust Channel Mixer
  command (Image menu), 72
Adjust command (Image
  menu), 194, 257
Adjust Hue/Saturation
  command (Image menu), 58

adjustment layers
  correcting high-key/low-key
    images, 231
  creating, 228-229
  shadows, 230
Adobe
  Color Management Wizard,
    306
  Illustrator, 238
    opening files, 13
    saving paths, 238
  PDF files
    inserting, 15
    opening, 14
Adobe Gamma command
  (Apple menu), 306
Adobe Gamma Utility, 306-308
algorithms
  Noise, 283
  Pattern Dither, 283
aliasing, 123
aligning
  color plates, 275
  layers, 136
All command (Select menu),
  207
alpha channels. *See* channels
anchor positions, 48
angles, measuring, 102
Animation palette, 301
animations, 293, 301-302
anti-aliasing, 123
  filling paths, 241
  options, 174
Apple menu commands
  Adobe Gamma, 306
  Control Panels, 306
applying
  artistic effects, 254-255
  blur, 250-251
  comic-book effects, 256-257
  depth-of-field, 252-253
  displacement maps, 260-261
  gradient fills, layers, 165-166
  History palette, 32

lighting effects, 262-263
Noise effects, 264-265
pattern fills, layers, 165-166
plug-ins, 248
saved images
illustration packages, 238
page-layout applications, 236-237
solid color fills, layers, 164
textures, 258-259
trapping, 275
Web palette, 291
areas
blurring, 210
copying images, 208-209
modifying saturation, 218
sharpening, 211
Art History brush, 126-127
Artistic command (Filter menu), 254
artistic effects, filters, 254-255
aspect ratios, constraining selection sizes, 80-81
Auto Contrast command (Image menu), 200
Auto Kern, 177
Automate command (File menu), 318
automating Photoshop, 315

B

Background Eraser tool, 119-120
backgrounds
creating glows, 161
creating Web pages, 292-293
drop shadows, 158-160
modifying, 48
baseline shift, modifying text, 179
Batch command (File menu), 322
Batch dialog box, 322

batch processes, executing, 322
Bevel and Emboss command (Layer menu), 162
bevel effects, creating, 162-163
Bézier path, 234. *See also* paths
bicubic interpolation method, 44
bilinear interpolation method, 44
bitmaps, converting, 75-76
blemishes, removing, 206-207
Blend If Property (layer), 134
blending, 112-113
Blending mode, 123
Layer Blend Mode, 138-139
Blur command (Filter menu), 250
Blur menu command (Filter menu), 59
Blur tool, 210
blurring
areas, 210
filters, 250-251
Gaussian, 250
objects, 243-244
BMP files, saving, 17
borders, selections, 90-91
boundaries, selection, 88
breaking layer effects, 162, 169
brightness, correcting, 201-205
Brush Options dialog box, 114
brushes
Art History, 126-127
customizing, 116-117
editing, 114-115
History, 124-125
Brushes palette, 117, 218
brushstrokes, paths, 242
bump plates, 272
Burn tool, 215
button rollovers, 299-300

C

calibrating monitors, 306-308
calibration bars, adding, 279
canvas, modifying size, 48. *See also* backgrounds
carved text, creating, 184-185
CD-ROM, opening Kodak PhotoCDs, 11-12
Channel Options dialog box, 191
channels
creating spot color, 272-274
editing, 193-194
merging, 195
Quick Mask mode, 193-194
selections, 95
loading, 190
managing, 191-192
saving, 188-189
splitting, 195
characterizing monitors, Adobe Gamma Utility, 306-308
circles, creating, 123
Clipping Paths, 236-237
cloning. *See also* copying
moving, 208
pixels, 208-209
CLUT (Color LookUp Table), 61
CMM (Color Management Module), 270, 305
CMYK
command (Image menu), 55
converting, 268-271
selecting colors, 268
Setup command (File menu), 268
Setup dialog box, 56, 311
Sponge tool, 218
CMYK Setup dialog box, 56, 311
Color Fill command (Layer menu), 164

Color LookUp Table (CLUT), 61
Color Management command (File menu), 309
Color Management Module (CMM), 270, 305
Color Picker, 164, 173
Color Range command (Select menu), 57, 86-88
Color Settings command (File menu), 9, 268, 311
Color Table command (Image menu), 67
Color Table dialog box, 62, 67
colors
  aligning plates, 275
  applying fills to layers, 164
  CMYK, 268
  Color Range command (Select menu), 86-88
  consistency, 306-312
  curves, removing, 222
  desaturating, 58
  glows, 161
  grayscale profiles, 311
  hue/saturation, 223-224
  ICC profiles, 9-10
  Indexed Color
    converting, 61-64
    ImageReady, 65-66
    RGB, 67
  Magic Wand, 83
  Magnetic Lasso, 84-85
  modifying profiles, 312
  removing
    Background Eraser tool, 119-120
    levels, 221
  replace color, 227
  RGB profiles, selecting, 309-310
  RGB/CMYK
    converting, 55
    modifying, 57-58
    previewing, 56
    saving, 59-60

  saturating, 58
  schemes, 130-131
  selective color, 226
  spot color channels, 272, 274
  tables, modifying in ImageReady, 70-71
  troubleshooting, 218-224, 226-231
  variations, 219-220
combining selections, 94
comic-book effects, filters, 256-257
commands. *See also* macros
  Apple menu
    Adobe Gamma, 306
    Control Panels, 306
  Edit menu
    Copy, 207
    Define Pattern, 121, 166, 293
    Distort, 107, 142
    Fill, 36, 121, 142, 244
    History, 36
    Master, 223
    Numeric Transform, 109
    Stroke, 123
    Transform, 103, 142
    Transform Numeric, 105
  executing, 317
  Extract, 96, 98
  File menu
    Automate, 318
    Batch, 322
    CMYK Setup, 268
    Color Management, 309
    Color Settings, 9, 268, 311
    Common Files, 175
    Conditional Mode Change, 318
    Export, 20
    Export Paths, 238
    File Info, 326
    Fit Image, 331
    General, 274
    Grayscale Setup, 311
    Jump To ImageReady 2.0, 65

    Multi-Page PDF to PSD, 335
    New, 8
    Open, 11
    Page Setup, 276
    Picture Packages, 333
    Place, 15, 238
    Place in Photoshop, 238
    Preferences, 56, 274
    RGB Setup, 309
    Save a Copy, 18, 29, 268
    Save As, 18
    Save As Optimized, 66
    Save for Web, 282
    Save Optimized As, 284, 295
    Saving Files, 295
    Transparency & Gamut, 56
    Units & Rulers, 102
    Web Photo Gallery, 334
  Filter menu
    Add Noise, 264
    Artistic, 254
    Blur, 59, 250
    Dust, 38
    Dust & Scratches, 206
    Embed Watermark, 329
    Fade Filter, 249
    Find Edges, 256
    Gaussian, 250
    Gaussian Blur, 59
    Lighting, 262
    Noise, 38, 264
    Offset, 292
    Other DitherBox, 68
    Pixelate, 249
    Render, 262
    Sharpen, 212
    Stylize, 256
    Texture, 258
    Texturizer, 258
    Unsharp Mask, 212
    Watercolor, 254
  History palette menu, New Snapshot, 33

Image menu
  Adjust, 194, 257
  Adjust Channel Mixer, 72
  Adjust Hue/Saturation, 58
  Adjust Threshold, 76
  Auto Contrast, 200
  Bitmap, 75
  Canvas Size, 48
  CMYK, 55
  Color Table, 67
  Crop, 50
  Curves, 203, 222
  Desaturate, 224, 257
  Duotone, 73
  Extract, 96
  Hue/Saturation, 223
  Image Size, 42
  Indexed Color, 61
  Invert, 156
  Level, 201
  Levels, 221, 257
  Mode, 8, 55
  Posterize, 257
  Profile to Profile, 312
  Replace Color, 227
  Rotate Canvas, 105
  Selective Color, 226
  Threshold, 257
  Trap, 275
  Variations, 219
Layer menu
  Add Layer Mask, 60
  Bevel and Emboss, 162
  Color Fill, 164
  Copy Effects, 168
  Defringe, 148, 252
  Drop Shadow, 159
  Effects, 159
  Gradient/Pattern, 165
  Group, 153, 181
  Inner Shadow, 159
  Layer Mask, 155
  Layer Options, 146
  Matting, 148, 252

New Adjustment, 228
New Background, 143
Paste Effects, 168
Render Layer, 179
Reveal, 60
Type, 179
Open menu, Show All Files, 17
Preferences, Displays & Cursors, 113
Select menu
  All, 207
  Color Range, 57, 86-88
  Deselect, 244
  Feather, 92
  Inverse, 89
  Modify Border, 90
  Modify Contract, 89, 184
  Modify Expand, 89
  Out Of Gamut, 57
  Save Selection, 59, 93
  Save Selections, 188
  Transform Selection, 88
Selection menu, Load Selection, 94, 190
Slices menu, Create Slices From Guides, 298
View menu
  Create Guides, 298
  Gamut Warning, 56
  Hide Edges, 57
  Preview, 55
  Show Rulers, 107
Window menu, Show Paths, 236
Common Files command (File menu), 175
components, breaking layer effects, 162, 169
compositing layers, 146-147, 154-155
compressing files
  GIF, 283
  Lossy, 66
  LZW, 24

Conditional Mode Change command (File menu), 318
configuring
  brushes, 116-117
  CMYK Setup, 268-271
  dither, GIF, 283
  halftone screens, 276-277
  highlighting, 203-205
  monitors, 306-308
  printing, 279
  profiles, 9
  transfer functions, 278
  Web pages, 294-295
consistency, color, 306-312
constraining selection sizes, 80-81
contact sheets, 332
Contract Selection dialog box, 89
contrast, correcting, 201-205
Control Panels command (Apple menu), 306
controlling
  dithering, 68-69
  user input, 317
Convert Point tool, 235
converting
  bitmaps, 75-76
  CMYK, 268-271
  duotones, 73-74
  ICC profiles, 9-10
  Indexed Color, 61-64
    ImageReady, 65-66
    RGB, 67
  paths, selections, 239-242
  RGB, 10
    CMYK, 54-55
    grayscale, 72
Copy command (Edit menu), 207
Copy Effects command (Layer menu), 168
copying
  images, 7, 208-209
  layers/layer effects, 145, 168

copyrights, 326, 328
correcting
    high-key/low-key images,
        231
    images
        dust/scratches, 206-207
        Eyedropper tool, 198-199
        Histogram, 200
        Sample tool, 198-199
        tonal range, 201-205
Create Guides command
    (View menu), 298
Create Slices From Guides
    command (Slices menu), 298
Crop command (Image menu),
    50
crop marks, adding, 279
Crop tool, 49-50
cropping images, 49-50, 284
curves
    removing color casts, 222
    tonal range, 203-205
Curves dialog box, 203, 222
Custom Colors dialog box, 74,
    272
customizing
    brushes, 116-117
    gradients, 130-131
    previous versions of images,
        126-127
    screens, 276-277
    Web pages, 294-295
customizing preferences, 116.
    See also configuring
cut-out effects, 158-160
CYMK/RGB
    converting, 54-55
    modifying colors, 57-58
    previewing colors, 56
    saving colors, 59-60

D

darkening images, 215
DCS 2.0 Format dialog box, 27
DCS (Desktop Color
    Separation), 16, 27
Define Pattern command (Edit
    menu), 121, 166, 293
defining patterns, 121
Defringe command (Layer
    menu), 148, 252
Defringe dialog box, 148
deleting. See also removing
    color casts, 201-205
        curves, 222
        levels, 221
        variations, 219-220
    dust/scratches, 206-207
    halos, layers, 148
    layer masks, 157
    layers, transparencies,
        119-120
    noise, 264-265
    Web page background
        seams, 292-293
depth-of-field, filters, 252-253
Desaturate command (Image
    menu), 224, 257
desaturating colors, 58
Deselect command (Select
    menu), 244
Desktop Color Separation
    (DCS), 16, 27
dialog boxes
    Add Noise, 264
    Batch, 322
    Brush Options, 114
    Canvas Size, 48
    Channel Options, 191
    Clipping Path, 237
    CMYK Setup, 56, 311
    Color Range, 57, 86-88
    Color Table, 62, 67
    Contract Selection, 89
    Curves, 203, 222
    Custom Colors, 74, 272

DCS 2.0 Format, 27
Defringe, 148
Displace, 260
DitherBox, 68
Duotones Options, 73
Duplicate Layer, 143
Dust & Scratches, 38, 206
Embed Watermark, 329
EPS Options, 25
Expand Selection, 89
Export Paths, 238
Extract, 96
Fade, 249
Feather Selection, 92
File Info, 326
Fill, 121, 123, 142, 244
Fill Paths, 241
Fill Subpaths, 241
Fit Image, 331
Gaussian, 250
Generic PDF Parser, 14
GIF89a Export Options, 20
Gradient Name, 130
Grayscale Setup, 311
Halftone Screens, 276
History Options, 35
Hue/Saturation, 58, 223
Image Size, 42
Indexed Color, 61, 291
Insert Menu Item, 321
JPEG Options, 18
Kodak ICC PhotoCD, 11
Layer Effects, 159
Layer Options, 134
Levels, 201, 221
Lighting Effects, 262
Load, 117
Load Selection, 94, 190
Make Layer, 152
Make Selection, 239
Message, 319
New, 8, 294
New Action, 318
New Adjustment Layer, 228
New Snapshot, 33
New Spot Channel, 272

Numeric Transform, 105
Offset, 292
Open, 11
Picture Packages, 333
Place, 15
Posterize, 257
Profile Setup, 9
Profile to Profile, 312
Rasterize Generic PDF, 14
Replace Color, 227
RGB Setup, 309
Rotate Canvas, 105
Save a Copy, 19, 29
Save As, 17
Save for Web, 282
Save Selection, 93
Save Selections, 188
Selective Color, 226
Texturizer, 258
TIFF Options, 24
Transfer Functions, 278
Trap, 275
Type Tool, 172-173
Unsharp Mask, 212
Variations, 219
Watercolor, 254
Web Photo Gallery, 334
Digimarc, 329-330
digital signatures, watermarks,
329-330
Direct Selection tool, 235
disabling layer masks, 157
Displace dialog box, 260
displacement maps, filters,
260-261
Displays & Cursors command
(Preferences menu), 113
distance, measuring, 102
Distort command (Edit menu),
107, 142
DitherBox, 68-69, 289
dithering, 64
configuring, GIF, 283
eliminating, 291
reducing, 291

documents
channels
loading, 190
saving, 188-189
copying layers, 145
EPS files, inserting, 15
file formats, saving, 16-17
saving copies of images, 29
selections, managing,
191-192
Web pages, laying out,
294-295
Dodge Options palette, 214
Dodge tool, 214
dot gain, 269
downsampling images, 42-43
drop shadows, 158-160. *See*
also **shadows**
droplets, 323
duotones, converting, 73-74
Duplicate Layer dialog box,
143
dust, removing, 206-207
Dust & Scratches command
(Filter menu), 206
Dust & Scratches dialog box,
38, 206
Dust & Scratches filter,
206-207
Dust command (Filter menu),
38

E

Edit menu commands
Copy, 207
Define Pattern, 121, 166, 293
Distort, 107, 142
Fill, 36, 121, 142, 244
History, 36
Master, 223
Numeric Transform, 109
Stroke, 123

Transform Numeric, 105
Transform, 103, 142
editing
actions, 319
brushes, 114-115
channels, 193-194
gradients, 130-131
layer masks, painting, 156
paths, 234-235
text, 175
Effects command (Layer
menu), 159
electronic publishing. *See*
Internet; Web
Embed Watermark command
(Filters Menu), 329
embedding
ICC color profiles, 9-10, 285
watermarks, 329-330
emboss effects, creating,
162-163
EPS (Encapsulated PostScript),
13, 236
inserting, 15
opening, 13
Options dialog box, 25
saving, 16, 25, 236-237
executing
action sets, 316, 321
Adobe Gamma Utility, 306
commands, 317
expanding selections, 89
Export command (File menu),
20
Export GIF 89a plug-in, 20
exporting paths, 238
Extract command (Image
menu), 96, 98
Extract dialog box, 96
Eyedropper tool, 198-199

F

Fade dialog box, 249
Fade Filter command (Filter menu), 249
fading
  filters, 249
  selections, 92
Feather command (Select menu), 92
Feather Selection dialog box, 92
feathering
  paths, 241
  selections, 92
File Info command (File menu), copyrights, 326, 328
File menu commands
  Automate, 318
  Batch, 322
  CMYK Setup, 268
  Color Management, 309
  Color Settings, 268, 311
  Common Files, 175
  Export, 20
  Export Paths, 238
  File Info, 326
  Fit Image, 331
  General, 274
  Grayscale Setup, 311
  Jump To Adobe ImageReady 2.0, 65
  Multi-Page PDF to PSD, 335
  New, 8
  Open, 11
  Page Setup, 276
  Picture Packages, 333
  Place, 15, 238
  Place in Photoshop, 238
  Preferences, 56, 274
  RGB Setup, 309
  Save a Copy, 18, 29, 268
  Save As, 18
  Save As Optimized, 66
  Save for Web, 282
  Save Optimized As, 284, 295
  Saving Files, 295
  Transparency & Gamut, 56
  Units & Rulers, 102
  Web Photo Gallery, 334
files. *See also* images; pictures
  Adobe Illustrator
    opening, 13
    saving paths, 238
  anchor positions, 48
  canvas size, 48
  copies
    creating, 8
    saving, 7, 29
  cropping, 49-50
  DCS, saving, 27-28
  EPS
    inserting, 15
    opening, 13
    saving, 25-26, 236-237
  extracting, 96-98
  formats, 7
    selecting, 276
  GIF
    compressing, 283
    saving, 20-21
    saving for Web, 282-283
  History brush, 36
    nonlinear, 38-39
  History palette, 32
    creating, 34
    nonlinear, 34-35
    saving snapshots, 33-34
  HTML, creating, 294-295
  ICC profile mismatch, 9-10
  interpolation method, resampling, 44
  JPEG
    saving, 18-19
    saving for Web, 282, 285
  Kodak PhotoCD, opening, 11-12
  LZW, compressing, 24
  PDF
    inserting, 15
    opening, 14
  PNG
    saving, 23
    saving for Web, 287-289
  prepress formats, saving, 16
  rasterizing, 14
  resolution
    modifying, 47
    selecting, 45-46
  saving, 16-17
  sizes, modifying, 42-43
  TIFF, saving, 24
Fill command (Edit menu), 36, 121, 142, 244
Fill dialog box, 121, 123, 142, 244
Fill Paths dialog box, 241
Fill Subpaths dialog box, 241
filling
  applying fills to layers
    gradient, 165-166
    pattern, 165-166
    solid color, 164
  areas with patterns, 121
  paths, 241
  text, images/objects, 152-153
Filter menu commands
  Artistic, 254
  Blur, 59, 250
  Dust, 38
  Dust & Scratches, 206
  Embed Watermark, 329
  Fade Filter, 249
  Find Edges, 256
  Gaussian, 250
  Gaussian Blur, 59
  Lighting, 262
  Noise, 38, 264
  Offset, 292
  Other DitherBox, 68
  Pixelate, 249
  Render, 262
  Sharpen, 212
  Stylize, 256
  Texture, 258
  Texturizer, 258
  Unsharp Mask, 212
  Watercolor, 254

filters, 247, 253
  artistic effects, 254-255
  blur, 250-251
  comic-book effects, 256-257
  depth-of-field, 252-253
  displacement maps, 260-261
  DitherBox, 68-69, 289
  Dust & Scratches, 206-207
  fading, 249
  lighting Effects, 262-263
  Noise, 264-265
  Offset, 292-293
  other, 247
  plug-ins, 248
  previewing, 253
  Smart blur, 251
  textures, 258-259
  Unsharp Mask, 212
  Watermark, 247
Finds Edges command (Filter menu), 256
finger painting, 118. *See also* painting
Fit Image command (File menu), 331
flat color images, dithering, 291
flattening layers, 137
fonts, selecting, 173
formats, 7. *See also* files
  saving, 16-17
    DCS, 27-28
    EPS, 25-26
    GIF, 20-21
    JPEG, 18-19
    PNG, 23
    TIFF, 24
  selecting, 276
functions, 278. *See also* commands

G

galleries, Web photos, 334-335
Gamut Warning command (View menu), 56
gamuts. *See also* colors
  modifying, 57-58
  previewing, 56
  saving, 59-60
Gaussian Blur, 250
Gaussian Blur command (Filter menu), 59
Gaussian command (Filter menu), 250
General command (File menu), 274
Generic PDF Parser dialog box, 14
geometric shapes, creating, 123
GIF (Graphics Interchange Format), 20, 282
  animations, 293, 301-302
  compressing, 283
  configuring dither, 283
  resizing, 284
  saving, 16
  transparencies, 290
GIF89a Export Options dialog box, 20
glows, 161
Gradient Name dialog box, 130
Gradient/Pattern command (Layer menu), 165
gradients
  customizing, 130-131
  layers, 165-166
  shaped, 128-129
Graphics Interchange Format. *See* GIF
grayscale
  profile selection, 311
  RGB conversions, 72

Grayscale Setup command (File menu), 311
Group command (Layer menu), 153, 181
grouped images, executing actions, 322

H

halftone screens, 276-277
halos, removing, 148
Hide Edges command (View menu), 57
high-key images, adjustment layers, 231
highlighting, configuring, 203-205
Histogram, 200
histories, previous versions
  customizing, 126-127
  painting, 124-125
History brush, 124-125
  files, painting, 36
  nonlinear files, painting, 38-39
History command (Edit menu), 36
History Options dialog box, 35
History palette, 32, 124
  files, creating, 34
  New Snaphot command, 33
  nonlinear, 34-35
  snapshots, saving, 33-34
horizontal text. *See* text
HTML files, creating, 294-295
Hue/Saturation command (Image menu), 223
Hue/Saturation dialog box, 58, 223
hues, 223-224

I

ICC (International Color Consortium), 305
color profiles, 9-10
embedding, 285
saving, 271
illustration packages, saving images, 238
Illustrator. files, opening, 13
Image menu commands
Adjust, 194, 257
Adjust Channel Mixer, 72
Adjust Hue/Saturation, 58
Adjust Threshold, 76
Auto Contrast, 200
Bitmap, 75
Canvas Size, 48
CMYK, 55
Color Table, 67
Crop, 50
Curves, 203, 222
Desaturate, 224, 257
Duotone, 73
Extract, 96
Hue/Saturation, 223
Image Size, 42
Indexed Color, 61
Invert, 156
Level, 201
Levels, 221, 257
Mode, 8, 55
Posterize, 257
Profile to Profile, 312
Replace Color, 227
Rotate Canvas, 105
Selective Color, 226
Threshold, 257
Trap, 275
Variations, 219
Image Size dialog box, 42
imagemaps, creating, 296-297

ImageReady, 7, 65-66
animations, 293, 301-302
button rollovers, 299-300
color tables, modifying, 70-71
Slice tool, 296-297
images
actions, executing, 322
adjustment layers
correcting high-key/ low-key, 231
creating, 228-229
shadows, 230
Adobe Illustrator files, opening, 13
anchor positions, 48
animations, 293, 301-302
areas
copying, 208-209
filling with patterns, 121
Background Eraser tool, 119-120
bevel effects, 162-163
bitmaps, converting, 75-76
blurring, 210, 243-244
brushes
customizing, 116
editing, 114-115
saving, 117
button rollovers, 299-300
calibration bars, adding, 279
canvas size, 48
channels
editing, 193-194
loading selections, 190
managing selections, 191-192
saving selections, 188-189
splitting, 195
CMYK, converting, 268-271
color consistency, 306-312
color profiles, modifying, 312
Color Range command (Select menu), 86-88

color tables, modifying, 70-71
colors, troubleshooting, 218-231
contact sheets, 332
copies, saving, 7, 29
copyrights, 326, 328
creating, 8
crop marks, adding, 279
cropping, 49-50, 284
curves, 222
darkening, 215
DCS, saving, 27-28
dithering, 68-69, 291
duotones, converting, 73-74
dust/scratches, 206-207
emboss effects, 162-163
EPS
inserting, 15
opening, 13
saving, 25-26
extracting, 96, 98
Eyedropper tool, 198-199
file formats, selecting, 276
filters, 247, 253
artistic effects, 254-255
blur, 250-251
comic-book effects, 256-257
depth-of-field, 252-253
displacement maps, 260-261
fading, 249
Lighting Effects, 262-263
Noise, 264-265
textures, 258-259
geometric shapes, creating, 123
GIF
saving, 20-21
saving for Web, 282-283
glows, creating, 161
gradients
applying gradient fills to layers, 165-166
customizing, 130-131

grayscale
converting, 72
selecting grayscale pro-
files, 311
halftone screens, 276-277
Histogram, 200
History brush, 36-39
History palette, 32
nonlinear, 34-35
saving snapshots, 33-34
hue/saturation, modifying,
223-224
ICC profile mismatch, 9-10
imagemaps, 296-297
Indexed Color
converting, 61-64
ImageReady, 65-66
RGB, 67
interpolation method, re-
sampling, 44
JPEG
saving, 18-19
saving for Web, 282, 285
keystoning, removing, 107
Kodak PhotoCDs, opening,
11-12
layer effects
breaking, 162, 169
copying, 168
layers
compositing, 146-147
copying, 145
layer masks, 154-155
removing halos, 148
levels, modifying, 221
lightening, 214
Lossy compression, 66
LZW compression, 24
Magic Wand, 83
Magnetic Lasso, 84-85
numeric values, 108-109
opening, 7
page lay-out applications,
236-237

painting
blending, 112-113
smudging, 118
paths, 234-236
converting into selections,
239-240, 242
filling, 241
stroking, 242
pattern fills, applying to
layers, 165-166
Pattern Stamp tool, 122
PDF
inserting, 15
opening, 14
perspective, adding, 103-104
pictures
creating picture packages,
333
merging, 195
pixels, modifying, 82
PNG
saving, 23
saving for Web, 287-289
predefined layer-effect
styles, 167
previewing, 21
previous versions
customizing, 126-127
painting, 124-125
registration marks, adding,
279
replace color, modifying, 227
resolution
modifying, 47
selecting, 45-46
retouching, 208-209. *See also*
Rubber Stamp tool
RGB, 67, 309-310
RGB/CMYK
converting, 54-55
modifying colors, 57-58
previewing colors, 56
saving colors, 59-60
Sample tool, 198-199
saving, 16-17

selection sizes, constraining,
80-81
selective color, modifying,
226
shaped gradients, creating,
128-129
sharpening, 211-212
sizes, 42-43
solid color fills, applying to
layers, 164
spot color channels, creating,
272, 274
straightening, 105
text
baseline shift, 179
carved, 184-185
editing, 175
filling, 152-153
inserting, 172-175
kerning, 177-178
metallic textures, 182-183
modifying leading, 176
special effects, 179
tracking, 177-178
wood textures, 180-181
thumbnails, creating, 331
TIFF, saving, 24
tonal range, 201-205
transfer functions, 278
transparencies, 290
trapping, 275
variations, 219-220
viewing, 282
watermarks, embedding,
329-330
Web pages
backgrounds, 292-293
laying out, 294-295
Web photo gallery, creating,
334-335
Indexed Color
converting, 61-64
ImageReady, 65-66
RGB, 67

Indexed Color dialog box, 61, 291

Info palette, 102, 198

Inner Shadow command (Layer menu), 159

Insert Menu Item dialog box, 321

inserting
EPS, 15
menu items into actions, 321
noise, 264-265
paths into actions, 320
PDF, 15
stops into actions, 319
text, 172-175

International Color Consortium. *See* ICC

Internet
animations, 293, 301-302
button rollovers, 299-300
GIFs, 282-283
imagemaps, 296-297
JPEGs, 282, 285
PNGs, 287-289
slicing images, 296-297
transparencies, 290
Web pages
creating backgrounds, 292-293
laying out, 294-295
Web palette, 291

interpolation method, resampling, 44

Inverse command (Select menu), 89

Invert command (Image menu), 156

isolating objects, Background Eraser tool, 119-120

J - K

JPEG (Joint Photographic Experts Group), 18, 285
format options, 19
resizing, 286
saving, 16
viewing, 282

Jump To ImageReady 2.0 command (File menu), 65

kerning text, 177-178

keystoning, removing, 107

Kodak
ICC PhotoCD dialog box, 11
PhotoCD, opening, 11-12
Precision Color Management System (KPCMS), 11

L

Layer Blend mode, 138-139

Layer Effects dialog box, 159

Layer Mask command (Layer menu), 155

Layer menu commands
Add Layer Mask, 60
Bevel and Emboss, 162
Color Fill, 164
Copy Effects, 168
Defringe, 148, 252
Drop Shadow, 159
Effects, 159
Gradient/Pattern, 165
Group, 153, 181
Inner Shadow, 159
Layer Mask, 155
Layer Options, 146
Matting, 148, 252
New Adjustment, 228
New Background, 143
Paste Effects, 168
Render Layer, 179
Reveal, 60
Type, 179

Layer Options command (Layer menu), 146

Layer Options dialog box, 134

layers
adjustment
correcting high-key/ low-key images, 231
creating, 228-229
shadows, 230
aligning, 136
bevel effects, 162-163
compositing, 146-147
copying, 145
effects
breaking, 162, 169
copying, 168
emboss effects, 162-163
flattening, 137
gradient fills, 165-166
halos, removing, 148
linking, 135
masks
creating, 154-156
deleting, 157
disabling, 157
editing, 156
moving, 157
painting, 155
merging, 137
pattern fills, 165-166
predefined layer-effect styles, 167
properties, modifying, 134
shadows, objects, 141-142
solid color fills, 164
text fill, 152-153
transparencies, preserving, 140

Layers palette, 119, 135, 228

laying out Web pages, 294-295

leading, text, 176

Lemple-Zif-Welch (LZW), 24

Level command (Image menu), 201

levels, removing color casts, 221

Levels command (Image menu), 201-202, 221, 257
Levels dialog box, 201, 221
lightening images, 214
Lighting command (Filter menu), 262
Lighting Effects
  dialog box, 262
  filters, 262-263
lines per inch. *See* **lpi**
linking
  layer masks, 157
  layers, 135
Load dialog box, 117
Load Selection command (Selection menu), 94, 190
loading
  action sets, 316
  selections, channels, 94, 190
Lossy compression, 66
low-key images, modifying adjustment layers, 231
lpi (lines per inch), 45
  modifying, 47
  selecting, 45-46
LZW (Lemple-Zif-Welch), 24

M

macros, 315
magenta, modifying, 226
Magic Eraser, 120
Magic Wand tool, 83
Magnetic Lasso tool, 84-85, 236
Make Layer dialog box, 152
Magnetic Pen tool, 236
Make Selection dialog box, 239
managing selections, 191-192
maps
  displacement, 260-261
  imagemaps, 296-297
marquee tools, constraining selection sizes, 80-81

masks
  creating, 96, 98
  layers
    creating, 154-156
    deleting, 157
    disabling, 157
    editing, 156
    moving, 157
  painting, 155
  transparency, modifying, 130-131
Master command (Edit menu), 223
Matting command (Layer menu), 148, 252
Measure tool, 102
measuring angles/distance, 102
menu items, inserting actions, 321
merging
  channels, 195
  layers, 137
Message dialog box, 319
metallic textures, text, 182-183
methods, 44
Mode command (Image menu), 8, 55
Mode property (layers), 134
modes
  Bitmap, 75-76
  Blending, 112-113, 123
  CMYK, 268-271
  Indexed Color, 61-64
    ImageReady, 65-66
    RGB, 67
  Layer Blend, 138-139
  Opacity, 123
  Quick Mask, 193-194
  RGB, 54-55, 67
Modify Border command (Select menu), 90
Modify Contract command (Select menu), 89, 184
Modify Expand command (Select menu), 89

monitors
  characterizing Adobe Gamma Utility, 306-308
  modifying color profiles, 312
  selecting
    grayscale profiles, 311
    RGB profiles, 309-310
moving. *See also* **copying**
  adjacent areas of images, 208-209
  layers, 135-137
    effects, 168
    masks, 157
  paths, 238
Multi-Page PDF to PSD command (File menu), 335

N

Name property (layers), 134
navigating, History palette, 32
nearest neighbor interpolation method, 44
New Action dialog box, 318
New Adjustment command (Layers menu), 228
New Adjustment Layer dialog box, 228
New Background command (Layer menu), 143
New command (File menu), 8
New dialog box, 8, 294
New Snapshot command (History palette menu), 33
New Spot Channel dialog box, 272
noise filters, 264-265
Noise algorithms, 283
Noise command (Filter menu), 38, 264
nonlinear files, History brush, 38-39

nonlinear histories, 35
Numeric Transform command
   (Edit menu), 109
numeric values, 108-109

O

objects
   blurring, 243-244
   filling text, 152-153
   layer shadows, 141-142
   masks, 96, 98
Offset command (File menu),
   292
offset filter, 292-293
Opacity mode, 123
Open command (File menu),
   11
Open dialog box, 11
Open menu, Show All Files
   command, 17
opening
   Adobe Color Management
      Wizard, 306
   Adobe Illustrator files, 13
   EPS files, 13
   images, 7
   Kodak PhotoCD, 11-12
   PDF files, 14
Optimization palette, 283
optimizing images
   ImageReady, 65-66
   saving for Web
      GIF, 282-283
      JPEG, 282, 285
      PNG, 287-289
options
   anti-aliasing, 174
   file formats, 276
Other DitherBox command
   (Filter menu), 68
other filters, 247
Out Of Gamut command
   (Select menu), 57

out-of-gamut colors, 271. *See
   also* **colors**
   modifying, 57-58
   previewing, 56
   saving, 59-60
output
   calibration bars, 279
   crop masks, 279
   file formats, 276
   halftone screens, 276-277
   registration marks, 279
   spot color channels, 272, 274
   transfer functions, 278
   trapping, 275
overlapping, pixels, 82

P

Page Setup command (File
   menu), 276
painting
   blending, 112-113
   brushes
      customizing, 116
      editing, 114-115
      saving, 117
   defined patterns, 122. *See
      also* Pattern Stamp tool
   layer masks, editing, 156
   masks, 155
   previous file versions,
      124-125
      History brush, 36
      nonlinear, 38-39
   Quick Mask mode, 193-194
   smudging, 118
palettes
   Actions, 180, 316
   Animation, 301
   Brushes, 117, 218
   Channel, 95
   Channels, 188-192
   Dodge Options, 214

History, 32, 124
   nonlinear, 35
   saving snapshots, 33-34
Info, 102, 198
Layers, 119, 135, 228
Optimization, 283
Paths, 234
Sharpen Options, 211
Smudge Options, 243
Sponge Options, 218
Web, 291
Pantone Matching System
   (PMS), 273
Paste Effects command (Layer
   menu), 168
Path Creation tool, 236
paths
   actions, inserting, 320
   Clipping, 236-237
   creating, 234-235
   exporting, 238
   filling, 241
   illustration packages, saving,
      238
   modifying, 234-235
   objects, blurring, 243-244
   saving, 236
   selections, converting,
      239-240, 242
   stroking, 242
Paths palette, 234
Pattern Dither algorithms, 283
Pattern Stamp tool, 122
patterns
   areas, filling, 121
   layers, applying, 165-166
PCX files, saving, 17
PDF (Portable Document
   Format) files, 14
   inserting, 15
   opening, 14
   saving, 16
Pen tool, 234
perspective, adding, 103-104
PICT files, saving, 17
picture packages, creating, 333

pictures. *See also* **images**
  actions, executing, 322
  adjustment layers
    correcting high-key/
      low-key, 231
    creating, 228-229
    shadows, 230
  Adobe Illustrator files, open-
    ing, 13
  anchor positions, 48
  animations, 293, 301-302
  areas
    copying, 208-209
    filling with patterns, 121
  Background Eraser tool,
    119-120
  bevel effects, 162-163
  bitmaps, converting, 75-76
  blurring, 210, 243-244
  brushes
    customizing, 116
    editing, 114-115
    saving, 117
  button rollovers, 299-300
  calibration bars, 279
  canvas size, 48
  channels
    editing, 193-194
    loading selections, 190
    managing selections,
      191-192
    merging, 195
    saving selections, 188-189
    splitting, 195
  CMYK conversion, 268-271
  color
    consistency, 306-312
    modifying color profiles,
      312
    modifying color tables,
      70-71
    troubleshooting colors,
      218-231
  Color Range command
    (Select menu), 86-88

  contact sheets, creating, 332
  copies, saving, 7, 29
  copyrights, 326-328
  creating, 8
  crop marks, adding, 279
  cropping, 49-50
  darkening, 215
  DCS, saving, 27-28
  dithering, 68-69, 291
  duotones, converting, 73-74
  dust/scratches, 206-207
  emboss effects, 162-163
  EPS
    inserting, 15
    opening, 13
    saving, 25-26
  extracting, 96, 98
  Eyedropper tool, 198-199
  file formats, selecting, 276
  filters, 247, 253
    artistic effects, 254-255
    blur, 250-251
    comic-book effects,
      256-257
    depth-of-field, 252-253
    displacement maps,
      260-261
    fading, 249
    Lighting Effects, 262-263
    Noise, 264-265
    textures, 258-259
  geometric shapes, creating,
    123
  GIF
    saving, 20-21
    saving for Web, 282-283
  glows, creating, 161
  gradients
    applying fills to layers,
      165-166
    customizing, 130-131
  grayscale conversions, 72
  grayscale profiles, selecting,
    311
  halftone screens, configur-
    ing, 276-277

  Histogram, 200
  History brush, 36-39
  History palette, 32
    nonlinear, 34-35
    snapshots, saving, 33-34
  ICC profile mismatch, 9-10
  imagemaps, 296-297
  Indexed Color
    converting, 61-64
    ImageReady, 65-66
    RGB, 67
  interpolation method, re-
    sampling, 44
  JPEG
    saving, 18-19
    saving for Web, 282, 285
  keystoning, removing, 107
  Kodak PhotoCDs, 11-12
  layer effects
    breaking, 162, 169
    copying, 168
  layer masks, 154-155
  layers
    compositing, 146-147
    copying, 145
    removing halos, 148
  lightening, 214
  Lossy compression, 66
  LZW compression, 24
  Magic Wand, 83
  Magnetic Lasso, 84-85
  numeric values, 108-109
  packages, 333
  page lay-out applications,
    saving in, 236-237
  painting
    blending, 112-113
    smudging, 118
  paths, 234-235
    converting into selections,
      239-242
    filling, 241
    saving, 236
    stroking, 242
  pattern fills, applying to
    layers, 165-166

Pattern Stamp tool, 122
PDF
    inserting, 15
    opening, 14
perspective, adding, 103-104
pixels, modifying, 82
PNG
    saving, 23
    saving for Web, 287-289
predefined layer-effect
    styles, 167
previewing, 21
previous versions
    customizing, 126-127
    painting, 124-125
registration marks, 279
resolution
    modifying, 47
    selecting, 45-46
retouching, 208-209. *See also*
    Rubber Stamp tool
RGB, 67, 309-310
RGB/CMYK
    converting, 54-55
    modifying colors, 57-58
    previewing colors, 56
    saving colors, 59-60
Sample tool, 198-199
saving, 16-17
selection sizes, constraining,
    80-81
shaped gradients, 128-129
sharpening, 211-212
sizes, modifying, 42-43
slicing, 296-297
solid color fills, applying to
    layers, 164
spot color channels, 272, 274
straightening, 105
text
    baseline shift, 179
    carved, 184-185
    editing, 175
    filling, 152-153

inserting, 172-175
kerning, 177-178
metallic textures, 182-183
modifying leading, 176
special effects, 179
tracking, 177-178
wood textures, 180-181
thumbnails, 331
TIFF, saving, 24
tonal range, 201-205
transparencies, 290
trapping, 275
transfer functions, creating,
    278
watermarks, embedding,
    329-330
Web pages
    backgrounds, 292-293
    lay out, 294-295
Web photo gallery, creating,
    334-335
PIXAR, saving, 17
**Pixelate command (Filter
menu), 249**
pixels
    cloning, 208-209
    displacement maps, 260-261
    downsampling, 42-43
    hue/saturation, 223-224
    interpolation method, re-
        sampling, 44
    layers, compositing, 146-147
    painting, blending, 112-113
    removing, 206-207
    resampling, 42-43
    selections, 82
    transparencies, 140
pixels per inch. *See* ppi
**Place command (File menu),
15, 238**
Place dialog box, 15
**Place in Photoshop command
(File menu), 238**

placing. *See* **inserting**
plates, color, 275
plug-ins, 248
    Export GIF 89a, 20
    filters, 247, 253
        artistic effects, 254-255
        blur, 250-251
        comic-book effects,
            256-257
        depth-of-field, 252-253
        displacement maps,
            260-261
        fading, 249
        Lighting Effects, 262-263
        Noise, 264-265
        textures, 258-259
**PMS (Pantone Matching
System), 273**
PNG
    saving, 16, 23, 287
    transparencies, 290
**PNG (Portable Network
Graphics), 23, 287**
Portable Document Format.
    See **PDF files**
**Posterize command (Image
menu), 257**
ppi (pixels per inch), 8
    modifying, 47
    selecting, 45-46
preferences, brushes, 116-117
**Preferences command (File
menu), 56, 274**
**Preferences menu, Displays &
Cursors commands, 113**
prepress file formats, 16
preserving transparencies, 140
**Preview command (View
menu), 55**
previewing
    colors, RGB/CMYK, 56
    filters, 253
    images, 21

previous versions
  History brush
    nonlinear, 38-39
    painting, 36
  images, 124
    customizing, 126-127
    painting, 124-125
printing
  calibration bars, 279
  crop marks, 279
  file formats, 276
  halftone screens, 276-277
  registration marks, 279
  spot color channels, 272, 274
  transfer functions, 278
  trapping, 275
Profile Setup dialog box, 9
Profile to Profile command
  (Image menu), 312
profiles
  configuring, 9
  grayscale, 311
  ICC color, 9-10
  modifying, 312
  RGB, 309-310
  saving, 271
properties, layers, 134
PSD, 7

Q-R

ranges, tonal, 201-205, 222
rasterizing files, 14
Raw, saving, 17
recording actions, 318
rectangles, creating, 123
reducing
  dithering, 291
  image size, 296-297
registration marks, adding, 279

removing
  color casts, 201-205
    curves, 222
    levels, 221
    variations, 219-220
  dust/scratches, 206-207
  halos, layers, 148
  keystoning, 107
  layer masks, 157
  layers, transparencies,
    119-120
  noise, 264-265
  Web page background
    seams, 292-293
Render command (Filter
  menu), 262
Render Layer command (Layer
  menu), 179
replace color, modifying, 227
resampling images, 42-43, 67
resizing
  GIFs, 284
  JPEG, 286
resolution, 8. *See also* ppi
  modifying, 47
  selecting, 45-46
retouching images, 208-209.
  See also **Rubber Stamp tool**
Reveal command (Layer
  menu), 60
RGB
  converting, 10
  CYMK
    converting, 54-55
    previewing colors, 56-58
    saving colors, 59-60
  DitherBox, 68-69
  grayscale conversion, 72
  Indexed Colors, resam-
    pling/text, 67
  profiles, selecting, 309-310
RGB Setup command (File
  menu), 309
rollovers, 299-300

Rotate Canvas command
  (Image menu), 105
Rubber Stamp tool, 208-209,
  292-293
running. *See* **executing**

S

Sample tool, 198-199
saturation
  colors, 58
  modifying, 218, 223-224
Save a Copy command (File
  menu), 18, 29, 268
Save a Copy dialog box, 19, 29
Save As command (File
  menu), 18
Save As dialog box, 17
Save As Optimized command
  (File menu), 66
Save for Web command (File
  menu), 282
Save for Web dialog box, 282
Save Optimized As command
  (File menu), 284, 295
Save Selection command
  (Select menu), 59, 93
Save Selection dialog box, 93
Save Selections command
  (Select menu), 188
Save Selections dialog box,
  188
saving
  actions sets, 316
  BMP, 17
  colors, RGB/CMYK, 59-60
  custom brushes, 117
  DCS files, 16, 27-28
  EPS files, 16, 25-26
  GIF files, 16, 20-21, 282-283
  History palette
    nonlinear, 34-35
    snapshots, 33-34

ICC profiles, 271
IFF, 17
images
　applying in page lay-out
　　applications, 236-237
　copies, 7, 29
　illustration packages, 238
JPEG files, 16, 18-19, 282, 285
paths, 236
PCX, 17
PDF, 16
PICT, 17
PIXAR, 17
PNG files, 16, 23, 287-289
prepress file formats, 16
Raw, 17
Scitex CT, 17
selections, 93
　channels, 188-189
　loading, 94
　managing, 191-192
TGA, 17
TIFF files, 16, 24
transparencies, GIF/PNG,
　290
**Saving Files command (File
　menu), 295**
Scitex CT, saving, 17
scratches, removing, 206-207
screens, halftone, 276-277
**SDK (Software Development
　Kit), 248**
**seams, Web page back-
　grounds, 292-293**
security
　controlling user input, 317
　copyrights, 326, 328
　watermarks, 329-330
Select menu commands
　All, 207
　Color Range, 57, 86-88
　Deselect, 244
　Feather, 92
　Inverse, 89
　Modify Border, 90
　Modify Contract, 89, 184

Modify Expand, 89
Out Of Gamut, 57
Save Selection, 59, 93, 188
Transform Selection, 88
selecting
　CMYK, 268-271
　commands, 317
　file formats, printing, 276
　fonts, 173
　grayscale profiles, 311
　layer masks, 154
　paths, 234-235
　resolution, 45-46
　RGB profiles, 309-310
**Selection menu, Load
　Selection command, 94, 190**
selections
　borders, 90-91
　boundaries, modifying, 88
　channels, 95
　　editing, 193-194
　　loading, 190
　　managing, 191-192
　　saving, 188-189
　contracting, 89
　expanding, 89
　fading, 92
　paths, converting, 239-242
　pixels, modifying, 82
　saving, 93-94
　sizes, constraining, 80-81
　tools
　　Color Range command,
　　　86-88
　　Magic Wand, 83
　　Magnetic Lasso, 84-85
selective color, modifying, 226
shadows
　adjustment layers, modify-
　　ing, 230
　drop, 158-160
　objects, 141-142
　points, configuring, 203-205
shaped gradients
　creating, 128-129
　customizing, 130-131

shapes, creating, 123
Sharpen Options palette, 211
sharpening
　areas, 211
　images, 212
shortcuts, History palette, 32
**Show All Files command
　(Open menu), 17**
**Show Paths command
　(Windows menu), 236**
**Show Rulers command (View
　menu), 107**
signatures (watermarks)
size
　canvas, 48
　images, reducing, 296-297
　selection, constraining, 80-81
Slice tool, 296-297
**Slices menu, Create Slices
　From Guides command, 298**
slicing images, 296-297
Smart Blur filter, 251
Smudge Options palette, 243
Smudge tool, 118, 243
snapshots
　History brush, 36-39
　History palette
　　creating files, 34
　　saving, 33
**Software Development Kit
　(SDK), 248**
solid color fills, layers, 164
solidity, 273
special effects
　bevel, 162-163
　cut-out, 158-160
　emboss, 162-163
　filters, 247, 253
　　artistic effects, 254-255
　　blur, 250-251
　　comic-book effects,
　　　256-257
　　depth-of-field, 252-253
　　fading, 249

layers
    breaking, 162, 169
    copying, 168
    predefined layer-effect
        styles, 167
    text, 179
splitting channels, 195
Sponge tool, 58, 218
spot color channels, creating,
    272-274
squares, creating, 123
stops, actions, 319
straightening images, 105
Stroke command (Edit menu),
    123
stroking, paths, 242
styles, predefined layer-effect,
    167
Stylize command (Filter
    menu), 256
subpaths
    modifying, 234-235
    saving, 236
subtracting, pixels, 82

T

tables, modifying color in
    ImageReady, 70-71
Tagged Image File Format. *See*
    TIFF
text
    baseline shift, 179
    carved, 184-185
    editing, 175
    images/objects, filling,
        152-153
    inserting, 172-175
    kerning, 177-178
    leading, 176
    metallic textures, 182-183
    RGB, 67

    special effects, 179
    tracking, 177-178
    wood textures, 180-181
Texture command (Filter
    menu), 258
textures
    carved text, 184-185
    filters, 258-259
        applying, 258-259
        displacement maps,
            260-261
        Lighting Effects, 262-263
        Noise, 264-265
    metallic, 182-183
    wood, 180-181
Texturizer command (Filter
    menu), 258
TGA, saving, 17
Threshold command (Image
    menu), 257
thumbnails, 331
TIFF (Tagged Image File
    Format), 24
    Options dialog box, 24
    saving, 16
tiled backgrounds, 292-293. *See*
    also **backgrounds**
tonal range
    curves, 203-205
    modifying, 201-202, 222
Toning tools, 58
tools
    Art History brush, 126-127
    Background Eraser, 119-120
    Blur, 210
    brushes
        customizing, 116
        editing, 114-115
        saving, 117
    Burn, 215
    Convert Point, 235
    Crop, 49-50
    Direct Selection, 235

    Dodge, 214
    Eyedropper, 198-199
    Fill, 121
    gradient, 128-131
    History brush, 124-125
    Magic Eraser, 120
    Magnetic Lasso, 236
    Magnetic Pen, 236
    marquee, constraining selec-
        tion sizes, 80-81
    Measure, 102
    painting, Quick Mask mode,
        193-194
    Path Creation, 236
    Pattern Stamp, 122
    Pen, 234
    Rubber Stamp, 208-209,
        292-293
    Sample, 198-199
    selection
        borders, 90-91
        channels, 95
        Color Range command,
            86-88
        contracting, 89
        expanding, 89
        fading, 92
        loading saved, 94
        Magic Wand, 83
        Magnetic Lasso, 84-85
        modifying boundaries, 88
        saving, 93
    Sharpen, 211
    Slice, 296-297
    Smudge, 118, 243
    Sponge, 58, 218
    Toning, 58
    Type, 172-185
    Type Mask, 172
    Vertical Type, 172
    Vertical Type Mask, 172
    Web Photo Gallery, 332
tracking text, 177-178

transfer functions, creating, 278
Transform command (Edit menu), 103, 142
Transform Selection command (Select menu), 88
transparencies
Magic Eraser, 120
preserving, 140
removing layers, 119-120
transparent masks, modifying, 130-131
Transparency & Gamut command (File menu), 56
Transparency property (layers), 134
Trap command (Image menu), 275
Trap dialog box, 275
trapping, applying, 275
Transform Numeric command (Edit menu), 105
troubleshooting colors, 218-231
Type command (Layer menu), 179
Type Mask tool, 172
Type tool, 172-185

U-V

Units & Rulers command (File menu), 102
Unsharp Mask commands (Filter menu), 212
Unsharp Mask filter, 212
user input, controlling, 317

values, numeric, 108-109
variations, color casts, 219-220
versions, files. *See* files
vertical text. *See* text

Vertical Type Mask tool, 172
Vertical Type tool, 172
View menu commands
Create Guides, 298
Gamut Warning, 56
Hide Edges, 57
Preview, 55
Show Rulers, 107
viewing
images, 282
watermarks, 329-330

W-Z

Watercolor command (Filter menu), 254
Watermark filters, 247
watermarks, embedding, 329-330
Web
animations, 293, 301-302
backgrounds, 292-293
button rollovers, 299-300
GIFs, saving, 282-283
imagemaps, 296-297
images
optimizing, 65-66
slicing, 296-297
JPEGs, saving, 282, 285
lay out Web pages, 294-295
palette, 291
photo gallery, creating, 334-335
PNGs, saving, 287-289
transparencies, 290
Web pages
contact sheets, 332
picture packages, 333
thumbnails, 331
Web Photo Gallery command (File menu), 334

Web Photo Gallery tool, 332
Window menu, Show Paths command, 236
wizard, Adobe Color Management, 306
wood textures, text, 180-181
work paths, saving, 236. *See also* paths